Parisian Architecture
of the
Belle Epoque

Parisian Architecture
of the
Belle Epoque

Roy Johnston

photography by
Steve Gorton

BICENTENNIAL
1807
WILEY
2007
BICENTENNIAL

WILEY-ACADEMY

Published in Great Britain in 2007 by Wiley-Academy, a division of John Wiley & Sons Ltd

Copyright © 2007 John Wiley & Sons Ltd, The Atrium, Southern Gate, Chichester,
West Sussex PO19 8SQ, England
telephone +44 (0)1243 779777

Photography © 2007 Steve Gorton unless otherwise stated
Anniversary Logo Design: Richard Pacifico

Email (for orders and customer service enquiries): cs-books@wiley.co.uk
Visit our Home Page on www.wiley.com

Other Wiley Editorial Offices

John Wiley & Sons Inc., 111 River Street, Hoboken, NJ 07030, USA
Jossey-Bass, 989 Market Street, San Francisco, CA 94103-1741, USA
Wiley-VCH Verlag GmbH, Boschstr. 12, D-69469 Weinheim, Germany
John Wiley & Sons Australia Ltd, 42 McDougall Street, Milton, Queensland 4064, Australia
John Wiley & Sons (Asia) Pte Ltd, 2 Clementi Loop #02-01, Jin Xing Distripark,
Singapore 129809
John Wiley & Sons Canada Ltd, 5353 Dundas Street West, Suite 400, Etobicoke,
Ontario M9B 6H8

Wiley also publishes its books in a variety of electronic formats. Some content that appears in
print may not be available in electronic books.

Executive Commissioning Editor: Helen Castle
Content Editor: Louise Porter
Publishing Assistant: Calver Lezama

ISBN 978 0 470 01555 1

Page design and layouts by Ian Lambot Studio, UK
Printed and bound by Conti Tipocolor, Italy

Contents

Preface
Continuity and Change in Paris 1889–1913

The Belle Epoque

The Belle Epoque is defined in Hachette's *Dictionnaire du français* as 'the years around 1900, retrospectively judged pleasant and without care'.[1] In this book the years 1889 to 1913 provide the overall time span, 1889 being the year of the International Exhibition marking the centenary of the 1789 Revolution and still represented by the Eiffel Tower; building virtually ceased in 1913 due to the threat of the coming World War. A few buildings started before 1889 have been included where this helps to explain the historical background.

Apart from marvelling at the artefacts themselves, for the average reader the study of the architecture of the past is of interest for two reasons: first, as a surviving record of daily life and, second, bearing in mind the degree of expenditure of both money and human effort involved, of a society's aspirations and ideals. The first may be seen most clearly from buildings designed for habitation, education and work which make up the greater part of any conurbation large or small, the second from more monumental constructions representing society as a whole.

The advantage of studying a relatively recent period in history is that the more mundane buildings are likely to have survived comparatively intact. Paris is ideal in this respect as, apart from destruction during the Commune of 1871 (of which more in Chapter One) and some rebuilding in the 1950s, the city

as built or rebuilt from the 1850s onwards is still there, although many of the buildings are little known and are unrecorded in currently available literature.

Continuity

Continuity in architectural design usually reflects stability in society: it was therefore inherent in France from the establishment of an official classical style in the seventeenth century as representative of a centralised authority. The political upheavals of the 1789 Revolution, the defeat of Napoléon I in 1814, the coup d'état by his nephew Louis Napoléon in 1848, 'the year of revolutions', his later defeat by the Prussians in 1870 and the subsequent Paris Commune in 1871, made it essential for successive French governments to embrace the continuation of French classicism as a symbol of national unity. The architectural success of Napoléon III's modernisation of Paris as a world-class capital, as carried out under Baron Haussmann and continued by the Third Republic, was largely due to the use of the classical system of design, which was generally understood by architects and builders and accepted by the public as a national style, and this continuity of design is the principal source of the city's harmonious character.

The establishment by the Second Empire and the Third Republic of International Exhibitions to stress how France remained a world power, having recovered from such a series of political and economic disasters, resulted in Paris becoming the world's tourist centre, as well as the European cultural capital. Chapter One of this book describes this historical background and the growth of a specifically Parisian public social life; the architectural fabric for this being outlined in Chapter Two. The two succeeding chapters are devoted to the two principal institutions whose existence ensured the continuation of the classical tradition up to the First World War: the apartment blocks which housed the bourgeoisie who were the governing class and the design training given by the Ecole des Beaux-Arts, which united the architectural profession despite any changes brought about by new functional requirements and foreign influences.

Change

The development of the railways and of the iron industry, of tourism and of manufacturing in general, including the establishment of Paris as the centre of the fashion industry, the increase in night life brought about by electric lighting and the resultant new types of building were all factors exerting major changes in architecture and are the subject of Chapter Five. The two following chapters describe how increased interest in foreign cultures resulting from the International Exhibitions and advances in communications made Parisian architects look for alternative approaches to the classical tradition, while the political necessity of improving the conditions of the working class produced design problems which could only be solved by a fresh approach, although one related to the 'rational' tradition within the Ecole des Beaux-Arts.

In the new century, Parisian cultural life was to be revolutionised by the influx of foreign artists, while architecture was changed irreparably by the adoption of reinforced concrete and by diminution of traditional hand craftsmanship, although the Exhibition of 1900 had failed to acknowledge this degree of change by either the design of its pavilions or their contents. The final chapter, however, shows that some Parisian architects, having absorbed the essentials of the 'rational' tradition enshrined in Beaux-Arts teaching, were able to create the beginnings of a true Modern architecture, which despite outward appearance was inherently a continuation of the Parisian tradition. The Belle Epoque may therefore be seen not as a mythical golden age separated from the present, but as an essential link between the past and the modern world.

1   *Le Dictionnaire du français*, Hachette, Paris, 1992: *'La Belle Époque: les années proches de 1900, jugées rétrospectivement agréables et sans soucis'*.

Part 1 Continuity

1823 · E. LALO · 1892

1 La Vie Parisienne
The Belle Epoque and its Historical Background

Introduction

The legend of the golden age is one of the most popular myths and the Belle Epoque, 'a time without care', perhaps the most recent. Strollers on the boulevards, night life in Montmartre with balls, cafés-concerts and circuses where aristocrats, tourists, the demi-monde and the working class mingled, young painters and seamstresses leading a bohemian life in garrets, boating on the Seine, all in the pleasure capital of the world: too good to be true, of course. The reality is more complicated and more interesting.

La Vie Parisienne is the title of an operetta by Offenbach, first performed in 1866, which still draws packed houses of foreign tourists and French provincials to the Opéra Comique, and the myth of the Belle Epoque relates to Paris's heyday as the world centre of pleasure, particularly for the newly rich who could afford to travel to the most famous city in the world for fashion, food and entertainments of all kinds, particularly those considered slightly risqué by foreigners and provincials. Yet a British art historian has recently written a book on the 'naughty Nineties' entitled *The Troubled Republic: Visual culture and social debate in France 1889–1900*,[1] which paints a very different picture of moral degeneration, fear of the crowd, religious differences and militarism.

Even the overall time span of the Belle Epoque appears unclear in many people's minds, often including, or being confused with, the Second Empire of 1853–70, a very different world in many respects from 'the years around 1900' and one which produced a very different architecture.

Because of architecture's essential nature as an immutable background to human life, it tends to change more slowly than the other arts (there are of course also economic reasons for this) and it is therefore necessary when studying the architecture of a quarter century to look first at the period immediately preceding it. In order to look for the reality behind the myth of 'a time without care' this chapter will therefore be devoted mainly to the growth of Paris during the nineteenth century. The allure of the city to the eyes of its foreign visitors cannot disguise the fact that they may only have seen the surface of a deeply divided society, but it is hoped that the following study of its architecture does show that it began to achieve a more harmonious solidarity in the years around 1900.

Paris 1789–1848

The political revolution of 1789 took place in a country with an agricultural economy and an established tradition of classical architecture. Paris was essentially a medieval city of narrow streets and individual family houses with shops on the ground

---

Opposite: **Restaurant Julien, 16 rue du faubourg-Saint-Denis, attributed to E. Fournier, 1902.** *Pâte de verre panel by Louis Trézel.*

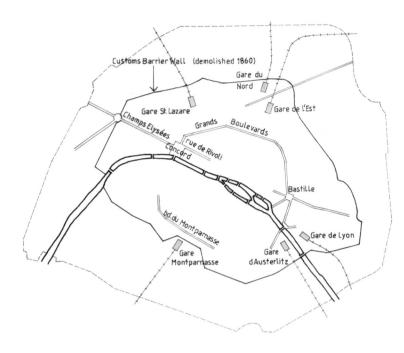

floor, the only wide streets or avenues being what are now the *Grands Boulevards* formed in the eighteenth century on the site of Charles V's fourteenth-century fortifications, plus a ring of boulevards on the Left Bank, curving round from Les Invalides to the Jardin des Plantes, the whole enclosed by Ledoux's customs barrier wall of 1784–7. The classical buildings within this area were national monuments, churches and aristocratic houses, plus a few squares or terraces such as the place Vendôme and the place de la Concorde.

The only important architectural addition made by Napoléon Bonaparte, apart from a few individual monuments, was the western section of the rue de Rivoli, whose historical importance is that it was the forerunner of the terraced streets built by Napoléon III and Haussmann: individual commercial and residential buildings behind a continuous government-imposed elevation or 'ordinance' of repetitive bays, its horizontal lines emphasising the continuity of the street, in contrast to the irregular rhythm of individual houses of varying heights.

Under the New Monarchies (Louis XVIII, Charles X and Louis-Philippe) of 1815–48 the first effect of growing industrialisation came with Paris becoming the hub of the French railway system: six new stations built between 1837 and 1848 in a ring around the city, into whose narrow streets they poured people and goods. Manufacturing moved into the area north of

the *Grands Boulevards*; its workers found accommodation where they could, the better off in comparatively new buildings east of the Bastille, the others mainly in the oldest and poorest parts of the city, which became densely populated slums. Map 1 shows the extent of Paris around 1846, the population at that date being 1,226,980, having grown from 861,436 in 1831.[2]

The character of Paris up to 1848 was therefore very similar to other more provincial French cities and towns: a medieval layout made up mainly of individual houses mostly three or four storeys high, of brick or timber-framed construction, the latter probably already leaning irregularly, having cream-painted rendered walls with louvred window shutters folding back on the wall surface and small family-owned shops on the ground floor. Parts of central Paris, for example north of the *Grands Boulevards* and to the east of the Marais, still have some of this character.

The principal difference from the provincial towns, apart from heavy horse-drawn traffic (merchandise had to be taken across the city from one terminal station to another, for example), was in the people. In addition to established residents, the increase in population of over 40 per cent in 15 years quoted above was due to the industrial revolution bringing in middle and working classes from rural areas in search of employment. In addition, newly rich foreign visitors were coming by rail from countries where the industrial revolution had preceded that in

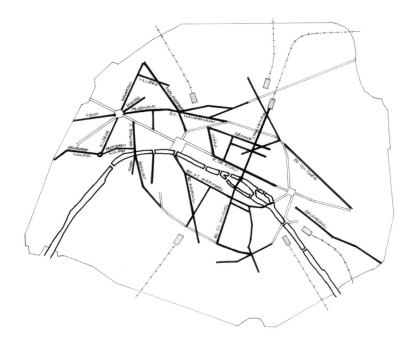

Right: **Map 2.** *The principal avenues and boulevards as laid out by Napoléon III and Baron Haussmann, some of which were completed by the Third Republic.*

France, descending in large numbers in search of pleasure, staying in hotels converted from previously aristocratic residences.

One of the first new industries to flourish was luxury fabrics, requiring specialist shops showing large stocks of *nouveautés*. These became a magnet for foreign visitors and increased Paris's reputation for *la mode*. Because the streets mostly did not yet have pavements, shopping arcades called *passages*, connecting two streets, were built to provide more comfortable conditions for shopping and promenading (some being especially popular with ladies of the town). The growth of the iron industry enabled them to have completely glazed roofs, this natural light being supplemented by the new gas lighting. Forty *passages* were built between 1779 and 1846,[3] but were later superseded by the new department stores and many have been demolished. The Galerie Vivienne and Galerie Véro-Dodat still have a little of their original architectural, but not social, character.

During the New Monarchies, Paris had an intense musical life: Liszt lived there in 1823–34 and Chopin in 1830, both performing mainly in fashionable salons; Rossini was director of the Théâtre Italien in 1824–36, his *Comte d'Ory* first performed at the Opéra in 1827, Bellini's *Norma* and *La Sonnambula* in 1831. Berlioz was the leading French composer. It was at this time that the north-eastern *Grands Boulevards* became the main district for popular theatres. Montmartre was still a village until the 1870s and many other outlying parts of the city also retained a rural character: for example the Champs-Elysées were not built up until the Second Empire, while the surroundings outside the customs barrier wall were rural in character until the 1860s, when the wall and most of Ledoux's gates were demolished.

The Second Empire

Louis Napoléon (Napoléon I's nephew) became President after a coup d'état in December 1848 and was declared Emperor as Napoléon III in 1853. He had been much influenced by the 'Utopian' philosophy of the Comte de Saint-Simon (1760–1825), who believed that social and economic progress involved massive investment in public works.

Realising that the existing city fabric was totally inadequate to deal with the economic, social and political pressures facing it, Napoléon III appointed Baron Georges-Eugène Haussmann (1809–91) as his *Préfet* (city administrator or mayor) in June 1853 to carry out the necessary improvements, and at his first interview Louis Napoléon handed him a map of Paris on which he, the Emperor, had drawn proposed new streets, in four colours indicating degrees of urgency. These streets are shown on Map 2: many were completed during the Third Republic, the boulevard Raspail not being finished until 1907.

Left: **Charles Garnier, The Opéra (now Palais Garnier), 1861–75.** *The Second Empire's greatest monument, the Opéra's scale and richness were designed to contrast with the adjacent terraces built to a repetitive government 'ordinance'.*

Very briefly, the urban work undertaken by Haussmann and later continued by the city council consisted of: the provision of new avenues and boulevards, which connected the main stations with one another and with the central market at Les Halles, and thereby improved circulation for the increasing quantity of goods and people (and, when necessary, troops), and greatly reduced congestion and delay in the rest of the city; the rebuilding of slum areas to remove centres of social unrest and physical disease; the provision of schools and hospitals; and the establishment of local public buildings, each of the *arrondissements* having its town hall, fire station and clinic.

Public buildings representing the state or the city were treated as individual free-standing monuments, sited at key points in the planning layout; private buildings formed parts of terraces whose overall elevational treatment was, during the Second Empire, the subject of a government-designed 'ordinance' of a repetitive nature so as not to compete visually with the monuments, each private developer having to comply with a standard design drawn up in 1860 by Charles Rohault de Fleury (1801–75). The best place to see this contrast today is in the place de l'Opéra, designed although not finished during Napoléon III's reign, of which the Palais Garnier, as the Opéra is now called, is the greatest monument, positioned at a focal point in the new commercial centre of the Right Bank.

The use of the repetitive ordinance did, however, mean that each city block, consisting of comparatively small individual buildings, now read as a single unit, thereby both increasing the monumental effect of the city as a whole and underlining the greater importance of private as against public building. In 1860, because density of population within the customs barrier wall had become intolerable, Haussmann demolished the wall, annexing the suburban areas which had grown up outside it to create eight new *arrondissements* (the 13th to 20th) thereby doubling the city's area.

Laws enabling the government to expropriate private property for reconstruction had already been passed in 1841 and 1852.[4] The cost of recompensing the owners was covered by the sale of the valuable lots having frontages on the new thorough-fares to property developers who erected at their own expense buildings for rent, usually as commercial premises with middle-class residential apartments over, occupied by *rentiers* living on their investments and by the professional and business class which proliferated with commercial growth. A large proportion of these and their living-in servants and of the workers employed by them were immigrants from the provinces. (Their life will be described in more detail in Chapters Three and Seven.)

Huge profits were to be made by the nouveaux riches, the 'industrial aristocracy', who were able to display their newly found wealth at Napoléon III's court, the most brilliant in Europe. The new avenues and boulevards, lined with shops, cafés and restaurants, the newly landscaped Bois de Boulogne, which was the fashionable rendezvous both for the 'respectable' leisured class (with chaperones as appropriate) and for the demi-monde, the establishment of Paris as the world capital for women's fashions, following the lead given by the Empress Eugénie, and the rapid growth of all forms of night life attracted the rich from all over the world. The new 'Palace' hotels built for them became centres also for the richer Parisians' social life. Paris's reputation as the world's pleasure capital, thus established, suffered only briefly with the Second Empire's downfall in 1870 and quickly revived, to be extended up to and including the Belle Epoque.

The Opéra

The new Opéra, commissioned by the Emperor and paid for by government funds, voted annually,[5] was intended to be the centre of this brilliant life of conspicuous consumption. Although designed in 1861, it was not completed until 1875, after the events to be described shortly had brought the Second Empire to a close and inaugurated changes in French life and architecture that were to herald the twentieth century. The building is the greatest example of the elaborate system of formal planning taught at the Ecole des Beaux-Arts (described in detail in Chapter Four), as enshrined in the extravagant designs produced for the Prix de Rome which the brighter students all hoped they might win. The architect, Charles Garnier (1825–98), a Rome prize-winner and probably the most decoratively brilliant French architect of the nineteenth century, employed in his Opéra *agence* a number of the most talented younger architects, thereby passing on his technical skills, but the architecture they eventually built was very different, due to changed social and economic conditions.

The building intentionally occupied the focal position in the new centre for commercial wealth on the Right Bank, being surrounded by department stores, banks and fashionable shops and restaurants, with the Grand Hotel and the Jockey Club – representing rich visitors and aristocratic exclusivity respectively – immediately to its west. The open loggia facing the place de l'Opéra therefore provides an intermediate zone between the public space used largely by the rich and an interior exclusive to them. The building's exceptionally rich modelling (indebted to Michelangelo) provides the maximum possible contrast with the surrounding commercial facades based on the approved government ordinance. Internally the decoration is even more opulent, with 30 per cent of the plan area given over to audience circulation, primarily for the social display more important to the patrons than the performance, the grand staircase being a theatre in itself with the public as actors. The overwhelming opulence of the design both externally and internally, totally at odds with the

traditional reticence of French classicism, led the Empress to complain that it was not in any known style, to which Garnier replied, '*Madame, c'est de Napoléon III!*'

The Opéra is therefore essentially a Second Empire and not a Belle Epoque building and is illustrated here to show how far Parisian architecture changed in appearance between 1861 and 1913. But it was a functional one, perfectly planned for its original purpose, with separate entrances for the Emperor, subscribers and the general public. Arrangements for buying tickets, depositing coats and meeting friends were all carefully planned by Garnier. Gentlemen from the Jockey Club were even provided with a private salon in which to meet poorly paid young dancers of the Corps de Ballet, to whom they wished to offer their protection. The grandiloquence of both scale and decoration may also be considered functional, being essential to the building's purpose as the centre of Second Empire society, a purpose never fully achieved, since the society for which it had been designed had largely come to an end before construction was completed.

The Franco-Prussian War and the Commune

In 1870 France declared war on Prussia, but the Emperor was defeated and captured at the battle of Sedan in December. The German siege of Paris lasted from September 1870 to January 1871, the city starved into surrender. The provisional French government had moved to Versailles, where it stayed until 1879, but Parisian workers, many of whom had been unemployed for a year and were bitter at a peace treaty which allowed German occupation, took control of the city, declaring it an independent Commune. (The treaty also ceded Alsace and most of Lorraine to Germany and required payment of reparations by France.)

The Prime Minister Adolphe Thiers sent an army of 130,000 to combat the Communards, who were suppressed by the end of May after violent street fighting and massacres, over 20,000 being killed or executed and some 38,500 arrested. Many important public buildings, including the Tuileries palace, the Hôtel de Ville and Préfecture de Police, had been set ablaze by the insurgents. The aftermath of these events was hatred of Germany and a deep distrust between the bourgeois and workers in the Third Republic which now succeeded the Empire. With the disappearance of the glittering Imperial court, power gradually passed from the nouveaux riches to the petits-bourgeois, essentially conservative and wishing to emphasise their social differentiation from the working class.

Recovery of the building industry was slow after the Commune, building trades being greatly depleted as a result of internment, deportation and executions. An amnesty was not declared until 1880, at which time some of the 238 buildings left in ruins still remained.

The Third Republic: Completing Hausmann's Work

The modernisation of Paris which Louis Napoléon had seen to be necessary if it was to be the capital of an industrialised nation was continued under the Third Republic. Haussmann resigned in 1870, but his assistants, the hydraulics engineer Eugène Belgrand (1810–78) and the landscape architect Adolphe Alphand (1817–91), remained in the City's employment and continued his work in the provision of water (the supply being divided into *eaux de source* for drinking, carried by aqueducts to reservoirs on the city's hills, and *eaux de rivière* for drainage and street cleaning); the building of sewers separating water and sewage; and forming parks and planting a total of 82,000 trees, mainly planes, chestnuts, elms and limes. These amenities were a principal factor in the re-establishment of the city's attraction as the greatest international tourist centre.

To an extent the rich had their own public spaces: the Bois de Boulogne for carriages and riders in the afternoon, the Tuileries and Champs-Elysées gardens for children and their nurses. Residents of the expensive houses surrounding the Parc Monceau had their own park enclosed by gates. The Seine north-west of Paris at Courbevoie and Asnières and the adjacent island of La Grande Jatte was the main playground of the working class at weekends, easily reached by train from the Gare Saint-Lazare and near the industrial suburbs around Saint-Denis. Like the dance halls and cafés-concerts of Montmartre, they were frequented also by middle-class men, with their mistresses or wishing to meet shop-girls. They feature in paintings by the Impressionists and Seurat, but from the 1880s artists became more interested in the boulevards, reflecting the successful progress of rebuilding.

Many of the outer *arrondissements* were developed largely during the Third Republic at a similar density to the city centre, so that all the local centres became metropolitan in character, whereas the 16th for example, now the district with the greatest preponderance of Belle Epoque buildings, had previously been mainly occupied by market gardens. In the centre, redevelopment was mainly as individual infill sites, a notable exception being the rue Réaumur, 2e, built as garment warehouses for the flourishing fashion trade between 1897 and 1902. With a few important exceptions noted later in the book, comparatively few buildings of the period have been demolished and most were in the outer *arrondissements*, pulled down during the 1950s to make way for larger-scale housing.

Fashionable members of the traditionally aristocratic faubourg Saint-Germain lived not there, but in the 8th *arrondissement*; the only aristocrats in the 'Seizième' were those married to 'new money'. As a solid bourgeois example, the Proust family lived for over 30 years at 9 boulevard Malesherbes, then

moved to the quieter and more fashionable 45 rue de Courcelles. After his parents' deaths, Marcel went to 102 boulevard Haussmann and only deserted the 8th *arrondissement* for the 16th in 1920. The much cheaper 9th *arrondissement* was popular with writers and painters, for example Mallarmé, Manet, Moreau and Seurat, while the main working-class areas were La Chapelle, 18e, Belleville and Menilmontant, 19e and 20e, Gentilly, 13e and Montrouge, 14e.

Under the Third Republic, the government ordinances were discontinued, but all new construction had to receive a building permission, involving design approval by the City's *architectes-voyers* who used regulations defined in 1882 to control building height and overall treatment (a building code relating heights to street widths had been first formulated in 1763). The 1882 code was revised in 1884 and again in 1902 to allow additional storeys, either set back or within a higher mansard roof than had previously been permitted. The aesthetic reasons for this will be explained in Chapter Six, with section drawings of the codes.

Economically, the larger scale reflects a growth in population and a change in political power, with individual developers being replaced by insurance companies. Architectural uniformity was further reinforced in practice by the general use of dressed limestone for the street facades, made economically available by rail transport and improvements in quarrying and cutting, and by the standardisation of components such as casement windows, balcony railings and metal shutters or *persiennes* folding into the window reveals, facade walls requiring to be 500mm thick under the building code. The traditional rendered elevations and wooden shutters, referred to earlier, had disappeared from new buildings by 1865, as the city took on an increasingly metropolitan character.

These residential blocks were *immeubles de rapport*, mostly having shops or cafés on the ground floor, bourgeois family apartments over – entered from a common staircase – and maids' rooms in the roof: these *immeubles* and the life they contained will be described in Chapter Three. The preponderance of private building for rent reflects change in power from a central authoritarian regime to large-scale private enterprise.

Political and Social Change 1871–1914

Political and economic stability was the main objective of the successive governments during the Third Republic against the backdrop of the continuing threat from Prussia; although there were 46 ministries between 1876 and 1914, they were mostly some form of coalition of centrist parties and pursued similar policies. Militarist attempts at coups d'état in the 1880s were unsuccessful. Despite free primary education becoming compulsory in 1881 and trade unions being legalised in 1884, workers' living conditions were generally wretched and the

Above: **François Saulnier, 15 rue Gay-Lussac, 1912.** *A later insertion into a typical Haussmannian street, after revised building regulations of 1902 had permitted greater height and a more picturesque silhouette, when the general introduction of lifts, together with increased traffic, had made the upper floor apartments the most desirable.*

Opposite: **Juste Lisch, 30 avenue de Villiers, 1891.** *Although built within the Belle Epoque, the exterior of this apartment block is more typical of the Second Empire in its reliance on the repetition of simple elements.*

Above: *The principal section of the 1900 International Exhibition on the Champ de Mars.*

Right: *The main entrance to the 1900 International Exhibition.*

problem of social housing was only seriously addressed when purpose-built blocks of low-rental flats (*habitations à bon marché*) were organised by philanthropic societies, starting in 1888 and increasing in size and number in 1904 with the establishment of the Fondation Rothschild (this will be described in detail in Chapter Seven).

Anarchist action in the 1890s, including bomb-throwing in the Chamber of Deputies in 1893 and the assassination of President Sadi Carnot at Lyons in 1894, reflected social unrest. Bourgeois complacency had been shaken by the threat of socialism and by a number of financial and political scandals, culminating in the Dreyfus Case of 1894–9, which did not affect the working class but tore conventional society apart. (Dreyfus, a Jewish army officer, had been wrongly convicted of passing secret information to the German government. The army, the press, the government, the courts, the monarchists, the right-wing 'League of Patriots' were all involved and all came badly out of the 'Affair'.)

The population of Paris increased from 1,851,792 in 1872 to 2,888,110 in 1911, mainly due to immigration from the provinces. This increase and the improved economic position, despite a slump following the crash of the Union Générale in 1882 and later periods of financial instability, resulted in a steady private building programme into the new century, although this eventually had to extend outside the city boundary due to

shortage of land. Building examples in this book have been confined to the 1st to 20th *arrondissements* and have therefore had to exclude, for example, Neuilly-sur-Seine, much developed during the Belle Epoque. Greater building density necessitated by population increase was partly catered for by the revised building regulations of 1884 and 1902 allowing greater heights, when the City encouraged a more picturesque treatment of the previously uniform *immeubles* by projecting bays and a varied skyline. This coincided with a desire among many architects for a 'new art' fitting a time of change.

The increasingly elaborate skyline, together with the amount and high standard of decorative sculpture on residential buildings, may be taken as a celebration of the city's life as well as of its economic prosperity. This applies also to some of the painters: having previously concentrated on landscape and portraiture, they now began to focus on the city and its pleasures. Pissarro, Béraud and Caillebotte were concerned with the life of the boulevards , Toulouse-Lautrec and Degas more interested in music halls and dance, and Seurat with the various aspects of city life. Pierre Bonnard and Edouard Vuillard, members of the group known as the Nabis or prophets, were mainly interested in interior scenes (they and Caillebotte will be mentioned again in Chapter Three), but all these were engrossed in the people and their life, rather than in the architecture as such.

The residential trend was westwards, with the centre increasingly given over to shops, banks and offices. Greatly proliferated street traffic eventually led to the provision of an underground railway system, although to those familiar with Paris today the first impression from contemporary photographs must be of the comparative emptiness of the wide avenues and the reliance on horses, which still pulled buses, carriages, cabs and vans in 1900, although mechanically powered trams were being introduced. Riverboats (*Bateaux Mouches*) were used by commuters: in the 1890s a fleet of 105 boats served an average of 25 million people per year, but after the establishment of the 'Métro', starting in 1900, the water service declined and was withdrawn entirely in 1914.[6]

The Tourist Capital of the World

Despite problems with the building industry and reparations payable to Germany, the generally swift economic recovery after 1871 was celebrated by International Exhibitions in 1878, 1889 and 1900 with spectacular buildings demonstrating the continuance of France's economic power established during the Second Empire. The European and American new rich enthusiastically adopted foreign travel and luxury 'Palace' hotels had to be built to accommodate them. The French were fascinated by foreign cultures as exhibited by the varied styles of national pavilions and their contents (the influence on Debussy of the Balinese Gamelan orchestra at the 1889 Exhibition is famous), but foreign influences on permanent Parisian architecture were rare. The exhibition pavilions were mostly of temporary construction, much more colourful than the permanent stone architecture, being mainly of iron framing either painted or covered with coloured brick, tiling or plaster. The use of the latter externally, plus the fanciful shapes it could cheaply assume, led to these buildings being referred to by French critics as '*pâtisseries*'. Their only influence on permanent Parisian architecture would appear to have been the fairly brief popularity of the Art Nouveau style around 1900.

The International Exhibitions of 1889 and 1900 enhanced the permanent holiday atmosphere which accompanied tourism (according to Theodore Zeldin's *France 1848–1945*, vol II, there were 39 million attendances at the Exhibition of 1889 and 50 million in 1900): this was aided by the existence of a leisured *rentier* middle class and by many aristocrats intermarrying with the new rich and spending much of their time in Paris rather than on their country estates. The reputation of the Belle Epoque as a time without care depends largely on this and on so much social life taking place in public on the boulevards and in cafés and places of entertainment, where both lonely newcomers and established Parisians could be *flâneurs* (strollers) who, Baudelaire

thought, could by being pure observers transform the spectacle of modern life into something poetic.[7]

The new phenomenon of electric lighting helped to create the fairy-tale atmosphere of boulevards and exhibitions. The boulevards were further animated by the wide pavements, initiated by Haussmann, that had been partly taken over by external café terraces and by ticket and newspaper kiosks displaying posters, particularly those of Jules Chéret (1836–1933) who invented new developments in colour lithography: these were later rivalled artistically by those of Toulouse-Lautrec. The theatrical light opera atmosphere was no doubt boosted by the authorities to encourage tourism. Because the newly redeveloped outer *arrondissements* were built up at a high density, each local centre shared in this lively urban character.

The Dark Side

The census figures show that about a third of the population would have been new to city life and would have consequently found its jostling crowds menacing. Edmond de Goncourt described Paris in his diary in December 1894 as *'the capital of a land of madness'*, and he continued, *'never has the Paris of my youth or the Paris of my maturity seemed as poverty-stricken as the Paris of this evening: never have so many women's pleading eyes asked me for a meal, never have so many men's weary voices asked me for a sou.'* [8]

Tourists probably did not see the more depressed working-class areas and certainly not the shanty towns surrounding the city: it was only during the Belle Epoque that the living conditions of the poor came to be seriously addressed. The 1890s, the *fin de siècle*, was a period of great political and social turmoil, much of it due to individual fears about the massive changes taking place in society and worry as to what the new century might bring: this explains the degree of alcoholism and drug addiction and the interest shown in such subjects as psychopathology and hypnotism.

The emergence of socialism brought about political realignment in the 1890s, leading to *Ralliement*, a political movement uniting the church and monarchists with republicans, who also moved towards addressing social problems in the movement known as *Solidarité*. Improvements in the life of the working class by architectural means will be described in Chapter Seven, 'The Social Aspect', and changes in architecture related to the *fin de siècle* in Chapter Six, 'The Search for a New Art'.

In retrospect, the year 1900 appears as a watershed in the arts. The Impressionist and Post-Impressionist painters and composers and the Symbolist writers were nearly all French, although affected by foreign, particularly Eastern, influences (the American painters Whistler, Sargent and Mary Cassatt, who came to Paris in the 1860s and '70s, worked within French traditions).

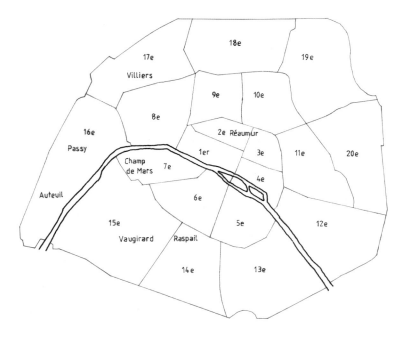

Right: **Map 3.** *The* arrondissements *as they are today, with those districts that developed most during the Belle Epoque noted.*

The international position of Paris as the world's artistic centre was consolidated after the 1900 Exhibition by an influx of foreign artists and writers. Picasso first arrived in 1900, sharing a garret with Max Jacob (after a visit to Barcelona he settled in Paris in 1904). Apollinaire arrived in 1902, Brancusi in 1904, Modigliani in 1906. Although Cézanne was French his work was virtually unknown in Paris until the retrospective exhibition in 1907. The Ballets Russes arrived in 1908.

Doubtless for most visitors the Belle Epoque appeared to continue unchanged. The *rapprochement* between classes encouraged by church and state and the improvement in the living conditions of the working class must have increased the feeling of 'a time without care' for many Parisians. Only the looming world war cast its increasing shadow. Despite this, Paris had now embarked on one of the greatest periods in its artistic life, a subject that can best be discussed in the second half of this book, along with the remarkable architecture produced at the end of the Belle Epoque, most of which is still almost unknown.

2   Census population figures in this book taken from Louis Chevalier, *La formation de la population Parisienne au XIXe siècle*, Presses Universitaires de France, Paris, 1950, p 284.

3   For complete list of *passages* see Paul Chemetov and Bernard Marrey, *Architectures à Paris 1848–1914*, Bordas, Paris, 1984, p 18.

4   David Van Zanten, *Building Paris*, Cambridge University Press, Cambridge, MA, 1994, p 19.

5   Christopher Curtis Mead, *Charles Garnier's Paris Opera*, MIT Press, Cambridge, MA and London, 1991, p 139.

6   Norma Evenson, *Paris: A Century of Change 1878–1978*, Yale University Press, New Haven, CT and London, 1979, pp 89–91.

7   Charles Baudelaire, *Le Peintre de la vie moderne*, 1863; translated by Jonathan Mayne, *The Painter of Modern Life*, Thames and Hudson, London, 1964, p 9.

8   Edmond de Goncourt, translated by Robert Baldick, *Pages from the Goncourt Journal*, Oxford University Press, London and New York, 1962, p 396.

1   Richard Thomson, *The Troubled Republic: visual culture and social debate in France 1889–1900*, Yale University Press , New Haven, CT and London, 2004.

2 Buildings for Public Life

The Ladies' Paradise

This is the title of an English translation of Zola's novel about a Parisian department store: it could equally well be a description of Belle Epoque Paris. The essential characteristic of Paris which emerged during the nineteenth century was its feminine glamour. Of all cities only Paris was in every sense *à la mode*. From *haute couture* through small speciality shops to the great department stores, the *Grands Magasins*, this was the place women wanted to go to shop for clothes and jewellery and where, having they hoped become more glamorous as a result, they could display their charms in restaurants and theatres and walking along the boulevards. Male visitors were attracted for the same reason, and, of course, for the city's reputation for night life of all kinds.

The buildings designed for public life described and illustrated in this chapter all display much of this glamorous character. This applies not only to restaurants and theatres: even a banking hall such as that of the Société Générale would be unimaginable in a more prosaic environment.

Opposite: **Louis Bernier, Opéra Comique, 1893.**
The past provided inspiration for the murals, busts and Baroque doorways in the Salon.

Entertainments

Although the theatre flourished, few new theatres were built during the Belle Epoque: the majority date from the Second Empire or earlier, or have been greatly altered during the twentieth century.[1] Many theatres had been set up after the Revolution of 1789 when censorship was temporarily abolished, but the early theatres, as elsewhere, were largely of timber construction and vulnerable to destruction by fire. The only one of major architectural importance built during the Belle Epoque, and this at its end, is the Théâtre des Champs-Elysées, to be described in Chapter Eight.

The Opéra Comique was won in competition by Louis Bernier (1845–1919) in 1893 because its predecessor had burnt down, but it was built on the same restricted site. It is therefore quite small, without any of the extensive spaces for public circulation provided at Garnier's Opéra: just two elegant stairs and a reception room or *salon* over the entrance foyer. Externally it looks rather like a town hall, but the auditorium has a good deal of gold leaf typical of most nineteenth-century theatres. Bernier did a thoroughly professional job in squeezing in as much accommodation as possible and the whole building is an excellent example of Beaux-Arts classicism without any attempt at originality. (Notable first nights included Charpentier's *Louise* in February 1900 and Debussy's *Pelléas et Mélisande*, April 1902.)[2]

Left: **Louis Bernier, Opéra Comique, 1893.** *French* Grand Siècle *bronze and marble for the bourgeois* Belle Epoque.

Above: **Louis Bernier, Opéra Comique, 1893.** *A very Beaux-Arts and perhaps slightly pompous facade for light opera.*

The enormously popular cafés-concerts and music halls (about 150 in 1900) were mostly in the boulevard de Strasbourg and Pigalle, in small theatres since demolished. In 1898 Baedeker thought *'the music and singing never of a high class, while the audience is of a very mixed character'*; and of the *salles de danse*, *'many of these entertainments are to a great extent "got up" for strangers'*.[3] Others were in Montmartre, where the rural atmosphere encouraged informal mixing between the classes (the Moulin Rouge opened in 1889). On the Left Bank a large proportion of social gatherings were in small cafés and cellars, centres for the consumption of absinthe and opium long since closed. More serious fare was provided in some small experimental theatres in the 1890s such as the Théâtre Libre and the Théâtre de l'Oeuvre, where the décor as well as the posters advertising the productions were mainly provided by Bonnard and Vuillard.

Circuses were a form of entertainment popular with all classes in Paris during the nineteenth century. At the Cirque Fernando for example, which is illustrated in Seurat's *Le Cirque* of 1890, petit-bourgeois families made up most of the audience, except on Wednesdays when it was taken over by 'high-life'. At the time the circus was frequently likened to the Roman amphitheatre.[4] The only circus building still remaining is earlier in date: the Cirque d'Hiver of 1852, designed by Jacques-Ignace Hittorff (1792–1867), featuring the external polychromatic decoration which was one of his principal contributions to Parisian architecture.

In the years after 1900 the cinema took over from the circus as the great form of popular entertainment. The first public film show by the Lumière brothers was given in the basement of the Grand Café, boulevard des Capucines, in December 1895. A theatre in the boulevard des Italiens was transformed into a cinema for three months in 1897 and the Cirque d'Hiver became a cinema in 1907. The Hippodrome-Gaumont-Palace, place de Clichy, also a former circus, became the largest cinema in the world in 1911, with five thousand seats; there were 37 cinemas in Paris by 1913, but unfortunately none survives in its original state.

Boutiques and Cafés

The development of poster art mentioned in the last chapter personifies a popular Parisian form of decorative art, which may also be seen in some happily extant small shops or boutiques, – *boulangeries* and *patisseries*, for example – some since changed to more fashionable uses, but having retained their decoration: painted ceilings and wall panels, tiles and mirrors, carried out by artists specialising in this work. This decoration is mainly floral and the paintings of a bucolic nature, derived from the eighteenth-century pastoral tradition. This is, in fact, a form of vernacular art which changed little between 1860 and 1900

Left: **Louis Bernier,
Opéra Comique, 1893.**
*Decoration throughout the
public spaces, as here in the
salon, is lavish.*

Below: **Louis Bernier,
Opéra Comique, 1893.**
*The view from the Presidential
box – traditional gold and red
in temporary contrast with the
latest stage set.*

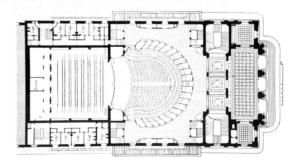

Right: **Louis Bernier,
Opéra Comique, 1893.**
*The entrance level plan:
a sensible division between
stage, auditorium and foyer.*

Left: **Au Petit Versailles du Marais, 1860.** *Painted glass ceilings were an essential part of boutique decoration.*

Left: **Au Petit Versailles du Marais, 1860.** *Eighteenth-century shepherds and shepherdesses provided inspiration for those artists specialising in the decoration of boutiques.*

Left: **Restaurant Chez Julien, 1 rue du Pont Louis-Philippe.** *A quiet pavement for outside lunch, with a medieval church next door and the Seine opposite.*

Below: **Restaurant Chez Julien, 1 rue du Pont Louis-Philippe.** *The ceiling here now provides a rural canopy for urban eating.*

(indeed Au Petit Versailles du Marais, 1 rue Tiron, 4e, dates from 1860, but is illustrated here because it is one of the few boutiques in central Paris still used as a *boulangerie*). However, since *Les décors des boutiques parisiennes* (see Bibliography) was published in 1987, a number of boutiques recorded therein have been allowed to deteriorate, or their decoration has been removed. Chez Julien, 1 rue du Pont Louis-Philippe, 4e, is a former *crémerie* now well preserved as a restaurant.

One of the principal effects of the creation of the Haussmannian boulevards and consequent acceleration of public life was the vast number of cafés established, the majority extending on to the pavement, allowed by 'temporary' licences if the extension was enclosed in glass. By the 1880s there were 30,000 cafés in the city. As early as November 1860, Edmond de Goncourt had been complaining in his diary: *'The home is dying, life is threatening to become public. The club for the upper classes, the café for the lower.'* [5]

In practice there were two grades of café, the first with waiters or waitresses, patronised by bourgeois men, occasionally accompanied by members of their family, but some also frequented by the demi-monde. In the 1898 edition of Baedeker's guide, he wrote, *'the best cafés may with propriety be visited by ladies, but some of those on the north side of boulevards Montmartre and des Italiens should be avoided, as the society there is far*

from select.'[6] There were many small local working-class cafés, run by the owner and his wife, where social life centred round the polished zinc-topped bar, the Parisian equivalent of a village pub: a subject to be considered in more detail in Chapter Seven, 'The Social Aspect'. Representative of a slightly more socially acceptable type of café is Angelina, 226 rue de Rivoli, 1e, which has always been a 'tea room'. Attributed to Edouard Niermans (1859–1928), it has paintings of Provençal landscapes by Heilbronn and was formerly called 'Rumpelmeyer's'.

Restaurants

The French aristocracy ate at home. After the Revolution, their chefs opened restaurants, providing the bourgeoisie with a standard of cooking hitherto unavailable to them: this and the resultant conviviality soon became an important attraction for foreign visitors. By the mid-nineteenth century there were about 2000 restaurants in Paris. The most expensive, mainly around the boulevard des Italiens, were highly fashionable, intimacy offered by their private rooms being an additional attraction. Brasseries (large restaurants originally serving beer and Alsatian food) multiplied after the arrival of refugees from Alsace-Lorraine, annexed by the Germans after the Franco-Prussian war. Two which survive are Le Bofinger, 5 rue de la Bastille, 4e, and Mollard (1895) at 113 rue Saint-Lazare, 8e, the only surviving brasserie by Niermans, where apart from the faience murals, coloured glass lay-lights and bronze grilles, nearly every surface is of mosaic. Niermans specialised in restaurants and other leisure buildings in Paris and the south of France.[7]

The cheapest restaurants, called *'bouillons'*, with shared tables for four or six persons, were patronised by unmarried male workers, students and commuters living in the suburbs. They originally only served broth and *pot-au-feu*: in *L'Oeuvre*, Zola described a student taking the 8-sous 'ordinary', a bowl of broth into which he broke up his bread and a slice of boiled beef and beans served on a plate still wet with washing-up water.[8] Although they existed in the eighteenth century, those now remaining were established during the Belle Epoque. They were mostly quite small and at first no attempt was made at 'decoration', the only fittings being small numbered drawers containing the regular clients' napkins to reduce laundry costs.

The largest and least changed in character is Chartier, 7 rue du Faubourg-Montmartre, 9e (1895), by Edmond Navarre (1848–1937), which has a glass roof and is decorated with just a few mirrors. The tables are still shared and the simple food is served quickly, mainly to students, tourists and elderly Parisians. Other *bouillons* which were much more expensively decorated and now attracting more prosperous customers are Bouillon Racine, 3 rue Racine, 6e (1907) attributed to J. M. Bouvier,[9] with

Above: **attributed to J. M. Bouvier, Restaurant Bouillon Racine, 1907.**
In the main room upstairs the mirrors and window glazing both show an Art Nouveau influence.

Right: **attributed to J. M. Bouvier, Restaurant Bouillon Racine, 1907.**
On the ground floor, mirrors are combined with pâte de verre *floral panels and a mosaic floor.*

Opposite: **attributed to E. Fournier, Restaurant Julien, 1902.** Pâte de verre *panels by Louis Trézel line the restauarant walls*

Below: **attributed to E. Fournier, Restaurant Julien, 1902.** *A mahogany counter by Louis Majorelle sits on the elegant tiled floor.*

Above: **attributed to E. Fournier, Restaurant Julien, 1902.** *Unlike Mollard, the whole interior can be seen as a single space, where the plasterers competed with the painters.*

Below: **attributed to E. Fournier, Restaurant Julien, 1902.** *An appropriate entrance to the most Art Nouveau of bouillons.*

pâte de verre panels (metal paintings on coloured glass) by Louis Trézel, the smallest in scale of the *bouillons*, with décor more typical of the boutiques; and Julien, 16 rue du faubourg-Saint-Denis, 10e (1902), attributed to E. Fournier, the most spacious and conventionally Art Nouveau, also with *pâte de verre* panels by Louis Trézel and a mahogany bar attributed to Louis Majorelle. (Others of similar character are Le Bistro de la Gare, 59 boulevard Montparnasse, 6e, Chardenoux, 1 rue Jules-Vallès, 11e, and Pharamonde, 24 rue de la Grande Truanderie, 1e.)

The most elaborately decorated restaurants of the period are Le Train Bleu in the Gare de Lyon (1901), patronised by the rich travelling on the Blue Train to the south of France, where the architect Marius Toudoire (1852–1922) employed 30 painters to depict towns and regions served by the railway in two huge vaulted rooms with some original furniture and much gold leaf, Mollard (described above) and the infinitely more expensive Lucas-Carton, 9 place de la Madeleine, 8e, with furniture and panelling by Majorelle (but a recent suspended ceiling), and Maxim's, 3 rue Royale, 1e, by Louis Marnez and Alexandre Brosset.

It has only been possible in this chapter to give a selection of the restaurants surviving from the period. (This book is not a restaurant guide, but readers should perhaps be warned that food and service are not always up to the standard of the decorations in a few Belle Epoque restaurants!)

Above: **Marius Toudoire,
Restaurant Le Train
Bleu, 1901.** *The clock,
essential in a railway-station
restaurant, is set in typically
Beaux-Arts joinery.*

Right: **Marius Toudoire,
Restaurant Le Train
Bleu, 1901.** *The vast
heavily decorated halls of Le
Train Bleu are a reminder
of the nouveaux riches who
dined there prior to taking
the night train to the Riviera.*

Above: **Juste Lisch, Hôtel Terminus St-Lazare, 1889.** *Standing opposite the entrance to the station, the hotel was built for the 1889 International Exhibition.*

Right: **Georges Chedanne, former Hôtel Elysée Palace, 1897–9.** *Bacchus, grapevines and Cupids suggest possible delights within.*

Hotels

The word 'hotel' in Paris up to 1789 signified a *hôtel particulier*: a large house occupied by one family, usually separated from the street by a courtyard and stables and with a large garden behind. After the Revolution, these were mainly converted to multiple use, but just as the chefs to the aristocracy had set up restaurants, so their former senior servants were able to run *hôtels à voyageurs*, providing elegant lodgings and good service and food: the latter normally a set meal, a communal *table d'hôte*.

The series of international exhibitions created a demand for much larger 'Palace' hotels, which first appeared during the Second Empire. A brief survey here of some hotels opened between 1889 and 1900 will indicate changes of taste during this period.

The Hôtel Terminus (now Concorde Saint-Lazare) of 1889 by Juste Lisch (1828–1910) is an island block standing in the forecourt of the station – which Lisch was then extending – connected directly to the station's main concourse by a pedestrian bridge. The hotel was straightforwardly planned: bedrooms around the perimeter – with some smaller rooms looking into internal courts – and a central hall three storeys high, originally containing a staircase connecting the two levels of access. The hall had arcades of twin cast-iron columns supporting semi-circular arches. There were originally 300 bedrooms (later increased by conversion of the mezzanine floor) served by two

lifts; the larger bedrooms had dressing rooms en suite: there were eight WCs per floor. The conservative external treatment follows the Haussmannian pattern of repetitious narrow bays, broken only by a central pavilion, but with a total of nine floors including the basement kitchens and the top-lit servants' rooms in the roof space. In the entrance hall, red granite columns with bronze Corinthian capitals supported a riveted cast-iron ceiling with decorative mosaic panels. The somewhat industrial nature of the interiors was perhaps in keeping with the contemporaneous International Exhibition's 'triumph of iron'.

Nothing could be more different from these than the interiors of the Ritz, 1896, by Charles Frédéric Mewès (1858–1928), a much smaller hotel, originally about eighty rooms but later enlarged, intended for the very rich and built behind a facade in the place Vendôme erected by Jules Hardouin-Mansart in 1699–1720. Mewès' only alteration to the front was to open up three blank arches to provide access to a porte-cochère. The eighteenth-century rooms at the front were retained for the grandest suites; by reducing storey heights for the remainder it was possible to erect a rear wing flanking a formal garden and having a total height of eight floors yet invisible from the place Vendôme. The design of the garden and interiors was based on eighteenth-century precedent: a return to the *hôtels particuliers* from which the 'Palaces' were descended. The furniture, silver

Left: **Georges Chedanne, former Hôtel Elysée Palace, 1897–9.** *Now a bank, what was formerly the grandest of the 'Palace' hotels has an elaborately sculptured front elevation, the whole enriched by high-quality decorative carving.*

Below: **Georges Chedanne, former Hôtel Elysée Palace, 1897–9.** *Ground-floor plan: a triumph of separating circulation for different uses.*

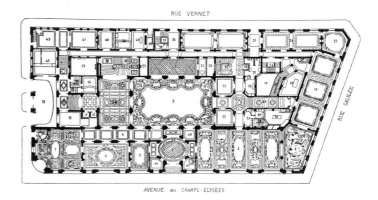

and linen were specially made, mostly in *Régence* style, the dining room had a carpet woven to a design based on an old engraving, the white panelled bedrooms all had their own bathrooms.

The area around the place Vendôme was now changing to business use. The Champs-Elysées on the other hand, where the 400-bedroom Elysée Palace, 1897–9, by Georges Chedanne (1861–1940) was situated, is in the 8th *arrondissement* – at that time the most fashionable residentially in Paris. Like the Ritz, the hotel's restaurant was consequently much used by Parisian society. Now the Banque Commercial de France, the hotel occupied a rectangular island site (like the Terminus Saint-Lazare) which allowed three separate entrances: the main social entrance in the centre of the Champs-Elysées frontage; a covered porte-cochère at the side where those checking in could go straight up to their rooms, by lift, without being seen in their travelling clothes by patrons in the main salons; and finally, an even more discreet entrance at the back for VIPs going to parties in the private dining rooms. A study of the ground-floor plan shows Beaux-Arts planning principles adapted perfectly to modern and complicated functional requirements.

It is very unfortunate that use as a hotel did not survive the First World War: this building was one of the masterpieces of the Belle Epoque and in every respect fit for its purpose. As at the Ritz, many rooms were decorated in a fairly restrained

eighteenth-century style, but the central hall and restaurant were more original: here artists from the Ecole des Beaux-Arts were employed, providing ceiling paintings, stained glass and Rococo-inspired plaster reliefs which were all firmly controlled by Chedanne's guiding hand and thereby related to the architectural whole. It is recorded, for example, that the plaster reliefs of *L'Histoire de Psyché* in the grand hall were thought out by the architect in the smallest detail.[10]

The 'Palace' hotels, like the banks and department stores, required a new design skill from their architects, one not taught at the Ecole des Beaux-Arts: the integration within the structure of mechanical and electrical services. An article in *La construction moderne* referred to Chedanne's minute studies for these.[11]

The exterior of the Elysée Palace departs much further from traditional precedent. The ground floor has elliptically arched windows alternating with narrower bays having small rectangular windows with circular *oeil-de-boeuf* windows over. Then comes a surprise: the smaller bays have corbels which support 'bow-windows' three storeys high, above which are two-storey Corinthian aedicules with segmental pediments. The bays between are comparatively plain: thus the principal vertical accents, not being above the ground floor arched windows as one would expect, provide a diagonal Rococo movement emphasised at the left-hand corner, where twin aedicules build up to another

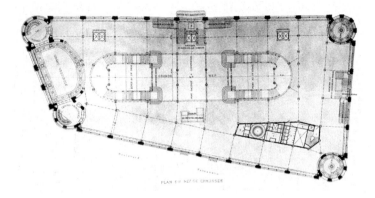

PLAN DU REZ-DE-CHAUSSEE

pediment curved on both plan and elevation, originally containing a sculpture by Boutry of *'Femmes Nues à leur Toilette'*, now removed presumably as being unsuited to a bank, even if one sited in the Elysian fields. At least three other sculptors were employed by Chedanne: the front elevation is much enriched by playing Cupids and by trailing garlands draped over windows, both popular motifs at the time, reflecting discontent with industrialisation and nostalgia for a largely imaginary past.

Many otherwise dull Belle Epoque buildings are enlivened by decorative sculpture of a high standard, the limestone used was ideal for delicate carving and achieved a unity of form and decoration unequalled in any later architecture. (Rodin, recognised at the time as the greatest sculptor of the age, preferred free-standing figures in bronze. The only exception, entrance doors for the Musée des Arts Décoratifs, were never used.) The increased elaboration of street architecture, of which the decorative sculpture was an essential part, may be read as a celebration of the city's public life. The ashlar stonework was mechanically cut into *'lits'* up to 1 metre high and 2.3 metres long by the full wall thickness (usually half a metre), an early example of prefabrication.

The Palais d'Orsay, 1900 by Victor Laloux (1850–1937), now part of the Musée d'Orsay, was also finished in time for the 1900 Exhibition, but although its interiors were also of eighteenth-century derivation, it has more in common with the Terminus Saint-Lazare in that, being a railway hotel, it catered for short-stay visitors and its public rooms were mainly used for middle-class functions including balls and commercial dinners. The dining and ballrooms can still be seen by visitors to the museum: here it is again recorded that the architect was concerned with every detail of the decoration.

Other 'Palace' hotels still in use are the Westminster, 1907 (M. Aubertin), the Lutétia, 1910 (H. Tauzin and L.-H. Boileau) and the Plaza-Athénée, 1911 (J. Lefevre). The Regina, 1903 (A. Sibien), the Meurice, 1908–10 (H.-P. Nénot) and the Crillon, 1908 (W. A. Destailleur) were all built behind existing facades. Many of the interiors have been redecorated.

The *Grands Magasins*

Of more economic and social importance than the small boutiques already described were the *Grands Magasins* or department stores, where married women and their daughters could pass their time 'just looking': respectable women couldn't go to cafés or restaurants without male chaperones. The bourgeois, newly enriched by industrialisation and property investment, needed to display their wealth by fashion and other forms of conspicuous consumption, and the *Grands Magasins* fulfilled this need by an overwhelming display of finished products that could be taken away immediately. By allowing free entry without obligation to buy, the experience of shopping was revolutionised, becoming for most women their principal leisure activity. They also marketed the bourgeois lifestyle, encouraging the less advantaged to aspire to its way of life.

These cathedrals of modern commerce, as Zola called them in his novel *Au Bonheur des Dames*, needed the assistance of new structural means of enclosing large internal spaces where, with the aid of artificial light and heat, unhurried customers could linger and be seduced by display techniques into buying items they hadn't realised they required. For this purpose one or more large naves (in modern parlance 'atriums'), filled with goods, colour and light, were surrounded by galleries to entice shoppers to explore the upper storeys. Clear access to the upper floors was therefore essential, either by open lifts or a grand staircase on which to see and be seen.

The principal early department store is Au Bon Marché, designed by Alexandre Laplanche in 1869 and extended in 1872–4 by Louis-Charles Boileau with Gustave Eiffel, on which (and its owners the Boucicaults) Zola based *Au Bonheur des Dames*. Au Printemps, rebuilt after a fire in 1881 by Paul Sédille, and its eastern extension by René Binet, were of much greater architectural distinction, but have unfortunately been considerably altered to provide more sales space: the naves have been filled in and additional storeys have been added.

Right: **Paul Sédille,
Au Printemps, 1881–5.**
*Decorative ironwork through-
out enhanced the excitement
of goods and movement.*

The corner domes and the use of external mosaic decoration, as well as the decorative ironwork internally (now destroyed) were influential in the design of La Samaritaine, 1905–10, which retains its central hall. Although closed at the time of writing, because of this building's exceptional technical as well as decorative interest it will be discussed in detail in Chapter Five, 'The Triumph of Iron'. Both Binet and Ferdinand Chanut, who extended the Galeries Lafayette in 1910–12, were enthusiastic admirers of Middle Eastern architecture, thereby able to endow their interiors with a suitably exotic bazaar-like quality. Chanut's circular hall – constructed in concrete, with balustrades by Majorelle and a glazed dome – survives but its grand stair from ground to first floors was demolished in 1974.

Covered markets were the principal retail venue for family food shopping, but the construction of these and of the covered arcades of small shops called *passages* date almost entirely from before the Belle Epoque.[12]

Banks

The private banks established in the eighteenth and nineteenth centuries were located in the *hôtels particuliers* of their proprietors. The Banque de France, created in 1800, was installed in the Hôtel de la Vrillière (designed by François Mansart in 1635) and has been altered and extended many times since. The industrial revolution created the need for new banks, accepting deposits from the thriving new industries and giving short-term credit to animate the financial market. During the Second Empire, the building works initiated by the Emperor under Haussmann's direction became a major source of investment. The banks quickly became intermediaries between *rentiers* and entrepreneurs needing capital, as well as dealing with small savers investing for their old age at a time when there were no retirement pensions. They also provided safe deposits for legal documents.

Banks had to convey to their customers both power and security, as well as needing to be fire-resistant for the storage of title documents and archives. Stone was therefore the principal building material and iron was only noticeably used for the construction of glazed roofs over banking halls, reliance on electric lighting not yet having become commonplace. In the earlier banks, the banking hall floors were also sometimes glazed to admit daylight to the lobbies of strong-rooms below. The hall's main artificial lighting was generally installed in the space, required for thermal insulation, between the outer roof glazing and the internal decorative lay-light; the hall was heated so that the customers, mostly male since women's financial affairs were handled by their husbands, could sit in the comfortable chairs and read the newspapers provided, there being few men's clubs of the English type.

Opposite: **E.-J. Corroyer, Comptoir d'Escompte, 1878–80.** *The portico completely fills the end of the side street by which the bank is approached; the contrast of solid and void, semi-circles and triangles create a true masterpiece of Beaux-Arts composition.*

Left: **J.-M. Cassien-Bernard and Paul Friesé, former Banque Suisse et Française, 1908.** *The demi-columns, three storeys high above a rusticated base, identify this as a typical bank.*

The headquarters of the Comptoir d'Escompte, 14 rue Bergère, 9e, 1878–80 by E.-J. Corroyer (1837–1904), extended 1894 by F. Constant-Bernard (1861–1930), now the Banque Nationale de Paris, is planned as offices around a top-lit rectangular banking hall and a small courtyard behind, with a monumental staircase – whose vaulted ceiling, walls and floor are all decorated with mosaic featuring birds and foliage designed by Charles Lameire – giving access to directors' offices on the first floor. The banking hall, heated by warm air, has a glazed floor to provide daylight to the basement documents storage: modernity also had to be part of the 'image'. The entrance is asymmetrically placed so that its portico, with tower over, dominates the vista down the side street, rue Rougemont, by which it is approached from the boulevard Poissonière. Corroyer had been a pupil of Viollet-le-Duc and restored the cathedral at Soissons and the abbey of Saint-Michel: this rationalist and medieval influence can be seen in the construction and composition, rendering this building less overtly classical than the majority of later banks.

The Banque Suisse et Française on the corner of rue Lafayette and rue Pillet-Will, 9e, 1908, by J.-M. Cassien-Bernard (1848–1926) and Paul Friesé (1851–1917) used Beaux-Arts planning principles on a triangular site, with a circular entrance hall leading to a hexagonal lobby, oval staircase and a fairly small *'hall du public'* or atrium. It is included here because the equally

Beaux-Arts external treatment, with its Ionic demi-columns, heavy stone cornice and dormers and slightly Baroque entrance, represents the preferred style for banks. It is untypical of Friesé and suggests that Cassien-Bernard, a former Premier Second Prix de Rome, was responsible for the design and that Friesé provided his greater practical experience on this, their only collaboration. The building is now (2006) being converted into a hotel.

The head office of the Société Générale, 29 boulevard Haussmann, 9e, was a conversion by Jacques Hermant (1855–1930) started in 1906–12 and completed in 1919, of a triangular city block that had been built as a series of apartment buildings behind a facade complying with the Haussmannian ordinance for buildings adjoining the Opéra, produced by Rohault de Fleury in 1860. Hermant kept only the facade, inserting a pedimented pavilion in the centre of the boulevard Haussmann frontage to mark the bank's entrance. This leads into a curved lobby, the curve enabling him to set up a cross axis at an angle to the entrance facade on which the staircase and banking hall could be aligned. The latter has one straight side, two concave and one convex, joined by small corner bays, above which glazed pendentives, between the four main bays, rise to a circular glazed dome.

The hall is one of Paris's great interiors, with its coloured glass, sculpted bronzes and mosaic floor. Five basements were

Above: **Jacques Hermant,
Société Générale, 1906
−19.** *The banking hall in
its heyday, a composition in
bronze, marble, mosaic and
coloured glass.*

Right: **Jacques Hermant,
Société Générale, 1906
−19.** *Hermant inserted this
pedimented pavilion into the
centre of a Haussmannian
'ordinance' facade to mark
the bank's entrance.*

constructed entirely in reinforced concrete, thereby maximising plan area available for the four levels of safe deposits, compared with the thick walls which traditional masonry would have required. The upper floors of perimeter offices are a very early example of the 'open-plan', any partitions being non-structural. (Permission was not given to photograph the banking hall for this book and an archive photograph has been used.)

The greatly increased elaboration of structure and mechanical services compared with earlier in the nineteenth century is a feature of the Samaritaine and the headquarters of the Société Générale, as may be seen from a talk given by Jacques Hermant in 1912, when in addition to crediting the sculptor J. Luc, he mentioned the designers of the reinforced-concrete structure, mechanical and electrical services, the metal vaulting of the banking hall, wrought iron balustrades, bronze medallions, stained glass, mosaics and internal relief sculptures.

Conclusion

Despite Paris's reputation for feminine glamour mentioned at the beginning of this chapter, department stores are the only building type included in it which were freely available to 'respectable' bourgeois women without chaperones. Their place was in the home, and the *immeubles* or apartment blocks that housed the bourgeois families, the subject of the next chapter, were the most important building type in Paris in the nineteenth and early twentieth centuries. Technically they provided both functionalism and flexibility, environmentally their extent is such that they still dominate most of Paris's 20 *arrondissements*.

1   New theatres built during the Third Republic include: Théâtre de la Renaissance, 1873 (C. de Lalande); Bouffes du Nord, 1876 (E. Lemenil); Antoine, 1880 (M. Deslignières: as Comédie Parisienne); Marigny, 1883, as a Panorama (C. Garnier), 1893, as a music hall (Niermans); Montparnasse, 1886 (Peignet and Marnez); Casino de Paris, 1890 (E. Niermans), altered in the 1920s; Paris (originally Nouveau Théâtre), 1891, altered in 1906 and 1955; L'Athénée, 1894 (L. Fouquiau); Théâtre Français: rebuilt 1900 after fire (J. Guadet), altered 1974; Théâtre Recamier, 1908 (C. Blondel).

2   Competition entries for the Opéra Comique by 30 architects, mostly similar in style to Bernier's, are illustrated in *L'Architecture*, 1893, pp 319 et seq.

3   Karl Baedeker, *Paris and Environs*, 13th revised edition, Karl Baedeker, Leipzig, 1898 (printed as English and French editions) pp 34–5.

4   Richard Thomson, *Seurat*, Phaidon, Oxford, 1985, p 221.

5   E. and J. de Goncourt, translated by Robert Baldick, *Pages from the Goncourt Journal*, Oxford University Press, London and New York, 1962, p 53.

6   Karl Baedeker, *op cit*, p 18.

7   Jean-François Pinchon, *Edouard Niermans, Architecte de la Café-Society*, Mardaga, Liège, 1991.

8   Emile Zola, *L'Oeuvre*, translated as *The Masterpiece* by Thomas Walton, Paul Elek, London and New York, 1950, p 77.

9   Four architects with the surname 'Bouvier' are listed in the *Dictionnaire des constructions élevées à Paris aux XIXe et XXe siècles 1876–99*. It has so far been impossible to obtain their birthdates, an indication of the difficulties of obtaining information on the 4871 architects listed in that work experienced by its indefatigable authors.

10 *La construction moderne*, 31 mars 1900: '*Si chacun des artistes que nous avons cités a en sa large part d'initiative, il n'en est pas moins vrai que la direction suprême était fournie par l'architecte, et que le thème de chaque motif était donné par lui. Trop souvent on laisse liberté entière aux sculpteurs et aux peintres, de là les disparates parfois choquants. M. Chedanne n'a pas voulu qu'il en fut ainsi, et les nombreuses études dont ses cartons sont pleins, témoignent de la part qu'il a prise à la composition de tous les oeuvres, qui se marient si heureusement avec le cadre architectural qu'il leur a donné.*'

Also article by V. Champier on Chedanne's hotel Dehaynin (since demolished) in *Revue des Arts Décoratifs*, 1901, pp 378–86, '*Tous composés, dessinés avec un soin scrupuleux par M. Chedanne*' [listing sculpture, paintings, wrought iron, window ironmongery, carpets].

11 *La construction moderne*, 21 mai 1900, '*Les installations mécaniques et techniques jouent un grand rôle dans le fonctionnement de cet hôtel, aussi la force motrice et électrique est-elle considérable. Tous les détails de ces services ont été étudiés par l'architecte qui a voulu en connaître lui-même le fonctionnement, afin d'être, jusque dans les plus petits détails, le maître de l'oeuvre.*'

12 See Paul Chemetov and Bernard Marrey, *Architectures à Paris 1848–1914*, Bordas, Paris, 1984, for complete lists of *passages*, p 18, and markets, p 42.

3 The Bourgeois Home
Private Life

Rentiers and Their Families

In Paris, as in most European cities, the middle class had originally lived in narrow terrace houses 'over the shop' on the medieval principle, with servants and apprentices living in. When Paris became more heavily populated after the death of Louis XIV in 1715, the court moving there from Versailles, the *immeuble de rapport* – consisting of superimposed apartments built to rent – was invented. The new bourgeois, who became the ruling class during the Third Republic, were mostly *rentiers* living mainly on investments and, although these may have been in property, with the exception of the most successful their financial position was usually too precarious to enable them to build individual houses (*hôtels particuliers*).

The demand for housing in Paris during the nineteenth century came from a socially mobile middle class, who wished to rent an unfurnished apartment, taking their movable furniture (*meubles*) with them when they moved on to something grander. The building was provided by the property developer and his architect, the furnishings by the tenant and his *tapissier-décorateur*, allowing the creation of an individual environment within a standardised system.

The best description of life in an apartment house in the years immediately before the Belle Epoque is Zola's novel *Pot-Bouille* written in 1882,[1] which emphasised the importance of keeping up appearances. The greatest expenditure was given to the facade and main staircase, although even here imitation marble was used, while cast-iron balustrades were treated to resemble old silver and bronze. Within the apartments, only the salons, used for entertainment, usually had plaster panelling, sometimes gilded. The remaining rooms, depending on the tenants' taste and finances, were usually treated much more simply, generally with patterned wallpaper.

The bourgeoisie were conscious of their recent ascent in society and anxious to consolidate their position by adopting the correct social habits. In *Usages du monde*, Baronne Staffe's guide to social behaviour, which had reached 105 editions by 1896, she counselled that at a time of rapid social rise it was as well for all classes to acquire good manners when young, in order to be equal to the demands of their next position, while also emphasising the importance of a happy family life.[2] It will be seen in this chapter that the apartment illustrates the successful establishment of the bourgeoisie and its consequent ease during the Belle Epoque, but that the apartment remained mainly a female preserve.

The Apartment

The *appartement* was introduced to France at Chambord in 1591 by Domenico da Cortona and was derived from the planning of

Above: **Charles Lefebvre, 239 boulevard Péreire, 1897.** *A typical apartment block of the late Belle Epoque period, with the upper apartments now the most important while the first floor is reduced to little more than a mezzanine over the ground-floor shops.*

Lorenzo de Medici's villa at Poggio a Caiano, remodelled by Giuliano da Sangallo in 1480.[3] The word comes from the Italian *a parte* (separate) and Chambord consisted of separate *appartements* grouped around a central hall, each containing a large room or *salle*, two smaller rooms and a closet (smaller apartments of one or two rooms were provided for members of the court). This unit was to be the basis of French aristocratic planning, both for chateaux and town houses, for the next 270 years, each principal member of the family occupying an apartment. The rooms were planned en suite, connected by a continuous line *(enfilade)* of double doors.

An early type of *immeuble*, such as that described by Proust in *Le Côté de Guermantes*, had a mixed population, with bourgeois tenants, shops and workrooms between street and court and an aristocratic family in the *hôtel* (probably older) behind. As already mentioned in Chapter One, segregation became largely geographical, with fashionable 'west-end' districts, petits-bourgeois in the north and south, and the more fortunate members of the working class in the outer eastern *arrondissements*, although even the most prosperous areas had back streets where tradesmen providing local services lived. During the Third Republic, the centre became increasingly commercial, but apartments in middle-class blocks were frequently used as professional offices and strict segregation by use did not exist.

The apartment floors were originally graded in value depending on the number of stairs to be climbed: this enabled storey heights and window sizes to be graded also, as in the Renaissance palace, with the first floor the *étage noble*. With increased traffic pollution the upper floors increased in value, especially after the introduction of lifts in the 1880s. The comparative equalisation of floors facilitated the use of mass-produced windows: only one example of how industrialisation speeded the massive building programme; others included the production of finished masonry blocks off-site, standardised services and mechanised site organisation.

As the rate of building increased and economic factors began to determine the building form, investors grouped together to purchase wider sites, facilitating the provision of two flats on each floor, both facing the street and thus of equal value (on a narrow site one would have to be at the back). The provision of a single apartment per floor was only economically feasible in the most expensive blocks, as the cost of a lift and concierge otherwise needed to be shared by as many tenants as possible. From the late 1870s onwards the larger blocks were mostly built by insurance companies: a typical example of an early Belle Epoque *immeuble* is 30 avenue de Villiers, 17e, 1891, architect Juste Lisch (1828–1910). The stairwell contains a lift in a metal cage: some later blocks have a separate lift shaft enclosed with masonry, but with metal gates. Hector Guimard installed the

Right: **Juste Lisch, 30
avenue de Villiers, 1891.**
*Virtually the standard plan
from the 1880s onwards, with
the lift in the stairwell.*

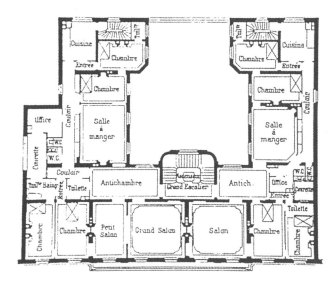

first glazed lift in his own house, because he said he didn't want to put his guests in a cage like animals.

Each flat has a tripartite arrangement of a salon next to the entrance, husband and wife's bed-sitting rooms facing the avenue (these three rooms being traditionally used for entertaining) and the family rooms (dining room, kitchen and children's bedrooms) in the rear wings overlooking the court. This block of 12 apartments, including two on the ground floor as this was a purely residential area, had 34 maids' bedrooms (sharing two WCs) in the roof. The external treatment (see Chapter One) is conservative for its date: its repetitive nature is relieved mainly by fairly chunky classical detailing, but the Baroque-inspired lintels at third-floor level are more typical of the Second Empire. Note the small rooflights indicating the maids' bedrooms.

Regulations introduced in 1884 fixed a minimum size of court in relation to the height of the block, and the elevations facing onto the court were frequently finished with white glazed tiles or bricks to reflect light into the family rooms. Kitchens and WCs were situated on courts or *courettes* (small light wells), which provided them with their only ventilation, drainage pipes being external. *Courettes* had to have a minimum area of four square metres under the regulations of 1884 if lighting only WCs and corridors, nine square metres if lighting kitchens – increased to eight and 15 respectively in 1902.

Good daylighting for dining rooms facing onto the inner courts was particularly desirable, as these were often used as the children's play room as well as for family lunch. At this time, lunch was usually the leftovers from the previous day's dinner, eaten cold and placed on the table for the family to help themselves. By 1900, lunch was at midday (it had been at 11 am in 1880) and dinner parties at 7 pm, but these got later as one went up the social scale. In 1903, in an article on '*the Salon of Her Imperial Highness the Princesse Mathilde*', Proust remarked that this was one of the few houses in Paris to which one was invited as early as 7.30.[4] Dinner parties were the only times when bourgeois couples entertained together: it was on these occasions that the double doors were thrown open.

Women and the Family

The husband's study or bed-sitting room could be used by male guests smoking after dinner. The minority of men who entertained business acquaintances at home usually did so in a work room next to the entrance hall. Up to the 1880s husbands had not been expected to be concerned with the daily life of the home. Wives did not work: their duty was to look after their home and family and make life agreeable for their husband. In return, they had a greater degree of freedom than before marriage. They still could not go to the theatre or a restaurant unless chaperoned

Opposite and below:
Charles Plumet, 21 boulevard Lannes, 1905–6. *The elevation clearly reflects the internal floor-plan (with its dining room and salon that can be used as one large living room), while the semi-circular gables relate it to the earlier studio house next door. The dormer windows of the former maids' rooms have been enlarged to make a penthouse flat.*

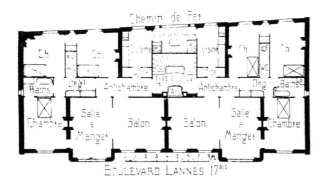

by their husband, father or brother, but in addition to shopping and churchgoing, bourgeois women had their own social rite to keep them in touch with others of their class: the *Jour*.

Each lady chose a day when she would be 'at home' to her friends in the late afternoon: she then dispensed tea in the salon (which even in the smallest of petit-bourgeois apartments therefore had to be the most expensively furnished room, even if only used for this purpose), assisted by her daughter if she had one of suitable age. When it was not her 'day' she would try to attend as many other tea parties as possible, ensuring that before the installation of telephones the latest news circulated quickly. As each 'tea' was only a short halt the ladies kept their hats on, giving the salons, Proust noted, an outdoor air.[5]

The *Jour* should not, of course, be confused with the 'Salon' held by aristocratic and haute-bourgeoise ladies, to which men were invited. This historic conversational institution also flourished in intellectual circles, notable examples being the weekly 'evenings' held by Mallarmé, the Goncourts and Georges Charpentier. Alphonse Daudet, who attended the latter, wrote a satirical essay, 'Les salons bourgeois', in 1878, describing *'salons comiques'*. These were often organised by professional men wishing to extend their practices by social contact, or given by parents with daughters of marriageable age – described by Zola in *Pot-Bouille* as having *'a ravenous appetite for sons-in-law'*.[6]

State-supported secondary education for women was established in 1880. This was largely an anti-clerical measure, girls being otherwise educated, if at all, in church schools, where they were trained to be wives and mothers. As a result, many chose to work – for example, as primary school teachers – rather than marry, and the government became concerned at the decline in the birth-rate. The marriage rate was one of the lowest in Europe and only a third of married couples had children.

The first international congress on women's rights was held in Paris in 1889 and others followed. The feminist journal *La Fronde* first appeared in 1897. The feminists' principal aims were teaching childcare to poor women, helping widows, orphans and prostitutes, and trying to give wives some legal control over family finance. Women were given the right to initiate divorce proceedings in 1884, but few took advantage of this as divorced women were not socially acceptable (women didn't get the vote until after the Second World War). The craze for cycling (many women cyclists even wore bloomers, known as 'rational dress') was only one example of the 'woman question' causing concern to all right-thinking family men: cycling gave them independence. The officially organised crafts movement of the 1890s encouraged women's participation in order to emphasise their place within the home, rather than taking up a profession. The first Exhibition of the Arts of Woman held in 1892 celebrated *'women from all enlightened classes of society who charm their leisure hours with the artistry of delicate needlework'*.[7]

Changes in Social Habits and Apartment Planning

In its aristocratic origin, husband and wife each had their own apartment, while the children were in separate nurseries, taken to see their mother once a day. The nineteenth-century apartment shows how the successful middle class aped aristocratic customs during the Second Empire, but by the Belle Epoque the apartment plan had changed to reflect the increased importance of children within the home and the husband's assumption of a social role within the family. The middle-class ascendancy meant that they no longer needed to defer to aristocratic precedent and the religious revival (largely a reaction to the Commune) encouraged family values. The home became a symbol of the stability and order which the Third Republic sought to establish. The pressures of social and business competition in a rapidly expanding metropolis no doubt resulted in drawing the family closer together, with increasing emphasis on the wife's role.

A comparison of the plans of 30 avenue de Villiers (slightly old-fashioned for 1891) with those of 21 (originally *17bis*) boulevard Lannes, 16e, 1905–6 by Charles Plumet (1861–1928), shows the effect of this social change: the latter being slightly smaller flats overlooking the Bois de Boulogne. The salon and dining room are now joined by wide folding doors, forming a

combined family living room. Children are now more important in the family than the entertainment of guests, and their bedrooms immediately adjoin those of their parents, who share a room. The plan of boulevard Lannes is recognisable to us as that of a modern block: it represents a less formal way of life than that of avenue de Villiers and this greater ease is reflected in Plumet's elevational treatment. It is clear that all floors are of equal importance, the overall design reflects the plan and the introduction of arched openings lightens the general effect.

Interior and Exterior

The interiors painted by Vuillard and Bonnard show a peaceful self-absorbed world, which seems far from the new Paris that succeeded the Prussian blockade and the Commune. The alchemy they learnt from Chardin and Vermeer in the treatment of familiar objects reminds us that a large proportion of Parisian citizens had grown up in the country, and would wish to retreat from the chaos of the industrialised city to the security of customary things whenever they could. Henri Havard, Inspecteur Général des Beaux-Arts, whose books on furniture and decoration were officially approved by the Third Republic, thought that decoration should provide repose for the spirit as well as pleasure for the eyes.[8] The country hearth, source of warmth and originally also of light, was replaced as the family centre by the dining-room

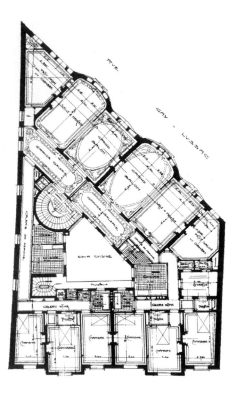

Left: **François Saulnier,
15 rue Gay-Lussac, 1912.**
*The standard plan adapted to
an irregular site – here the lift
is in an enclosed shaft.*

table with its hanging lamp. Oil lamps had largely replaced candles in the nineteenth century and gas was now widely used, being replaced by electricity from about 1910.

Away from the tree-lined boulevards, most rooms in the new tall apartment blocks looked onto narrow streets and courtyards; from the lower floors it is often difficult to see the sky. The lace curtains diffused the light falling on patterned walls creating a world of shade. (The interest of the Impressionists in shadows and their colours was dispensed with by the later painters of interiors, where the whole room was in shade.) These interiors show people in an environment created by themselves by means of décor and belongings: a class socially and environmentally mobile, needing the reassurance and immutability that accumulated personal possessions could provide.

This was a society in which the Goncourt brothers, in their writings and the decoration of their home,[9] revealed the nervous relationship between the self and its internal environment. In the same vein Proust wrote that the things in his room in Paris were 'an enlargement of myself' and that *'we alone, by our belief that they have an existence of their own, can give to certain things we see a soul which they afterwards keep and which they develop in our minds'*.[10] Apart from the Nabis, the greatest artistic manifestations of this life centred within the Parisian home are probably the chamber music of Fauré and Debussy and Symbolist literature: Mallarmé's influence was disseminated not only by his poetry but also by his 'Tuesdays' in the rue de Rome.

The constriction of small shadowy rooms was partly overcome by various means. One has already been referred to: the *enfilade*. In addition, this provided functional flexibility: when doors were closed individual members of a family could have privacy and rooms could more easily be heated; when open, the connected rooms could be read as a single space. This effect was emphasised towards the end of the century, when the doors were frequently glazed, with a mirror at the end of the vista. Mirrored false doors were also added to formalise a room and increase apparent size. Henri Havard, writing in *Les arts de l'ameublement*, thought that the degree of cheerfulness in a room was directly related to the number of real and apparent openings.[11] Another essential feature was the *porte-fenêtre*, inward-opening windows reaching to the floor with a balcony or guard-railing, thereby lighting the floor and linking interior and exterior. The *portes-fenêtres* being the same width as internal double doors, the city became an external room.

Unlike the traditional window with a waist-high sill, where one views the world but remains cut off from it, the *porte-fenêtre*, especially with a balcony, encouraged the occupant to look down into the street or boulevard. While still an onlooker, he became closer to the life observed below. The ambivalence of the

Left: **Clément Feuguer, 31 avenue Félix-Faure, 1912.** *A well-proportioned and highly decorated stone facing to a petit-bourgeois immeuble.*

onlooker is an essential feature of Caillebotte's paintings of views from balconies, which take into account the same vertiginous aerial perspective that must also have influenced the high-level townscapes by Monet and Pissarro.

Bourgeois and Petit-Bourgeois

The difference between bourgeois and petit-bourgeois apartments was one mainly of accommodation size and services provided; it was important that class difference should not be obvious externally. Two *immeubles* built in 1912 are illustrated here, the facades of both displaying the elaborately modelled treatment generally thought typical of the Belle Epoque. (This will be discussed in more detail in Chapter Six.) During the Second Empire the cheaper blocks had frequently been barrack-like in appearance, but in the Belle Epoque, Paris had become sufficiently prosperous for the petit-bourgeois to expect and afford the latest in Rococo-inspired external decoration.

15 rue Gay-Lussac, 5e, by François Saulnier (*b* 1875) is an example of a fairly expensive block with two apartments per floor, adapted to an irregular site, a planning problem resulting from many of the Haussmannian avenues being positioned at an angle to existing street patterns. Here, its being between two streets made a large courtyard unnecessary, as all main rooms could face outwards. The late date is reflected not only in the provision of a separate lift shaft and a family bathroom, but in the integration of *galerie*, salon and dining room into a single unit by sliding-folding doors – entertaining and family rooms are no longer separated.

The adjacent position of the main bedroom, which could double as a boudoir, is a relic of the aristocratic *chambre de parade* (a principal bedroom in which visitors were received), which by now would have disappeared from less expensive blocks. A service stair still connects kitchens with maids' attic bedrooms. The size of the children's rooms reflects the greater attention now paid to them, older children each having their own room capable of use as a study. The *office*, or pantry, acts as a barrier to prevent cooking smells penetrating into the apartment. The exterior view (see Chapter One) shows the contrast in scale and decorative treatment with the adjacent Second Empire buildings. The external emphasis on the fifth floor reflects its now fashionable status and the first floor, by now the least desirable, is really only a mezzanine, but all floors have equal storey heights.

Turning to a petit-bourgeois block, 31 avenue Félix-Faure, 15e, by Clément Feuguer, on a large site where the three main apartments face the avenue and another three look into the court behind, the better flats are not dissimilar from those in more fashionable blocks, except for the absence of lifts, bathrooms and service stairs. They also have smaller rooms: the dining rooms are

about 4.3 x 3.6 metres compared with 6.9 x 4.3 metres in the Saulnier block. In the cheaper flats behind, the double living room is omitted.

To our eyes, the elaborately sculptured elevation contrasts strangely with the lack of amenities and the confined position of the rear flats, which have a view solely of the opposite wall only seven metres away. Outward appearances were still the most important consideration. Incidentally, Feuguer, probably because his large practice was confined to the less fashionable districts, is one of many architects of the period not mentioned in standard history books. He did not study at the Ecole des Beaux-Arts and his birth and death dates appear unrecorded.

Decoration: True and False Luxury

The nineteenth century was marked by very great social mobility, with wealth acquired by a class with no tradition of culture, but wishing to exhibit its new status and distinguish itself from the class out of which it had arisen. This could most easily be achieved both inside and outside the home by ornamental richness. The neo-classical tradition's aristocratic restraint did not appeal to the new rich and only returned to fashion after 1900.

The 'cluttered' look was at its height about 1885–90, with draped chimneypieces and door curtains. Luxury was divided by writers of the time into *le mauvaix luxe* and *le véritable luxe*. False luxury (kitsch) was concerned primarily with ostentation, whereas true luxury was considered to give an interior an agreeable aspect. The return to purer styles of decoration was started by the Goncourt brothers in the 1870s, and a bedroom in pure Empire style was shown at the Exhibition of 1889. Slightly later, Proust described how a single rose in a long-necked crystal vase replaced the profusion of flowers in Mme Swann's salon, with walls painted white instead of sombre colours and curtains sprinkled with Louis XV garlands in place of Chinese dragons.[12] By 1900 period reproduction was no longer so much in fashion and a simplified version of Art Nouveau was in vogue. A similar simplification was taking place in women's dress.

The development of fibrous plaster, invented in 1845, together with the industrialised standardisation of carpentry and joinery, facilitated the mass reproduction of moulded motifs once the domain of only the most talented craftsmen. The middle classes could, within their limited financial resources, enjoy what they believed to be the luxury of highly decorated interiors, only available before to the very rich. Mechanical duplication on this scale could only result in thoughtless debasement, whether of historical styles or of Art Nouveau and other new modes. Objects that had once emanated organically from production and use were now trivialised by mimicry. More important still was the sterilisation of artistic invention, which played a critical part in the trend to reduce all productive activities to the status of making a living – coming to define labour as the opposite of play. Work and leisure were divorced, making each less enjoyable and adding to the breakdown in social cohesion resulting from the Commune and its aftermath.

Masters and Servants

The apartment building shows how a combination of social and spatial separation could alienate servants and employers. In 1906 there were 206,000 servants in Paris, 11 per cent of the population, five-sixths of them female. In the aristocratic *appartement* servants were near at hand, in vestibules adjoining the main rooms, ready to be summoned by a hand-bell. With the introduction of electric bells, however, in 1885, servants were relegated to the kitchen by day and climbed the back stairs to the attics at night. There they slept in small cubicles lit by rooflights, without washing facilities other than a communal tap and with one Asiatic WC shared by a dozen or more maids.

The unheated bedrooms under uninsulated zinc roofs were freezing in winter and scorching in summer. The kitchens, looking onto rear courts, had no refrigeration or artificial ventilation and the odours of cooking, laundry, boxes of refuse waiting to be carried downstairs and from WCs ventilated into the court prevented sensitive employers even entering them. (Among the petit-bourgeois, single maids were even worse off as they slept in an alcove off the kitchen and had little contact with other servants in the block.) Solidarity among the servant class was such that markets had separate prices for employers and servants. In Zola's *Pot-Bouille* the more intelligent employers are stunned by the hatred shown by the servants at their exploitation and at their contempt for bourgeois moral hypocrisy.[13]

Services

Not only were the maids' rooms unheated, but the other bedrooms, although provided with fireplaces, were usually only heated in cases of illness. The provision of flues necessitated by the multiplication of fireplaces was a constricting factor in planning, but by the Belle Epoque it had become usual in the more expensive apartments to heat the reception rooms and principal bedroom by warm air. The apartments were connected to a calorifier in the basement by terracotta pipes concealed in the floors and partitions, with a grille in each room just above floor level. In order to increase air movement in the ducts, ventilators were installed in external walls at ground level, and in many luxury blocks decorative metal grilles can still be seen just above the pavement. Radiators were first used about 1895: where some form of central heating was installed, the fireplace was frequently omitted in the dining room, though never elsewhere. The kitchens, paved with hexagonal red tiles, had a stoneware sink near the window and below the window a projecting larder with louvred external ventilation. Cooking was usually on a cast-iron stove, heated by coal and fitted with hot-plates, an oven and a water-filled reservoir.

The reason that bathrooms were not installed until the end of the century is that it was usual to have an all-over wash standing in a circular zinc tub in the *toilette* or dressing room adjoining the bedroom, the water carried from and to the kitchen by a maid. The *toilette* usually had a scrubbed softwood parquet floor, walls covered with varnished paper and a marble-topped table for the basin and water jug. A wall cistern providing hot and cold water was only introduced around 1900. Among the upper classes, women's *toilettes* were more highly decorated, often hung with muslin which sometimes extended to a tented ceiling. Even in their private boudoir, however, respectable women kept their modesty by wearing a chemise while in the tub. Rich courtesans had been the first to possess a bath, which therefore did not become socially acceptable until campaigns by hygienists were successful in the years after 1900. Bathrooms, when provided, had wall and floor tiling, cast-iron baths with chrome taps and gas water heaters.

Gas had been in general use for domestic lighting in the 1870s, so it was sometimes economically advantageous to light the main staircases permanently by this means, meaning that they did not have to be on an external wall to receive daylight. The light bulb, invented by Thomas Edison in 1878, was in relatively common use by the 1890s – a central ceiling fitting integrated with the decorative mouldings in living rooms, usually wall lights in bedrooms. The general lightening of colour schemes at the end of the century was partly the result of the new modes of illumination, raising the occupants' expectations of lighting levels.

The increase in the number of floors in apartment blocks was linked to the development of lifts. First exhibited by Elisha Otis at the New York Exhibition in 1853, the first shown in France was a hydraulic hoist by Léon Edoux in 1867. From the 1880s lifts started to be installed in *immeubles*, by the end of the century operated by pneumatic pressure. A private company had obtained the concession to provide compressed air to industries and workshops in return for supplying the city with pneumatically operated clocks at the main crossroads. At an apartment building on the quai d'Orsay built in 1905, condensed air points adjacent to the lift were available for carpet cleaning. By this time, increased traffic pollution combined with the availability of lifts to make the upper floors the most desirable: usually the fifth was the most expensive, with maids' rooms in the roof above.

One of the first modern penthouses was designed by Léon Chesnay (*b* 1869) for himself at 85 rue de Courcelles, 8e, in 1907, with reception rooms on the sixth floor and his *atelier* on the seventh. (The first *immeuble* with a penthouse flat and maids' rooms on the lower floors seems to have been 7 rue Le Tasse: see Chapter Six.) A car lift had been invented about 1898, but as the basements, which would have been useful for this purpose, were divided up by load-bearing walls, parking was normally in the court. The telephone came into domestic use in the late 1880s, being automatically installed in luxury apartments by 1910.

Studios

One type of accommodation associated with Paris is the artist's studio, or *atelier*: many apartment blocks incorporated ateliers on the top floor, although the majority of purpose-built ateliers in Montmartre and Montparnasse were cheaply constructed timber-framed workshops, since demolished – the most famous being the Bateau-Lavoir in Montmartre where Picasso painted *Les Demoiselles d'Avignon* and gave a banquet in honour of the Douanier Rousseau. The more expensive multi-storey blocks of *ateliers* were occupied not so much by artists as by childless bourgeois, particularly writers and intellectuals, to whom the *vie bohème* (but with lifts and servants) appealed. These were known as *studios*, a term now used in Paris for one-room flats (the *studettes* now advertised by Parisian estate agents are former maids' bedrooms).

One of the best-known is the block at 31 rue Campagne-Première, 14e (1911), by André Arfvidson (1870–1935), where the *atelier*, which is really a double-height living room, has a separate dining room adjoining, and the gallery above (used as storage space in an artist's studio) was labelled 'salon' on the original plan. The elevation is clad in faience tiles, providing a permanent and colourful finish, although the general treatment, as in most of Arfvidson's buildings, is rather heavy-handed. The use of ceramic tiling will be described in more detail in Chapter Six.

Right: **André Arfvidson, 31 rue Campagne-Première, 1911.** *Four floors of double-height ateliers – the main facade finished with small tiles, while the top floor is rendered.*

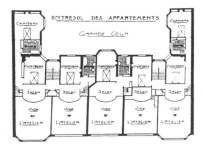

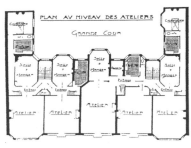

Left: **André Arfvidson, 31 rue Campagne-Première, 1911.** *Separate dining rooms allowed the double-height 'studios' to be used as salons by the artistic bourgeoisie.*

Although in 1894 nearly a third of the population were recorded as being single, there seem to have been few bachelor flats: a large proportion of single people were probably too poor to rent an apartment.

Houses

The rising cost of land reduced considerably the number of individual terrace houses popular early in the nineteenth century, particularly with those commercially successful in the arts and what would now be called the media, who wanted something different from the stone *immeubles*. A few sites, usually about six to eight metres wide, were available, but the accommodation was no greater than in a large apartment, where one would have a lift and a concierge.

The 'difference' extended, of course, to contrast with the adjacent houses, as shown by 14 rue Eugène-Flachat, 17e (1895) by Charles Girault (1851–1932), which is in every respect superior to its neighbours – in height, scale, delicately coloured brickwork and finely balanced proportions. There were some much grander houses (the Musée Nissim de Camondo is a perfectly preserved example), usually in a purer classical style, but they are far outnumbered by the most luxurious type of *immeuble*.

The Apartment: *Grand Luxe*

The extent of accommodation and degree of grandeur possible in an apartment block may be illustrated by a plan of *23 bis* avenue de Messine, 8e (1906), designed by Léon Chesnay in the most fashionable location near the Parc Monceau, with a suite of five reception rooms, including a corner salon and four large bedrooms, the two principal with bathrooms en suite. (This building is currently being converted to commercial use.)

The external composition, with its dome (which has unfortunately now lost its pinnacle and therefore seems too small) supported visually by the corner chimney, provides exactly the appropriate amount of plain wall surface to contrast with the curved bays and beautifully placed sculptural detail. Moreover, the introduction of projecting balconies at second-floor level means that, despite the single-storey rusticated base aligned with the smaller building on the right, the five main floors below the cornice 'read' as two plus three, a happier relation than one plus four. Lastly, the decorative treatment of the top floors reflects their greater desirability than in earlier years. All these elements combine to produce one of the most perfect domestic buildings of the period. The classical system of design, to be described in the next chapter, is here applied with very little period detail.

The apartment plans illustrated in this chapter are both functional (in relation to the requirements of the time) and flexible (within the confines of a load-bearing structure). As a result, with updated services they remain suitable for family use today.

Above: **Charles Girault, 14 rue Eugène-Flachat, 1895.** *Beautifully detailed and proportioned, the duality inherent in this delicately coloured two-bay elevation is overcome by the placing of the door.*

PLAN DES ETAGES

1   Emile Zola, *Pot-Bouille*, Paris, 1883, current French edition GF
    Flammarion, Paris, 1979, translation *Pot Luck* by Brian Nelson,
    Oxford University Press, London, 1999.

2   Baronne Staffe, *Usages du monde, Règles de savoir-vivre dans la
    société moderne*, Victor Havard, Paris, 1896, *l'avant-propos* p 9:
    'Toutes les classes feraient bien d'ajouter aux autres cette étude facile, car
    nous sommes à l'époque heureuse des fortunes rapides et des promptes
    élévations. Il est utile d'acquérir les belles manières au temps de la
    jeunesse, pour être complètement à la hauteur des positions prochaines.'

3   Anthony Blunt, *The Art and Architecture of France 1500–1700*,
    Penguin Books, London, 1953/1973, ch 1.

4   Marcel Proust, 'A Historic Salon: the Salon of Her Imperial Highness
    the Princesse Mathilde', included in *Against Sainte-Beuve and other
    Essays*, translated by John Sturrock, Penguin Books, London,
    1988.

5   *The Guermantes Way*, translated by C. K. Scott-Moncrieff and
    Terence Kilmartin, , *Remembrance of Things Past*, Penguin Books,
    London, 1983, p 210: 'they waft into a succession of salons the
    quality of the fresh air outside'.

6   E. Zola, *Pot-Bouille*, GF Flammarion, Paris, 1883, ch 3, p 80: '*un
    furieux appétit de gendre*'.

7   Debora L. Silverman, *Art Nouveau in Fin-de-Siècle France*,
    University of California Press, Berkeley, 1989, p 189.

8   Henri Havard, *Les arts de l'ameublement, la décoration*, Paris 1891,
    p 19: '*Le rôle d'une décoration bien comprise était, avant tout, de créer
    un plaisir pour les yeux en même temps qu'un repos pour l'esprit. Il
    faut, par conséquent, renoncer en principe à ces figurations qui simulent
    un effort persistant, et dont la contemplation ne manquerait pas de
    devenir fatigant à la longue.*'

9   Edmond de Goncourt, *La maison d'un artiste*, Paris, 1881, and
    see Debora L Silverman, *Art Nouveau in Fin-de-Siècle France*,
    University of California Press, Berkeley, 1989, pp 20–3.

10 Marcel Proust, *A l'ombre des jeunes filles en fleurs*, translated by
    C. K. Scott Moncrieff and Terence Kilmartin, *Remembrance of
    Things Past*, vol 1, p 581.

11 Henri Havard, *Les arts de l'ameublement, la décoration*, Paris, 1891,
    p 151 : '*Le degré de gaieté d'un appartement étant en raison directe du
    nombre de ses ouvertures apparentes ou réelles, en multipliant le chiffre
    des fenêtres et des portes apparentes, on peut arriver à augmenter la
    gaieté d'une pièce*'.

12 Marcel Proust, *A l'ombre des jeunes filles en fleurs*, translated by
    C. K. Scott-Moncrieff and Terence Kilmartin, *Remembrance of
    Things Past*, vol 1. See pp 580, 637, 640, 662 and 663 for changes
    in Madame Swann's drawing room.

13 *Pot-Bouille*, translated as *Pot Luck* by Brian Nelson, Oxford
    University Press, London, 1999, p 262.

4 The Ecole des Beaux-Arts

The French Classical Tradition

The architectural success of the new Paris, built under Haussmann, depended on the general use of the classical system of composition, possible on such a large scale because most of the architects involved had been trained at the Ecole des Beaux-Arts in Paris, until 1903 the sole official architectural school. (Regional schools were set up in 1905, but the better students still preferred to complete their training in Paris, which offered more professional opportunities.) This did not change under the Third Republic, whose main aim being the restoration of stability, encouraged continuance of the French classical tradition, which was officially believed to be superior to the architecture of other countries. Lucien Magne (1849–1916), Professor of the History of Art at the Ecole, wrote in *L'Architecture française du siècle* in 1889, '*To shine forth, as in the past, throughout the western world, French art must conserve and develop the qualities which are appropriate to its genius: clarity, sobriety and taste. It must not adapt to the exaggerations of other countries and other centuries.*'[1]

The first government school of architecture had been run by the Académie Royale d'Architecture, founded by Louis XIV and Colbert in 1671 as part of their policy to centralise authority and reduce the power of the guilds, in this case by establishing an architectural profession trained in an official style, a synthesis of Italian and French elements created by Lemercier, François Mansart and Le Vau, rather than architects being craftsmen learning by apprenticeship. Drawing replaced construction as the basis for architectural education. From 1819 to 1958 this official school was the architectural section of the Ecole des Beaux-Arts, for most of this time under the control of the Académie des Beaux-Arts, one of the four academies constituting the Institut de France. The Académie had five sections (painting, sculpture, architecture, engraving and music). The eight architect members were appointed for life, ensuring a conservative policy. The fact that the Académie was part of the Institut underlines the links between the arts forged by classicism.

The term 'classicism' usually refers to art ultimately derived from ancient Greece and Rome, as adapted during the Renaissance and therefore excluding Gothic and the Romantic tendencies developed in northern Europe. It does, however, usually imply both a harmonious simplicity and a gravitas born from lasting values. French classical architecture of the nineteenth century may therefore be compared with the paintings of Ingres, Puvis de Chavannes and Georges Seurat, the writings of Anatole France, Heredia and Leconte de Lisle, and the music of Camille Saint-Saëns and César Franck. All have been described as classicists, classicism forming a bond between all the arts.

Opposite: **Charles Girault, Petit Palais, 1896–1900.**

The Educational Tradition

Design work was carried out entirely in studios or *ateliers* of 20 to 70 students. There were three *ateliers officiels* under 'Patrons' appointed by the school, but in addition an *atelier libre* could be created by a minimum of 20 students asking a well-known architect to act as their *Patron*, the *ateliers libres* being rented and organised by the students in the cheapest premises available near the school. Zola described one in *L'Oeuvre* as '*a hut of lath and plaster, formerly occupied by a packing agent, approached through two filthy courtyards at the back of an old weather-beaten building*'.[2] New students (men aged 15 to 30: women were not admitted until 1897), who were called *aspirants*, studied for exams, held half-yearly, in maths, history, drawing and architectural design. When they had passed these, they entered the Second Class.

All students were free to attend lectures by the professors of theory, history, construction (the most highly attended), perspective, mathematics, descriptive geometry, physics and chemistry, stereometry, building legislation and ornamental design: there were no lectures on lighting, heating or ventilation. Students in the Second Class undertook design programmes for which, if successful, they were awarded credits or '*valeurs*'. They usually needed to stay there for two to four years in order to obtain a sufficient number of *valeurs* to qualify for the First Class, which was solely in the art of composition, monthly competition programmes being set by the Professor of Theory, who was the most influential of the professors, because in this way he controlled the building types studied.[3] Typical subjects were monuments, schools, baths and luxury houses: no industrial buildings, department stores or social housing. Each student had to enter at least two monthly competitions in a year.

Each competition (including the annual Prix de Rome, judged by members of the Académie) started with a 12-hour sketch design '*en-loge*' (the student working alone in a cubicle). The design then had to be developed in detail for a period of one to three months, resulting in rendered drawings ('*rendu*') conforming with the *en-loge* sketch. The 12-hour sketch tested the student's ability to grasp the essentials of a design problem by analysing a given programme without help from his *Patron* or from other students, and to arrive at the most fitting solution by means of the formal design system taught by the school. The principal planning device was the axis: both a line of physical movement linking separate spaces and a means of relating the volumes containing those spaces.

The students learnt to draw the classical orders: the classical system of design is essentially a configurative and proportional exercise in which each part is in its right place and related to the whole. This order can most simply be achieved by numerical ratios, in the case of the classical orders based on the column diameter. The Golden Section – most beautiful of proportional ratios, because the smaller part is always related to the larger as the larger is to the whole, thereby providing, for example, the basis for window pane proportions in Renaissance architecture generally – does not appear to have been emphasised in the Ecole's teaching, although Seurat is thought to have used it for compositional purposes.

The use of columns or pilasters (the orders) was, in practice, generally reserved for representational buildings – that is those personifying church or government – but despite this nearly all the apartment blocks, for instance, have a base and attic with two or three floors in between representing the order and windows marking regular bay widths equivalent to those which would otherwise be established by column or pilaster spacing. This regular rhythm is perhaps the most notable characteristic of Haussmannian facades (earlier examples are the Palais Royal, 1784 and the rue de Rivoli, 1802); the change to a freer method of composition in the 1890s will be considered in Chapter Six.

In the atelier, which the *Patron* visited two or three times a week, the students ranged from new *aspirants* to those 25 to 30 years old hoping to win the Prix de Rome. Junior students not entering competitions helped the seniors with their large and elaborate final drawings, which were mounted on boards and carried in a noisy procession to the Ecole on a cart, or *tumbril*. The juniors therefore learnt from the more experienced, including how to work to a deadline, and the seniors learnt how to delegate. In addition, once students had gained some experience, they took time off between competitions to earn money working for their *Patron* or other architects, thereby obtaining practical training not provided by the school's system.

A government diploma was introduced in 1867, being granted to students who, having studied for six years, passed a combined design and practical knowledge examination: this only became popular after 1887, when the diploma was awarded to all winners of the Prix de Rome and diploma students were allowed to choose their own design programme. It was particularly favoured by foreign students: an indication of the international prestige of the Ecole as the leading architectural school in the world during this period.

The Prix de Rome winners spent five years at the Villa Medici: the first four on the study of ancient monuments, the last on the design for a 'project for a public monument of his own conception and conforming to French habits'.[4] This requirement was determined by the practice of offering a junior appointment on a government project to the returning prize-winner and, later on, a major government appointment. During the Third Republic it gradually became more usual to hold open competitions for public buildings, but the experience gained in the design and presentation of elaborate schemes usually ensured that a First or Second Prix de Rome was the winner.

Right: **Charles Lefebvre, 170 boulevard Haussmann, 1909.** *A very large but lively building in scale with both the main boulevard and the side street, the corner successfully treated with a dome of just the right size.*

The Profession

The Congrès des Architectes Français held in 1895 adopted the definition of an architect given in the *Dictionnaire de l'Académie* (1878 edition): *'The architect is the artist who creates buildings by determining their proportions, arrangement and decoration, superintends their construction and regulates their cost.'* [5]

The architectural profession was essentially centralised: in 1880 there were about 2000 architects in Paris, only about 700 elsewhere in France. [6] Over half of those who called themselves architects (there was no registration) had learnt by apprenticeship rather than at the Ecole, but they mostly either worked as assistants or designed minor private or commercial buildings.

The Monuments Historiques and the Edifices Diocésains (responsible between them for the maintenance of existing and design of new churches) employed their own architects, but lycées, colleges, theatres and hospitals, all under government control, normally appointed an architect for each project – although they tended to be specialists in this work. As the proportion of private building increased, the only government architectural departments to grow were those responsible for enforcing regulations on new buildings and ensuring the safety of existing ones.

Architects unsuccessful in winning one of the open competitions had to rely on private contacts to obtain commissions from private clients or small property developers, mainly contractors. The more successful, including former Prix de Rome winners, designed large projects for banks and insurance companies. The preparation of elaborate design drawings had become an essential part of architectural publicity: a separate section of the annual Salon was devoted to these, including imaginary projects submitted by those hoping to attract clients (unfortunately for them, it was the room least frequented by the public).

Many architects working exclusively for private clients received little publicity in professional journals at the time and are still generally unknown. The high quality of the work of the following, for example, has only been illustrated slightly in the *Dictionnaire des constructions élevées à Paris aux XIXe et XXe siècles* (see Bibliography) and nowhere else in current literature: Charles Lefebvre, 1867–1923 (80 buildings listed in the *Dictionnaire*); Albert LeVoisvenel, *d* 1905 (67 buildings listed); Albert Sélonier, 1858–1926 (111 buildings listed). Of these only Lefebvre was educated at the Ecole, but the others designed in the Beaux-Arts manner. One typical building by each is illustrated here and contrasting examples by Lefebvre and LeVoisvenel appear in later chapters.

The camaraderie of the *atelier* with its attendant celebratory parties was continued later in functions held by a number of professional associations, such as the Société Centrale (founded

Above: **Albert LeVoisvenel, 1–3bis quai aux Fleurs, 1898.** *These four adjacent immeubles have sufficient variation for their separate identities to be visible, while the horizontals provided by* balconies and cornices give a scale suitable to the situation, facing the Seine.

in 1843). These were needed to protect the position of architects trained as artists in the face of a rapidly changing building industry, with the new engineering profession often more able to deal with industrialisation. (This will be considered in the next chapter.) Despite this, architects generally were proud of their professional standing as artists: there appears to have been little 'ghosting' even in the larger commercial practices, although a senior assistant was occasionally employed as a chief designer by exceptionally busy principals. For example, Paul-Ernest Sanson (1836–1918), one of the most successful architects specialising in luxury domestic work, employed René Sergent (1865–1927) as his chief designer from 1884 to 1897 and after that date his son Maurice may have acted in that capacity.

The Ecole's Theory

Emphasis in Beaux-Arts teaching was on the plan. The *Dictionnaire de l'Académie des Beaux-Arts*, for example, stated '*it is the plan which reconciles all the requirements of the programme, which contains the architect's creative idea; it is the criterion used by knowledgeable people to judge the true value of the composition*'.[7]

Eléments et théorie de l'architecture by Julien Guadet (1834–1908), based on his course as Professor of Theory started in 1894, became the school's official design manual. Guadet wrote, '*the axis is the key to the design and will also be the key to the*

composition … it extends itself into the whole of the vertical plane separating the two halves symmetrically'.[8] The words 'axis' and 'symmetry' represent the basic procedures of Beaux-Arts design used by all architects trained at the school, irrespective of their stylistic preferences.

The repetition of exactly similar parts either facing one another or on either side of a centre line – an axis – is one of the two definitions of 'symmetry' given by most dictionaries. The other is the harmonious relationship of parts within a whole, the latter agreeing roughly with Vitruvius, the author whose precepts were generally followed by classical architects up to the nineteenth century. He wrote: '*Symmetry also is the appropriate harmony arising out of the details of the work itself; the correspondence of each given detail among the separate details to the form of the design as a whole.*'[9]

Strict bilateral symmetry had always been the main feature of single-cell monuments from Greek temples to Gothic and Renaissance churches (an extreme example being the centralised Greek cross church plan symmetrical about both axes), while more complex palace-type buildings usually had symmetrical main facades, but plans which departed from strict symmetry for functional reasons. Guadet thought that '*symmetry with variety should be sought*' and defined symmetry as '*the regularity of which one is aware at a glance*'.[10]

Above: **Eugène Viollet-le-Duc, design for a covered market.** *A mixture of stone and iron, emphasising an interest in truth rather than beauty. Guimard adapted the V-columns for a school – see Chapter Six.*

Right: **Henri Labrouste, Bibliothèque Nationale reading room, 1860–7.** *A great interior, both for the control of daylight entering through the domes' glazed oculi and for the lightness of the iron structure, which contrasts with the solidity of the side walls' buttresses.*

Left: **Julien Guadet, Hôtel des Postes, 1880–7.** *The corner pavilions, containing small offices, relate in scale to the neighbouring buildings and frame the more industrial and therefore less traditional central bays.*

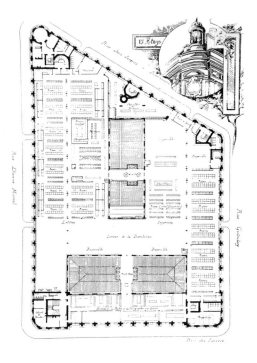

Right: **Julien Guadet, Hôtel des Postes, 1880–7.** *The plan is completely open inside its stone exterior: an entirely functional design.*

Rationalism

Diderot's *Encyclopédie* of 1751 had emphasised *'convenance'* (suitability to rank and function) as the basis for architectural design,[11] and there had always been an undercurrent within the Ecole in favour of a more rational design system than complete reliance on the orders. This was usually led by former Prix de Rome winners, in the mid-nineteenth century by Henri Labrouste (1799–1875). Labrouste had been *Patron* of an *atelier libre* from 1830 to 1856, although, not having been elected to the Institut because of his radical views, none of his students had a chance of winning the Prix de Rome. His principal buildings, the Bibliothèque Sainte-Geneviève (1839–50) and the Bibliothèque Nationale reading room (1860–7), are remarkable for their originality of detail, frank use of iron construction and absence of classical reference. When he gave up his *atelier*, his students persuaded Eugène Viollet-le-Duc (1814–79) to take it over.

Viollet-le-Duc had refused to study at the Ecole because of his passion for Gothic architecture, which eventually resulted in his restoration of Gothic abbeys and cathedrals including Notre Dame. He persuaded Napoléon III to reform the Ecole and in 1863 was appointed Professor of the History of Art and Aesthetics. The senior students, led by Julien Guadet (1834–1908) and Jean-Louis Pascal (1837–1920), were unhappy at the school coming under government control and at Viollet-le-

Duc's proposal to reduce the age limit for Prix de Rome entrants from 30 to 25 (Guadet and Pascal both eventually won the prize at 30 and 29 years respectively). Student noise wrecked Viollet-le-Duc's lectures and he resigned in 1864. The Academy regained control of the Prix de Rome in 1871, but Viollet-le-Duc's *Entretiens* (the lectures he had been unable to give) became the most influential book of the period; in it he emphasised that form should follow function.

Labrouste's influence continued at the Ecole through the medium of Jules André (1819–90), *Patron* of an *atelier officiel* from 1867 until his death, who had been his assistant at the Bibliothèque Nationale and whose Galerie de Zoologie, 1877–89 (now the Grande Galerie de l'Evolution of the Muséum National d'Histoire Naturelle) has a cast-iron main hall and minimal classical detailing (see Chapter Five); and then through Julien Guadet, who despite his opposition to Viollet-le-Duc's reforms, had been a pupil of both Labrouste and André. His Hôtel des Postes (Poste Paris-Louvre, 48 rue du Louvre, 1e) of 1880–7 is a straightforward iron-framed industrial building, providing large spaces with a minimum number of columns, enclosed by load-bearing stone walls with projecting buttresses, the large windows of the first-floor sorting hall having iron central mullions supporting stone lintels; only the small offices at the corners of the site are encased in simple classical forms. The smaller-scale here was intended to relate the building to adjacent *immeubles*, but integration of corners and centre is unsatisfactory, because although the continuous entablatures of the corners are echoed on the buttresses, the effect of the latter is entirely vertical when seen in perspective. Guadet's published lectures, like those of Viollet-le-Duc, emphasised rational planning and use of materials, and were not concerned with 'style'. Rather, he insisted that architecture was an art of creation and not of imitation and that the architect must be guided above all by fidelity to the programme.

Viollet-le-Duc, influenced by the Positivism of Auguste Comte (1798–1857) with its subordination of beauty to truth (Guadet quoted Plato's *'Beauty is the splendour of truth'*,[12] was succeeded as Professor of Aesthetics by Comte's disciple the philosopher Hippolyte Taine (1828–93), with whose theory of *'la race, le milieu et le moment'* being the determining conditions for art Viollet-le-Duc was in agreement. (Taine's first series of lectures dealt with the history of Renaissance art.) It is necessary to mention philosophy here because the senior classes in French schools were *'classes de philosophie'*, teaching skills in classification and synthesis: skills used by the Ecole-trained architects whose mode of thought would therefore be appreciated by those of their clients and by civil servants, writers and politicians who had the same educational background. Charles Garnier, architect of the Opéra, for example, who came from a Parisian working-class family, wrote profusely on architecture and included among his friends the writer Théophile Gautier, the chemist Louis Pasteur and the politician Léon Gambetta. Several of the Belle Epoque's leading architects had worked as Garnier's assistants on the Opéra,[13] and learnt their technical skills from him. The Opéra was the most influential building among all classically motivated young architects studying in the 1870s, but even those fortunate enough later to obtain commissions with generous budgets produced designs considerably more restrained and chastely classical, due to changes in society and in public taste.

The Sorbonne and Axial Planning

The two most remarkable monuments of the Belle Epoque in a purely classical style are the Sorbonne and the Petit Palais, both the subject of public competitions, both won by architects possessing remarkable creative and practical skills.

Henri-Paul Nénot (1853–1934) won the competition for the Sorbonne (now occupied by the University of Paris IV) in 1882, having gained the Prix de Rome at the early age of 25. His only practical experience had been in the Opéra office, but his appointment at the Sorbonne was confirmed because Garnier was able to vouch for his exceptional abilities. Construction started in 1884 and the project was completed in 1901. Nénot then went on to design 16 large apartment blocks, two hotels, four office blocks

Right: **Henri-Paul Nénot, La Sorbonne, 1882–1901.**
The restrained seventeenth-century inspiration does not prevent the appropriate modification in scale for different rooms, or a subtlety in surface variation.

Below: **Henri-Paul Nénot, La Sorbonne, 1882–1901.**
An outline plan, with axes controlling circulation routes, and a sketch elevation to rue Saint-Jacques showing how the heights are adapted to the sloping ground.

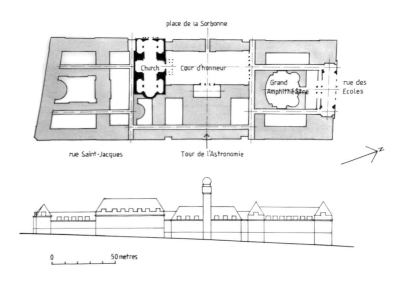

and a 'Palace' hotel, as well as laboratories and country châteaux.

The new Sorbonne eventually covered a complete island site apart from the only original building to remain, the church by Lemercier, built in 1635–42, two-thirds of the way uphill on the west side, centred on the place de la Sorbonne. The university is otherwise surrounded by narrow streets except at the lowest, north end, where the rue des Ecoles opens out into a small square opposite the main entrance. The northern third of the site, the first to be built, is occupied by a virtually solid block centred on the Grand Amphithéâtre (with 2700 seats). Between this and the church, whose length is only half the width of the site, is the Cour d'Honneur.

The interest of the Sorbonne lies largely in the application of Beaux-Arts planning principles to a very large and complex late nineteenth-century building, containing units of diverse purpose and scale and uniting them into a lucidly organised entity. This can only be appreciated by a close study of the planning, and the

fairly long description that follows should be read in conjunction with the outline plan and elevation provided.

The church has a pedimented portico on the centre of its north side and Nénot used this to position the long axis of his court, the axis continuing beyond an open loggia through a corridor which connects with the barrel-vaulted main entrance hall, parallel to the entrance facade. At the other end of the entrance hall a parallel corridor runs south to connect with the east-west axis of the loggia, forming an enclosing rectangle for the Grand Amphithéâtre and its monumental stair. The Cour d'Honneur's cross axis is marked by an entrance arch from the rue de la Sorbonne on the west side; opposite is a raised central pavilion, three bays wide, with a five-bay vestibule leading to lecture halls on its east, north and south sides.

The 246 metre-long site is broken down into three parts, each approximately square, the main block at the north end being five storeys high plus a high pitched roof. The central third

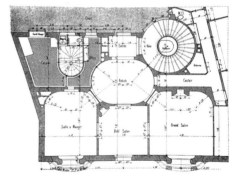

Below: **Adolphe Bocage, 95 boulevard Raspail, 1902.** *This masterpiece of classical planning uses diagonal axes to connect near-symmetrical rooms, with every detail perfectly considered and related to the whole.*

Left: **Adolphe Bocage, 95 boulevard Raspail, 1902.** *The flowing curves derived from the internal planning are echoed by the segmental arches over the windows and the curved corner pediment over a sculpted figure.*

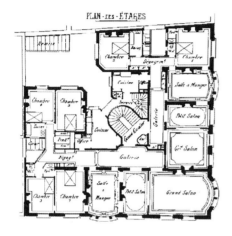

Right: **Georges Pradelle, 5 rue de Luynes, 1904.** *A smaller-scale building in a side street, the rectangular forms are crisply carved, but provide an excellent contrast to the plain areas and the variations in balcony form.*

Left: **Georges Pradelle, 5 rue de Luynes, 1904.** *The two interlocking apartments per floor, each with well-proportioned rectangular rooms, are entered from a staircase positioned on the diagonal in the square block.*

contains the Cour d'Honneur and an eastern block centred on the Tour de l'Astronomie with its clock and dome. The southern third is at the highest end of the site and contains the fewest number of storeys: the three parts are demarcated on the long elevations by single recessed bays. Looking along the rue Saint-Jacques, what would otherwise have been an interminably long elevation is broken by the two principal features of the Tour de l'Astronomie and the high block to its south backing onto the church. Starting from the south wing – which has a low base, two storeys and dormers – a strong horizontal line formed by string courses above the base continues through the connecting link and the high block where, due to the sloping ground, the base has by now become a full two storeys high.

The cornice of the south wing repeats on the high block, but with an attic floor above so that the roof is a storey higher. The link between has only one floor, cornice and roof dormers above the base: this cornice then reappears north of the high block as the main cornice line of the major two-thirds of the site. On the north front this cornice continues, with a total of four storeys below it at the ends. Equal to two double-height storeys in the centre, this incorporates the arched main entrance doors and above them a large hall whose windows are separated by Corinthian pilasters articulating the order. This elevation, at the furthest point from Lemercier's church, is more nineteenth-

century in character than the remainder of the ensemble. The only other use of a classical order is in the Cour d'Honneur, where Tuscan half-columns enclose arches to emphasise entrances.

By means of axes marking circulation routes on plan and by a careful balancing act between sizes and heights of blocks – related to one another by string courses and cornices – Nénot achieved a coherent whole. This was treated very simply throughout but with the same care taken in every detail, including such practical matters as the excellent acoustics of the Grand Amphithéâtre. This, the principal interior, is decorated by Puvis de Chavannes' mural *Le Bois Sacré*. Puvis said that he wanted to be more and more sober, more and more simple, to try to say as much as possible in a few words.[14] His consummate synthesis of form and content by the elimination of all inessentials is perfectly in accord with Nénot's architecture, which derives mainly from François Mansart and achieves that master's seventeenth-century grace and subtle restraint.

Beaux-Arts Principles and the Apartment Block

Plans of apartment buildings designed by Adolphe Bocage (1860–1927) at 95 boulevard Raspail, 7e, in 1902, and by Georges Pradelle (1865–1935) at 5 rue de Luynes, 6e, in 1904, show how axial planning could be adapted to a domestic scale. By the use of axes, cross axes and axes positioned on the diagonals of curved

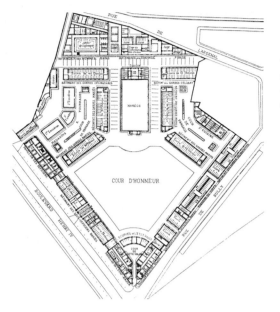

spaces, and by the skilful juxtaposition of slightly varied rooms, Bocage, one of the best architects of the Belle Epoque, was able to create out of a bourgeois apartment an ingeniously related sequence of elegantly proportioned spaces equal to the finest eighteenth-century interior planning.

The formalisation of domestic rooms by the use of symmetrical wall treatments, if necessary by the addition of false doors, has already been mentioned in Chapter Three. In contrast, in Pradelle's building only the staircase is set on the diagonal and, apart from the curved 'bow-windows', the rooms are rectangular. Although there are two flats per floor, one larger than the other, they interlock neatly. The external treatment reflects this difference, Bocage's elliptical curves flowing harmoniously, while Pradelle's crisper forms are tied together more closely by horizontal cornices and balconies (note how the fourth floor acts as a frieze), and by the Greek key patterns and the vines that emphasise the central bay.

The Caserne des Celestins: Type Character

Charles Blanc, writing in the *Grammaire des arts du dessin*, gave Proportion, Character and Harmony as the three necessary conditions for beauty in architecture, and thought that the sublime stemmed from grandeur of dimensions, simplicity of surfaces and from rectitude and continuity of lines.[15] To quote Charles Blanc: *'The artist's responsibility is to remind us of the ideal, to reveal to us the fundamental beauty of things, to discover their eternal character, their pure essence.'*[16] Proportion and Harmony are present in the Sorbonne, as in the two examples that follow – the Caserne des Célestins and the Petit Palais – but their character is different because in each case appropriate: scholarly, military or celebratory. Guadet defined character as *'identity between the architectural and moral effects of the programme'*.[17] Donald Drew Egbert in his book on the Grand Prix designs refers to this as 'type character',[18] implying that all military barracks should have a similar basic character.

The Caserne des Célestins is a public building, intentionally 'traditional' in style but without the use of the orders, won in open competion in 1889 by Jacques Hermant (1855–1930), who had been the second prize-winner for the Prix de Rome in 1880. A barracks for the Garde Républicaine on an irregularly shaped site, where one corner (between the boulevard Henri IV and the rue de Sully) faces the Seine, it consists of separate blocks grouped round courtyards, with the main entrance into the Cour d'Honneur being on the centre line of the symmetrical frontage to the boulevard. The administration building (Pavillon de l'Etat-Major) is placed on the corner and its importance is emphasised by its entrance, establishing the main planning axis about which all the principal buildings are

Left: **Charles Girault,
Petit Palais, 1896–1900.**
*The series of recessions
around the main entrance –
generated by the relationship
of the three semi-circles of
door, arch and dome, as well
as the brilliant placing of
sculpture – lead the eye into
the building.*

symmetrically arranged. The infirmaries at the quiet rear of the site are insulated from the remainder by a tree-lined internal boulevard.

Hermant said he wanted to give the building a feeling of strength suitable to its use. A high ground storey forms the base, the order (but without pilasters or columns) above consisting generally of two storeys, but three on the corner block and a mansard roof containing the top floor. Wide corner quoins of white stone tie together the cornice (dentilled on the corner block where additional emphasis is required by the greater height of the order, and plain elsewhere) and the white stone Florentine rusticated base. The remaining wall surfaces (in pictorial terms the 'ground'), which in a domestic building might have been brick, are of brown stone.

The problem of providing three levels of windows of approximately equal size within the order in the corner block, which arises because there is no *étage noble*, is addressed – though probably not solved – by giving the second-floor windows a straight hood on brackets at the same level as the cornice on the lower blocks to each side, this horizontal line being emphasised by sculptured cartouches between the windows. The dormer windows are tied firmly into the wall plane by being set in a stone parapet half their height: a motif derived from the château at Azay-le-Rideau of 1518.

Jacques Hermant, like Nénot a highly successful commercial architect, had already designed another barracks, the Caserne Monge, 5e, in 1884, in partnership with his father Achille. Architectural families were a feature of the profession at this time: for example there were four generations of Vaudoyers, the third in line being half-brother of the architect William Bouwens van der Boijen (whose son was also an architect). He also married a niece of Viollet-le-Duc, making at least seven architects in one family, which only sheds further light on the close-knit nature of the profession.

The 1900 Exhibition and the Petit Palais

The 1900 Exhibition can be seen as the pivotal point of the Belle Epoque, artistically as well as figuratively. As will be seen in Chapters Six 'The Search for a New Art', and Eight 'Towards a New Architecture', it clearly marked the change from the *fin de siècle* to what is still recognisable, a century later, as the modern world.

Architecturally, the Exhibition consisted of numerous temporary buildings and two permanent ones: the Grand and Petit Palais. The temporary pavilions generally constituted the last of the pastiches and '*Pâtisseries*' (finished in fibrous plaster rather than icing sugar), which had been a feature of the 1889 Exhibition (see Chapter Five), the area on the banks of the Seine being mostly devoted to 'Old Paris'.

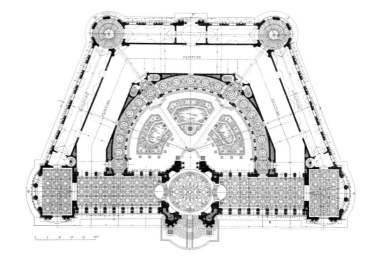

Above: **Charles Girault, Petit Palais, 1896–1900.**
The culmination of elegant Beaux-Arts planning, with perfect attention to every detail. As in the previous examples, the use of diagonal axes is essential here, too.

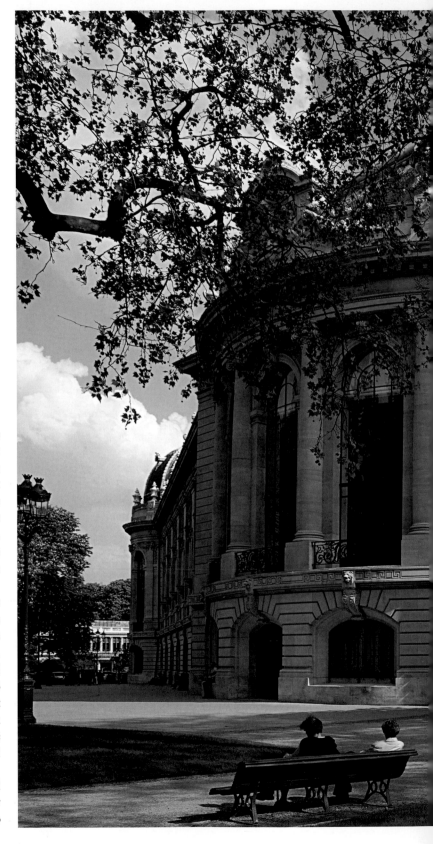

In 1880, the year that Jacques Hermant came second in the Prix de Rome competition, the prize was won by Charles Girault (1851–1932), who in 1896 not only received the fourth prize in the competition for the Grand Palais des Beaux-Arts to be built as part of the 1900 Universal Exhibition, but also came first in the competition for the Petit Palais. This latter building was designed to house the Exhibition's retrospective of French art. Since 1902 it has contained historical collections owned by the Ville de Paris, as well as hosting temporary exhibitions. It has recently been re-opened after restoration.

Girault had, after his return from Rome, been appointed to design the Palais de l'Hygiène at the 1889 Exhibition, more chastely classical than the average exhibition pavilion of the period, but lightened with Pompeiian painted decoration. Between then and his 1896 competition successes he had designed *immeubles* at 12 *bis* place Henri-Bergson, 8e, and 36 avenue Georges-Mandel, 16e (in which he lived), and a house at 14 rue Eugène-Flachat, 17e, faced with cream and green decorative brickwork, illustrated in Chapter Three. All three have asymmetrical elevations reflecting the internal planning and are far less conventionally classical than his better-known work.

The Grand and Petit Palais face each other across a broad avenue formed on the axis of the Jardins des Invalides, a new bridge (the Pont Alexandre III) being built across the Seine to

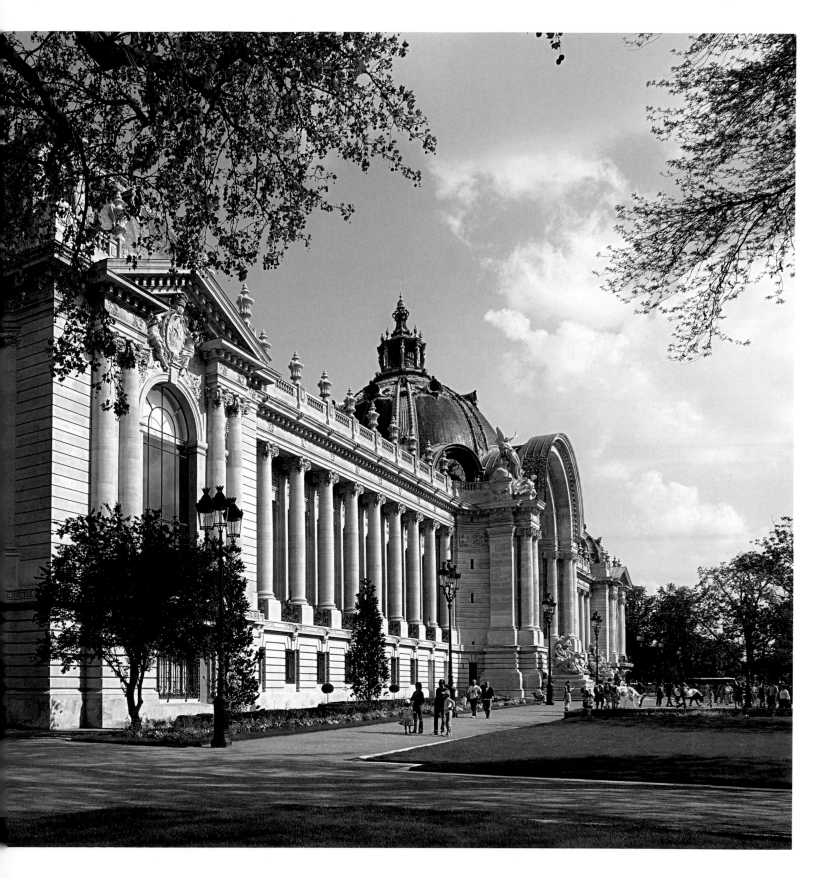

Above: **Charles Girault,
Petit Palais, 1896–1900.**
*The newly restored garden
partly enclosed by an elegant
Tuscan colonnade, smaller in
scale than the external order.*

Right: **Charles Girault, Petit Palais, 1896–1900.**
Although the inspiration of the staircases is the eighteenth century, their elegant lightness could only be achieved with reinforced concrete construction.

connect the Invalides with the Champs-Elysées. Both the new buildings have irregularly shaped sites as the outline of each building was defined in the competition conditions. The principal entrances are centralised on the avenue frontages.

The given plan form for the Petit Palais was a trapezium, with the entrance on the longest side. An oval hall connects through arches to two naves, each of which is nine bays long, with further arches at the end of each nave leading to the end pavilions. What would otherwise have been awkward corners to the trapezium are resolved by giving these pavilions shallow bows, while the two rear corners became circular staircases connecting with galleries on the lower ground floor. (The elegant helical stairs are in reinforced concrete.)

On the main level, the three rear sides are lined with sculpture galleries with arched windows; behind these is a continuous top-lit gallery for paintings. The centre of the building is occupied by a semi-circular garden court with a colonnade on the curved side. The centre point of the court is determined by where the axes at right angles to the centres of the three rear elevations meet, while the circular staircases are on the axes bisecting the corner angles. The colonnades connect into the centre bays of the two front naves, the painting galleries into the outer three bays, the sculpture galleries into the centre of the front corner pavilions.

The suitably horizontal external expression of this plan form is provided by a Roman Ionic order on a low rusticated base, its height beautifully proportioned in relation to that of the order, with a balustrade above crowned by urns. The cornice line, which converts to broken pediments on the end pavilions and at the centre of the rear elevation, is interrupted only at the entrance, by a semi-circular pedimental form framing the entrance below – a motif first seen in French architecture on the entrance wing, now destroyed, of the château at Ecouen (Jean Bullant, 1555), and then at the Temple Sainte-Marie in the rue Saint-Antoine (François Mansart, 1632).

This semi-circle both relates happily to the oval dome above it and to the scale of the much larger entrance of the Grand Palais opposite, and the problem of its junction with the balustrade on each side is solved by the sculptural groups which appear to support it. The staircases at the rear are crowned by smaller domes, the front corner pavilions by rectangular domed roofs. On the rear elevations, where the bay width is greater, semi-Palladian windows with Tuscan columns are set between piers which are also a form of Tuscan, being too wide for Ionic caps. (The Tuscan colonnade of the central courtyard echoes the columns of the external arched windows.)

Perhaps more than any other building, the Petit Palais gives the impression of the Belle Epoque as having been a period

Left: **Albert Louvet, Henri
Deglane and others, Grand
Palais, 1896–1900.** *The
elevational design, obviously the
work of a Prix de Rome winner,
and the dress of the bystanders
contrast with the glazed roof of
the great hall, underlining the
transitional nature of the Belle
Epoque.*

'without care'. It is heartening to record that its success was generally recognised at the time,[19] and that it was so much admired by the King of the Belgians when he visited the 1900 Exhibition that he invited Girault to undertake several important projects in Brussels. His buildings in Brussels are, at Royal insistence, somewhat overblown in scale, but generally Girault's work, like Nénot's, combines classical principles with a spontaneous adaptation to contemporary functional requirements.

The success of the Petit Palais was never shared by the Grand Palais, largely because the programme for the latter introduced conflicting elements which the winning architects were never able to resolve fully. The two buildings occupy the site of the Palace of Industry constructed for the 1855 Exhibition, which since 1866 had been used for the annual Concours Hippique. The Grand Palais had therefore to include a hall large enough to contain a *grande piste*, measuring 190 x 40 metres, for equestrian and agricultural shows, a space which could only be covered by an iron and glass domed roof. To complicate matters, however, the building also had to incorporate 40,000 square metres of galleries – mainly to house the annual Salon, which the Republic believed to exhibit 'the glory of French Art' — so the building had to be 'of monumental aspect and solid and durable materials', such as stone.

The opening of the annual Salon was one of the most important social events in the bourgeois calendar and the section devoted to modern French art in 1900 included the Salon's favourite artists, such as Gérôme, Bouguereau and Meissonier. Bonnard, Degas, Gauguin, Maillol, Matisse, Pissarro, Renoir, Redon, Rousseau, Seurat (who had died in 1891), Signac and Vuillard were excluded by the exhibition jury, while Cézanne and Monet were represented only by a couple of early works. The choice by clients of architects for important buildings tended to be equally conservative, although the permanent nature of the buildings and extent of financial investment has to be taken into account. The more progressive architects, although occasionally appointed for commercial or purely utilitarian buildings, as will be seen later, were also hampered by the conservationist lobby which was reacting against the destruction of much of old Paris produced by Haussmannian improvements.

Five prizes were awarded in the competition for the Grand Palais held in 1896. First place was awarded to Albert Louvet (1860–1936), second Prix de Rome 1885 and 1886, who had worked on the great Palais des Machines for the 1889 Exhibition and whose father had been Garnier's chief assistant at the Opéra. Second went jointly to Henri Deglane (1855–1931), Prix de Rome 1881, and René Binet (1866–1911), and third to Albert Thomas (1847–1907), Prix de Rome 1870. Charles Girault was

placed fourth and Lucien Tropey-Bailly (1846–1920), fifth. Because of the size of the project and shortage of time if construction was to be completed for 1900, the winning architects were asked to join forces. Binet and Tropey-Bailly sensibly declined and were awarded other smaller exhibition projects. Deglane was asked to be responsible for the front portion of the building, containing the great hall, Louvet the centre and Thomas the rear wing. Girault, who would otherwise be busy building the Petit Palais, was asked to co-ordinate the others' designs, incorporating the jury's comments (design by committee), which he succeeded in doing in the amazingly short time of 10 days.

Development of the elevations took a little longer: mainly the work of Henri Deglane, they were finally approved in February 1897 and show the strong influence of Girault's Petit Palais design, as well as reflecting the use in the Grand Palais design office of illustrations of French classical masterpieces of the seventeenth and eighteenth centuries – contrasting with the Baroque qualities of much of the external sculpture. A lot of the internal decoration was altered later, and further damaged by fire in 1944. The building has since been subdivided for various uses and only the exterior can be seen in its original state. However, restoration is also taking place here and the main central hall, or *nef*, with its cast iron structure and Art

Nouveau staircase designed by Albert Louvet may again be seen. Its huge scale is a reminder that Louvet had been Dutert's assistant on the 1889 Palais des Machines, to be described in the next chapter.

This section must end with another smaller building by Girault: 21 rue Blanche, 9e (1901–3), built as an *hôtel particulier*. Its carefully modulated facade combines a Palladian central pavilion, slightly recessed, with plain side bays, but the ground and first floors, including curved bows, combine Rococo and Art Nouveau elements. The combination would have been bizarre in the hands of a lesser architect, but is here delightfully original. Unfortunately, at the time of writing (2006) this building has been empty and neglected for several years.

Reaction and Innovation in a Time of Change

The Grand and Petit Palais are the last important Parisian buildings in a full-blown classical style and represent the culmination of traditional nineteenth-century architecture. The second half of this book is devoted to work which, although rooted firmly in the Rational tradition within the Ecole des Beaux-Arts, attempts to solve the new architectural problems set by a changing society, incorporating the foreign influences brought by the increased international contacts which the 1900 Exhibition represented.

Right: **Albert Louvet, Henri Deglane and others, Grand Palais, 1896–1900.**
An architecture in transition, the otherwise rational iron structure is adorned at every turn with decorative flourishes.

1   *L'architecture française du siècle*, Firmin-Didot, Paris, 1889, p 99 (translation by Anthony Sutcliffe, quoted in A. Sutcliffe, *Paris: An Architectural History*, Yale University Press, New Haven, CT and London, 1993, p 108.

2   E. Zola, *L'Oeuvre*, 1886; translation by Thomas Walton, *The Masterpiece*, Paul Elek, London, 1950, p 73.

3   The most influential Professors of Theory were Edmond Guillaume 1884–94 and Julien Guadet 1894–1908. The three *ateliers officiels* were run during this period by Jules André from 1867, succeeded by Constant Moyaux in 1890; Léon Ginain from 1890, succeeded by Louis Scellier de Gisors in 1898 and Louis Bernier in 1905; and by Julien Guadet from 1871, succeeded by Edmond Paulin in 1895. The most popular *ateliers libres* were those of Honoré Daumet 1860–85, Henri Deglane 1894 onwards, Victor Laloux 1890 onwards, Jean-Louis Pascal 1872–90, Gustave Raulin 1875–1910 and Gaston Redon 1891 onwards.

4   David van Zanten, *Building Paris 1830–70*, Cambridge University Press, Cambridge and New York, 1994, pp 47 and 289, note 5.

5   *'L'architecte est l'artiste qui compose les édifices, en détermine les proportions, arrangements et décorations, les faits exécuter sous ses ordres et en règle les dépenses'*. Quoted in *La carrière de l'architecte aux XIXe siècle*, Les Dossiers du Musée d'Orsay, 1986, p 7.

6   E. & J. Charton, *Dictionnaire des professions*, 1880. Quoted in *La carrière de l'architecte aux XIXe siècle*, Les Dossiers du Musée d'Orsay, 1986, p 59, note 24.

7   *'C'est le plan qui concilie toutes les exigences du programme; c'est le plan qui contient la pensée créatrice de l'architecte; c'est le plan qui est le critère par lequel les gens spéciaux jugent avant tout de la valeur réelle de la composition'*, Dictionnaire de l'Académie des Beaux-Arts, 1884, Institut de France, vol 4, p 204.

8   *'L'axe est la clef du dessin et sera celle de la composition'*, J. Guadet, *Eléments et théorie de l'architecture*, Aulanier et Cie, Paris, 1901, vol 1, book I, ch 3, p 40.

9   *Vitruvius on Architecture*, translated by Frank Granger, 1931, W. Heinemann Ltd, London, book 1, ch 2, 4.

10 *'La symétrie, avec cependant, la variété, devra généralement être cherchée. Mais il est bon de définir la symétrie. La symétrie est la régularité de ce qui doit se voir d'un seul coup d'oeil. La symétrie est la régularité intelligente,'* J. Guadet, *Eléments et théorie de l'architecture*, Aulanier et Cie, Paris, 1901, vol 1, book 2, ch 4, p 128.

11 Architectural section of Diderot's *Encyclopédie*, written by J.-F. Blondel, see Allan Braham, *The Architecture of the French Enlightenment*, Thames and Hudson, London, 1980, p 38.

12 *'Le beau, a dit Platon … est la splendeur du vrai'*, Eléments et théorie de l'architecture, Aulanier et Cie, Paris, 1901, vol 1, book 2, p 99.

13   Garnier's chief assistant was Louis-Victor Louvet (1822–98), Prix de Rome, 1850. Junior assistants with notable subsequent careers included Joseph Cassien-Bernard, Julien Guadet, Henri-Paul Nénot, Jean-Louis Pascal, Gustave Raulin and Louis Scellier de Gisors.

14   Quoted in G. H. Hamilton, *Painting and Sculpture in Europe 1880–1940*, Penguin Books, Harmondsworth, 1967/72, p 80 and Bernard Dorival, *Les étapes de la peinture française contemporaine*, Paris, 1943, I, pp 43–4.

15   Charles Blanc, *Grammaire des arts du dessin*, Jules Renouard, Paris, 1867, p 104: '*Proportion, caractère, harmonie, telles sont les trois conditions générales du beau dans l'architecture,*' p 71: '*Le sublime de l'architecture tient à trois conditions essentielles: la grandeur des dimensions, la simplicité des surfaces, la rectitude et la continuité des lignes.*'

16   *Ibid*, p 14: '*L'artiste est chargé de rappeler parmi nous l'idéal, c'est-à-dire de nous révéler la beauté primitive des choses, d'en découvrir le caractère impérissable, la pure essence.*'

17   '*Le caractère, identité entre l'impression architecturale et l'impression morale du programme*', *Eléments et théorie de l'architecture*, book 2, ch 3, p 132.

18   Donald Drew Egbert, *The Beaux-Arts Tradition in French Architecture*, Princeton University Press, Princeton, NJ and Guildford, Surrey, 1980, pp 122–3.

19   P. Planet, *Construction Moderne*, 1901, p 392, '*Le Petit Palais des Champs-Elysées a été le grand succès de l'Exposition; c'est une vérité que tout le monde à peu près s'accord à reconnaître*'.

Part 2 Change

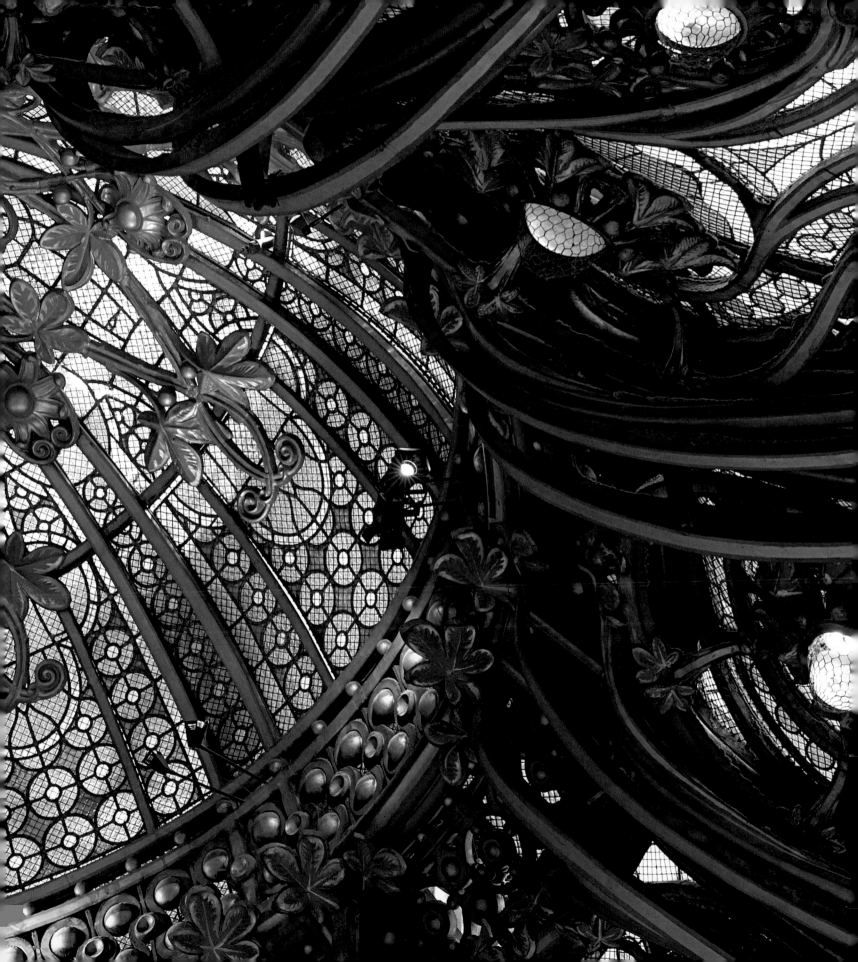

5 The Triumph of Iron

The 1889 International Exhibition

It may seem strange to the reader that a chapter devoted partly to the 1889 International Exhibition should follow one which ended with the Exhibition of 1900. The reason is that the Grand and Petit Palais are the last important buildings of pure Classicism in a stylistic sense, whereas the 1889 Exhibition was essentially a celebration of the changes brought about by industrialisation, which would eventually render the reproduction of classical detail on a large scale both economically prohibitive and artistically inappropriate.

The 1878 and 1889 International Exhibitions were mainly staged to show the world how remarkably France had recovered from its troubles of 1870–1 and how, despite the annexation by Germany of Alsace and Lorraine, its consequent loss of mineral resources as well as the payment of reparations, it had become a fully industrialised nation.

The Grand and Petit Palais and the adjacent Pont Alexandre III are the only surviving structures from the 1900 Exhibition; the sole survivor of the previous Exhibition of 1889 is the Eiffel Tower, a masterpiece, but a work of engineering rather than of architecture. The greatest building of the 1889 Exhibition was the Palais des Machines, which was demolished in 1909. There is only space in this book to describe those buildings that

can still be seen in Paris, and therefore the temporary pavilions intended only for the duration of the International Exhibitions cannot be properly included, although some reference to their nature will follow later. An exception must be made for the Palais des Machines, however, because of its importance in the history of architecture on three counts: the inevitable development of new structural forms made both necessary and possible by industrialisation; the relationship between architects and engineers which this entailed; and the aesthetic dilemmas facing architects trained in the use of forms derived from pre-industrial construction.

Early Iron Buildings

The 1889 Exhibition was described by Louis Rousselet as representing *'the resounding triumph of iron in modern construction'*.[1] The ability of metal construction to be assembled on site from elements produced more effectively elsewhere made it particularly suitable for buildings needing to be incombustible and having to be completed promptly. The roof of the Théâtre Français (Victor Louis, 1786), since rebuilt, was an early example of iron being used for reasons of fire-resistance. In this situation, of course, the structure was concealed behind a ceiling, but in more prosaic structures, such as the early railway stations and markets, the iron trusses were exposed to view.

Opposite: **Ferdinand Dutert, Galerie de Paléontologie, 1892–8.**

Cast iron had been successfully produced for the first time in France at Le Creusot in 1785, the first entire cast-iron structure in Paris being the Pont des Arts of 1801 (rebuilt and modified in 1980). Wrought iron had been used as reinforcement in masonry structures since the seventeenth century, but the development of coal mining and railways early in the nineteenth century had made iron cheaper and more easily available. As a result cast iron came generally into use as a constituent material in commercial structures – for example, I-beams at one metre centres supporting small brick vaults to create fire-resisting floors, or iron columns in ground-floor shops to provide uninterrupted floor space, even though the *immeubles* above were of load-bearing brick and stone.

Early iron buildings still standing include the dome of the Bourse de Commerce (a circular stone structure built as the grain market), where in 1806–11 (architect F.-J. Bélanger, engineer F. Brunet) it replaced an earlier timber dome destroyed by fire. It was originally covered with copper, replaced by glazing in 1888. The greenhouses of the Jardin des Plantes were built in 1833 to a design by the architect Charles Rohault de Fleury, but had to be replaced by a replica after being damaged in the Franco-Prussian War. The main Paris market at Les Halles, entirely in exposed iron and glass, was built in 1854–66 by Victor Baltard and Félix Callet, engineer César Jolly, and demolished in 1971. Smaller markets and shopping arcades *(passages)* have been mentioned in Chapter Two.

The most important early public buildings where exposed iron was consciously designed as a decorative element by the architect were the Bibliothèque Sainte-Geneviève, 1854, and the reading room of the Bibliothèque Nationale, 1858–68 (see Chapter Four), both by Henri Labrouste (1801–75), where forms derived from classical precedent were elegantly modified to express their material. The Bibliothèque Sainte-Geneviève is essentially of stone. The exterior reflects a ground floor used mainly for storage and the reading room above has solid walls for the height of the bookcases, while internally the lattice beams in the entrance hall and the central cast-iron columns and semi-circular openwork beams in the reading room emphasise the lightness possible with iron. The nine domes with their central oculi and supporting attenuated columns do the same in the Bibliothèque Nationale reading room. The prime architectural importance of these two buildings, designed two to three decades before the birth of Le Corbusier but 60 years after Boullée's studies in the architecture of shadows, is however something different: their forms, derived wholly from the purpose and structure of the building, were then moulded to shape space and control light.[2]

Exterior walls of permanent buildings continued to be of masonry for thermal as well as aesthetic reasons and the facade walls of all *immeubles* had to be half a metre thick, although building regulations were somewhat relaxed in this respect in 1878.

Unlike London's Crystal Palace of 1851, most iron buildings at the 1855, 1878 and 1889 Paris Exhibitions had their construction largely disguised by elaborate decoration in fibrous plaster, usually referred to by later French architectural critics as '*pâtisseries*'. Colour was provided by glazed brick and faience, any exposed iron usually being painted green, in festive contrast to the Parisian tradition of cream stucco, grey stone and zinc roofing. The use of painted polychromaticism in nineteenth-century French architecture was introduced by J.-I. Hittorff's coloured plates in his *Architecture antique de la Sicile* (where he had measured the Greek temples), published in Paris in 1827–30, and in Henri Labrouste's reconstruction of the Temple of Neptune at Paestum in 1829, undertaken while he was a Grand Prix *pensionnaire* at Rome.[3] It was later furthered by Viollet-le-Duc's medieval restorations and by the reconstruction in 1845, by Duban and Lassus, of the fragments of original wall paintings in the Sainte-Chapelle.

The principal iron building of the 1855 Exhibition had been the Palace of Industry in the Champs-Elysées (architects Victor Viel and Alexis Cendrier, engineer Alexis Barrault), which remained there until 1898 when it had to be demolished to make way for the Grand and Petit Palais, but this was encased in stone. The main building of the 1878 Exhibition, by Léopold Hardy (1829–94), had elaborate exposed ironwork, which may have influenced Victor Horta – generally thought of as the founder of Art Nouveau – who was then studying in Paris, as will be described in the next chapter.

Science and Engineering

The scale of both industrial construction and machinery exhibited in 1889 was an essential demonstration of France's prominence as a modern nation, and most visitors to the Exhibition were fascinated by mechanisation and the novelty of machines. To them the greatest revelation was probably the use of electricity as the main form of illumination and as an alternative source of power to steam. Stemming from the eighteenth-century Enlightenment, writers and philosophers (Saint-Simon, Zola and Taine, for example) thought of science as a guide to everyday conduct as well as a form of knowledge, while the International Exhibitions of 1855, 1878 and 1889 served to emphasise the extent to which science and engineering were affecting daily life.

Viollet-le-Duc, whose love of Gothic had made him understand the extent to which its forms were related to the development of constructional technique, had written in his published lectures: *'Few ages can compete with our own in the glory of its scientific achievements. Do our architects, like their predecessors, eagerly avail themselves of this source of aesthetic revolution? No; they prefer to ignore the close connection of science with art and to give us public buildings of a hybrid style … If they persist in refusing that aid which science would gladly give them, the function of the architect is obsolete; while that of the engineer is commencing – that of men really devoted to construction, who will make purely scientific knowledge their starting point to constitute an art deduced from that knowledge and from the requirements of the times.'*[4]

The foundation of the Ecole des Ponts-et-Chaussées in 1747, to facilitate the design of bridges and roads for military purposes, had marked the recognition by the State of engineering as a separate profession. This was extended by the formation of the Ecole Centrale des Travaux Publics in 1794 (which was renamed the Ecole Polytechnique a year later), and of the Ecole Centrale des Arts et Manufactures in 1829, where Gustave Eiffel (1832–1923) had been a student and where architecture was also taught.[5] Emile Trélat (1821–1907), who studied architecture there, was critical of the Ecole des Beaux-Arts' emphasis on the design of large expensive buildings, resulting in its more

mediocre students, inevitably employed on lesser projects, compromising the architectural profession by their lack of practical knowledge. He founded the Ecole Centrale (later renamed Ecole Spéciale) d'Architecture in 1856: here students attended daily lectures, completing their training in three years and receiving more instruction in practical subjects than the Ecole des Beaux-Arts students.

In 1845 a number of architects, concerned at the threat to their profession from engineers being employed to design railway buildings, had formed a promotional body called the Société Centrale des Architectes, to explain to the public that architects were still needed to provide imaginative solutions to architectural design problems.

Railway Stations

The earliest large Parisian structures constructed in iron were the railway terminals, where roofs, glazed to admit daylight but high enough for the engine smoke to escape, needed to be supported by the minimum number of columns. Most of the Paris stations had been built before the Belle Epoque,[6] the most distinguished architecturally being the Gare du Nord, 1842–6, by J.-I. Hittorff, where the Greek classical facade (now spoilt by a modern cantilevered canopy) clearly echoes the form of the elegantly simple iron shed behind.

Left: **Victor Laloux, Gare d'Orsay, 1898.** *In its original form, the ground floor acted as a balcony from which the lines below could be seen.*

The Gare de Lyon, originally built in 1847–52, had to be enlarged in 1895–1901, when the number of lines was increased from seven to 13. Although the train shed was a straightforward engineering job in iron, the architect Marius Toudoire – designer also of stations at Bordeaux and Toulouse – masked this by a stone frontage. This contained the main entrance, a hotel, a restaurant and a clock tower at one end that terminated the view along the rue de Lyon. This was all finished in the Third Republic's official classical style, with much external sculpture by Prix de Rome winners.

The Gare d'Orsay (now the Musée d'Orsay) was the subject of an architectural competition, won in 1898 by Victor Laloux (1850–1937), who had already designed a remarkably fine station for the Orléans company at Tours. Together with its associated hotel, the new station was completed in time for the 1900 Exhibition. There was one complication in that it had to be built over existing lines running along the side of the river at basement level. The station shed is therefore placed parallel to the Seine, with the hotel terminating it at its west end. The station was originally entered directly from the Quai, through seven glazed and arched openings into a vaulted entrance hall that overlooked the platforms beyond. Because the tracks were electrified, the absence of smoke enabled the main engine shed to be enclosed and toplit by rooflights, with its iron vault encased in fibrous plaster. Originally the ground-floor concourse formed a balcony from which the platforms below could be seen.

The competition was held because an earlier more mundane design had been criticised as an *'usine de transports'* unworthy of facing the Louvre and the Tuileries gardens. Laloux therefore faced the building with stone topped by statues representing Toulouse, Bordeaux and Nantes, while inside the fibrous plaster eliminated any industrial character. The size and number of the arched openings and the scale of the two mansard-roofed end bays, where the arches are echoed by semi-circular gables enclosing clocks, are nicely calculated to provide a restful effect from the Right Bank. From there, the plain horizontal line of the station hall's roof can be seen, although its size – which would have been overwhelming if a greater number of smaller bays had been used – can only be appreciated when one realises that the hotel at the end has seven floors.

The Tour Eiffel

Much of the interest of the Eiffel Tower – designer and contractor Gustave Eiffel, engineers Maurice Koechlin (1856–1946) and Emile Nouguier (*b* 1839) – lies in the fact that contemporary attitudes to it reflected Parisian society's reactions to the huge scale of industrialisation. The 1889 Exhibition was intended to celebrate the centenary of the political revolution of

1789, as well as demonstrating scientific and industrial progress, and it was opposed by both political and artistic conservatives. A number of leading Academicians, including the leading Salon painters Gérôme, Meissonier and Bouguereau, the writers Dumas fils, Leconte de Lisle and Sully-Prudhomme and the architects Daumet, Questel and Guillaume, wrote to *Le Temps* objecting to the 'useless and monstrous' tower.

The only artists who admired and painted it at the time were Georges Seurat (1859–91) and Jean Béraud (1849–1935), both of whom were essentially concerned in their work with contemporary Parisian life. The tower was always popular with the general public, however, and Seurat thought of it as an image of the future. Béraud wrote to the actor Constant Coquelin, '... *it's very beautiful. When one is inside this complicated metal construction, it becomes a very bizarre work of art: it gives one a notion of what today's Gothic might be.*' He added, '*the galerie des machines is also very beautiful.*'[7] Albert de Lapparent wrote about the Eiffel Tower in 1890: '*By this example one acquires proof that true beauty in architecture resides essentially in perfect adaptation of means to purpose.*'[8] The un-noteworthy architectural adornments at the base of the tower are by Stephen Sauvestre (1847–1919).

The Palais des Machines
The Palais des Machines, built of steel (the Eiffel Tower is iron),

was designed not by an engineer, but by an architect Premier Prix de Rome, Ferdinand Dutert (1845–1906), with Victor Contamin (1840–98) as his engineering consultant. The vast single nave was spanned by a series of three-pin trusses, essentially Gothic in shape, to create a space measuring 429 metres long, 43 metres high and 115 metres wide (excluding the two-storey side aisles). Dwarfing all rivals, it was an astonishing 50 per cent wider than the previous record for a single-span truss, held by the St Pancras Station train shed in London (1868, engineers Barlow and Ordish), which had a width of 74 metres. (For a modern comparison, the internal diameter of the Greenwich Millennium Dome is 320 metres, with a height of 50 metres.)

The Palais des Machines was first designed with apsed ends, but these were omitted for reasons of expense, being replaced by glass curtain walls braced externally with openwork vertical trusses. The omission of internal columns (included in Dutert's preliminary sketches) significantly reduced foundation costs on poor-quality ground, while providing more flexible exhibition space and improved visibility. The building was essentially a celebration of industrialisation: most of the machines were in motion, a foretaste of Charles Chaplin's *Modern Times*. Electrically powered mobile viewing platforms running the length of the hall on elevated tracks enabled visitors to view the machines from above.

Left: **Ferdinand Dutert, Galerie de Paléontologie, 1892–8.** *Pink and white stone and a Romanesque- (or Bostonian-) inspired entrance, but no 'period' details.*

Above: **Jules André, Galerie de Zoologie, 1877.** *The exposed iron structure as seen when the building first opened. It is now the Grande Galerie de l'Evolution.*

Most visitors entered this vast cathedral (its plan was basically a nave with a row of side chapels on each side) at its central point, having approached it from the *Dôme Central* on the axis of the Eiffel Tower, through a highly decorated vestibule whose coloured glass dome was lit from above at night by electricity. The Palais' steel frame was painted a warm ochre, contrasting with the green, blue and red highlights in the (otherwise mainly clear) glazing, and the spandrel walls of red and yellow brickwork. External decorative elements were in green and yellow faience.

From photographs, the contrast to modern eyes between the revolutionary and highly functional overall design and somewhat eclectic polychromatic Beaux-Arts detail led early modern historians to assume that Contamin had been the designer and Dutert the decorator. In fact, as Stuart Durant has shown in *Lost Masterpieces*, 'Palais des Machines, Paris 1889', the building was a heroic endeavour by one of the Ecole des Beaux-Arts' most brilliant disciples to unite art and science, tradition and modernity. (Le Corbusier photographed both the Palais des Machines and the Eiffel Tower in 1908–9, while working for Auguste Perret.)

Dutert's poor health only enabled him to complete one other major building: the Galerie de Paléontologie in the Jardin des Plantes, 5e (1892–8), which has a very solid stone exterior,

totally without period detail. The simplicity of the entrance facade is emphasised by the massive scale of the surrounding arch, windows and stone mouldings, as well as the use of small square blocks of pink sandstone to accentuate the contrast with the ashlar dressings. The side elevations reflect the simple interiors – with large windows for the lower floors, while the upper floor is top-lit – the only decoration provided by the moulded cast-iron balustrades designed by the assistant architect Louis Bonnier (1856–1946), whose leaf motifs are perfectly in accord with the skeletons of prehistoric animals displayed in the galleries. In many ways, the elevation is reminiscent of the work of Bostonian architect Henry Hobson Richardson, of the 1870s and 1880s, which Parisian architects would have known from illustrations. (Richardson had been a pupil of Jules André 1858–60 and had also worked for Théodore Labrouste, Henri Labrouste's brother.)

Also in the Jardin des Plantes is the Galerie de Zoologie, 1877 (now the Grande Galerie de l'Evolution), designed by Jules André (1819–90) who had been Labrouste's assistant at the Bibliothèque Nationale. This Galerie mainly consists of a top-lit iron hall with galleried sides. Although the stone facade facing the gardens is of a rather dull classicism, the smaller rooms behind it have virtually no period detail apart from Tuscan pilasters in the lobbies.

Above: **Ferdinand Dutert, Galerie de Paléontologie, 1892–8.** *The upper floor is largely top-lit, and accommodates a balcony supported by delicately detailed brackets, its cast-iron balustrade designed by Louis Bonnier.*

Left: **Ferdinand Dutert, Galerie de Paléontologie, 1892–8.** *The ground-floor gallery is lit by large windows, on either side, the space spanned by beams with curved ends that are echoed by small plastered vaults in the ceiling.*

The Eglise de Notre-Dame-du-Travail

In 1892 Jules Astruc (1862–1935), a pupil of André and Laloux, was asked to design a new church for the parish of Plaisance, a working-class area where most of the building workers for the 1889 and 1900 Exhibitions, as well as many railworkers, lodged. The church, Notre-Dame-du-Travail, 59 rue Vercingétorix, 14e, at first sight stone Romanesque, had to be built very cheaply and only the front is of ashlar, the side walls being rendered over a mixture of rubble stone and brick. The interior structure, however, including the galleries in the double-width side aisles, is entirely of metal, and unlike the earlier iron churches – notably the Eglise Saint-Eugène of 1854, by L.-A. Boileau (1812–96) which is entirely Gothic – there is no attempt at period styling.

The structural slenderness made possible with metal, and later reinforced concrete – often utilised in commercial buildings to provide maximum usable space – here serves a different function. Its transparency, particularly in contrast with the solid exterior, must have provided some degree of spiritual delight, while the choice of material would have had particular relevance to those in the congregation who worked on metal structures during their daily lives. Built partly by popular subscription, the church contains murals depicting the patron saints of carpenters and metal workers, while its first *curé*, the Abbé Soulange-Bodin, founded a mutual help society, workers' club and co-operative.

The Métro

The number of visitors to the 1889 International Exhibition proved that a radical improvement to public transport facilities was becoming necessary, and in 1897 the development of an underground *chemin de fer métropolitain* was approved, having been discussed since 1872. (The station entrances by Hector Guimard (1867–1942), with their iron steps, railings and occasional glazed canopies, being primarily of decorative rather than structural interest, will be included more appropriately in the next chapter.) The main lines were usually built close below ground level, under the centres of wide streets, but two lines (numbers Two and Six) were built partly above ground and known as *métro aérien*. The architect for these was Jean-Camille Formigé (1845–1926), while the engineer for the whole Métro was Fulgence Bienvenue (1852–1936), known as *le Père métro*. Formigé had been responsible at the 1889 Exhibition for the Palais des Beaux-Arts and the Palais des Arts Libéraux, both of iron construction but much smaller and more highly decorated than the Palais des Machines.

The iron bridges of the *métro aérien* are supported on a mixture of stone and iron columns, the latter of particular interest. Made of cast iron in the style of Doric columns, these needed to support the ends of two bridge sections capable of separate movement, which was achieved by the introduction of a

brilliantly original iron 'padstone' – vaguely Assyrian in character, but with Ionic volutes – with a rectangular top plate wide enough to provide bearing for two rollers to move independently. The simply designed, cantilevered and canopied station platforms are entirely constructed in iron. As Bernard Marrey and Paul Chemetov have elegantly phrased it, the details *'sont aériens comme le métro'*.[10]

Sub-stations

Electricity sub-stations, required for lighting streets and buildings, the provision of compressed air and running the Métro, were a new industrial building type for which an engineer was more likely to be appointed than an architect. However, most of the Paris sub-stations were designed by an architect, Paul Friesé (1851–1917), who had entered into partnership in 1885 with an architect-engineer, Jules Denfer (1838–1914), whom he had assisted in the reconstruction of the Ecole Centrale des Arts et Manufactures, where Denfer was a professor. Because of his subsequent experience of the industrial work carried out by the partnership, he was appointed joint architect, with J.-C. Formigé, to the Compagnie du Chemin de Fer Métropolitain in 1898, going on to design the company's power station and administrative building between the rue de Bercy and the quai de la Rapée – a remarkable building now sadly demolished[11] – as

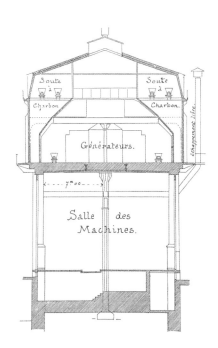

Left: **Paul Friesé, former generating plant, 132 quai de Jemmapes, 1895.** *A typical section through the machine and generator halls*

Above: **Paul Friesé, former generating plant, 132 quai de Jemmapes, 1895.** *The main facades are a mixture of metal framing and load-bearing brickwork.*

well as nine sub-stations, of which only the earliest, built in 1902, has since been destroyed.

He designed a further nine for the Compagnie Parisienne de l'Air Comprimé and three for public electricity companies. The majority occupy infill sites, having elevations three bays wide with exposed riveted columns. They generally consist of one double-height machine hall, glazed for maximum ventilation with straight lintels, above which is an upper floor containing smaller items of plant. This usually has arched metal windows, between which are brackets supporting a plain cornice. The sub-station at 41 rue Caumartin, 9e, has a further storey added later by Friesé himself, which was treated as a classical attic by enlarging the cornice, introducing dentils and providing six windows above.

The sub-stations at 14 avenue Parmentier, 11e (currently in poor condition), and 36 rue Jacques-Louvel-Tessier, 10e, had an additional floor from the beginning. The main upper floor glazing is combined with the machine room windows under semi-circular arches, while the top floor, above a dentilled cornice, has three groups of triple round-arched windows. These facades have brick side piers or wings (although in terrace formation, the sub-stations had to be structurally independent of existing party walls to avoid vibration). The small arched doors and windows in the side wings at avenue Parmentier, with their rounded reveals, contrast with the sharper texture of the riveted metal stanchions.

Friesé also increased the areas of brickwork at the last and largest sub-stations for the Métro: those at *2 bis* rue Michel-Ange, 16e (1912), and at the Bastille on a prominent corner site between boulevard Bourdon and rue de l'Arsenal, 4e (1911). The latter was treated more monumentally and almost entirely in brick with very little stone, its forms possibly inspired – like the exterior of Dutert's Galerie de Paléontologie – by the architecture of H. H. Richardson. Here, where the building is exposed on three sides, a more sculptural approach was employed using contrasting round-arched openings of at least four different sizes, ranging from small slits lighting the corner spiral staircases to the two huge windows of the machine room. The corbelling and solid balustrades at the top, although ultimately derived from classical precedent, only serve to emphasise the fortress-like aspect, reminiscent of Vanbrugh's castles.

The generating plant for the Air Comprimé company at 132 quai de Jemmapes, 10e (1895) – of which only a part was built and which is now a garment factory (Vêtements Labor) – combines brickwork with metal framing on the front administration block, while the ground-level machine hall behind has stone piers supporting corbels that carry the exposed metal frame of the generator hall over. The projecting external balcony was provided should the workers need to escape from burning hot vapour if the boilers overheated.

Left: **Paul Friesé, 20 rue Duphot, 1898 and 1910.** *When the building was first completed, its principal source of elegance derived from the wrought-iron balustrades silhouetted against full-length windows and white curtains.*

Left: **Paul Friesé, 20 rue Duphot, 1898 and 1910.** *Although the balustrades remain on two floors, their effect has been lost by the insertion of new glazing and spandrel panels behind.*

Glazing for the Fashion Industry

In 1898 Paul Friesé also designed – entirely in glass with metal framing to provide maximum daylight – a three-bay facade at 20 rue Duphot, 1er, as an extension to the department store Aux Trois Quartiers. (In 1910, this was doubled in width with an identical repeat.) Although extant, removal of decorative arches on the top floor and the insertion of modern glazing with solid spandrel panels in place of delicately curvilinear railings has robbed the facade of its original fragile elegance, so appropriate to its purpose.

The use of extensive glazing enabled the colour of fabrics to be examined and if necessary exactly matched in daylight. It was therefore an essential feature of multi-storey workshops built at this time for the fashion trade, mostly in the second *arrondissement*. The establishment of Paris as the world centre of fashion during the Second Empire and the success of the *Grands Magasins* turned dressmaking into big business, requiring large-scale purpose-built accommodation. The standard plan was for a deep rectangle with glazed front and rear facades and a central atrium roofed over with glass, providing daylight to the centre of the building. A good example is 13 rue d'Uzès by Gustave Raulin (1837–1910), built in 1885. This is clearly a metal-framed commercial building but, being a *Patron* at the Ecole des Beaux-Arts, Raulin also used elaborately sculpted stone piers.

Nos 23 and 25 rue du Mail are an interesting pair. No 23 by Jacques Hermant, 1884, is the more eclectic, with Romanesque arches surmounted by stone piers (with incorrect Corinthian capitals), which have side brackets supporting metal beams. No 25, 1886, by Paul Héneux (1844–1909), has its iron frame exposed, creating a more industrial structure with larger glazed areas, above which 'Gothicky' dormers peep incongruously.

The most complete collection of architect-designed garment factories, however, lies on rue Réaumur between rue Notre-Dame-des-Victoires and rue Saint-Denis. This was formed in 1895–6 on land owned by the city as a profitable replacement for a slum area, and illustrates perfectly how different architects found different ways to resolve the external treatment of buildings of identical height and purpose. The most satisfactory design, faced entirely with stone, is no 103 (1896) by Jean-Jules Despras (*b* 1850), where workshops on the first to third floors have large full-height windows with shallow arches or flat metal lintels. It is clear from the elevation that the three floors above these are occupied by apartments: two per floor. It is even obvious that the vertical windows behind the continuous balconies light three rooms per apartment. In this serene facade, where nothing is superfluous, the entrance is marked simply by linking the doorway with the arched window over, protected by a projecting balcony supported on stone brackets.

Left: **Gustave Raulin, 13 rue d'Uzès, 1885.** *The wide side bays with their full-height glazing and central columns emphasise the 'rational' tradition within the Ecole des Beaux-Arts, although the fourth floor acts as a frieze.*

Above: **Jacques Hermant, 23 rue du Mail, 1884, and Paul Héneux, 25 rue du Mail, 1886.** *No 23 (on the left) is essentially stone with a two-storey base and three-storey order, while no 25 is wholly metal, but with a residential fourth floor.*

Left: **Jean-Jules Despras, 103 rue Réaumur, 1896.**
The most successful of the all-stone facades: the architect has created an 'order' four storeys high including the ground floor – an original adaptation of classical principles.

With one exception, the other architects combined stone and metal with varying degrees of success, usually treating the ground floor and mezzanine as a stone base, then the next three floors as the order with vertically linked metal windows between stone pilasters and an 'attic' of two domestic storeys at the top; in other words, they were adapting the classical system taught at the Ecole des Beaux-Arts to a new type of multi-storey building. The most spectacularly Baroque example is no 118 (1900) by Joseph-Charles Guirard de Montarnal (1867–1949), where the order has been replaced by a giant arch filled with a three-storey curtain wall, the whole overbearingly pompous for a piece of street infill. The most charming, designed for a printing firm, is no 69 (1898) by Ernest Pergod (1844–1912), where a two-storey conservatory has been inserted into a traditional four-storey house.[12]

The sole exception to a design based on French tradition is no 124, the last to be built, in 1904–5, and designed by a former winner of the Prix de Rome, Georges Chedanne. This amazing building, in which the five main floors are totally clad in steel and glass, is so revolutionary that its attribution to Chedanne has been queried, especially – as Paul Chemetov and Bernard Marrey have pointed out[13] – since the built design does not correspond with that submitted for building permission in April 1903.

The original design is preserved in the Archives de Paris, including Chedanne's pencil sketch for the elevation. The original proposal was for a building four bays wide: the subsequent reduction to three bays had the advantage of reducing the width of the central court to about a third of the plot width, thereby increasing floor area available for workspace. (As the sketch elevation, obviously hastily prepared, is too fragile for reproduction, the author has produced his own drawings for comparison with the scheme as built.)

Apart from the omission of brick piers against the party walls, the elevation is basically the same except that small areas of brickwork were originally proposed between the fourth-floor bay windows and the exposed metal stanchions. The brick recessed wall to the fifth-floor apartments (metal not being thermally suitable for domestic walling) is identical except that the original sketch showed larger windows, perhaps better related to the window bays below but less flexible for domestic subdivision.

Paul Chemetov and Bernard Marrey have suggested that Chedanne may possibly have been busy with more prestigious projects and employed a 'ghost', but contemporary accounts of the degree of personal involvement by Chedanne in every detail of the Elysée Palace Hotel, which has already been quoted,[14] suggest that this would have been unlikely, and we do not know of any other contemporary architect who might have produced such a design. Since the original proposal was produced quickly

Left: **Georges Chedanne, 124 rue Réaumur, 1903 –1904.** *Art Nouveau meets Mies van der Rohe, with a complete facade in bronze-painted steel and glass that extends down to pavement level.*

Above: **Georges Chedanne, 124 rue Réaumur, 1903–4.** *As the author's sketch of Chedanne's preliminary pencil elevation indicates, the original design included four bays in place of three as built.*

Right: **Georges Chedanne, 124 rue Réaumur, 1903 –4.** *Plans of the fourth floor, comparing the original four-bay proposal put forward for building permission with the scheme as built.*

As originally proposed   As existing

Below: **GeorgesChedanne, 124 rue Réaumur, 1903 –4.** *On the ground floor, mullions curve out on each side of the main columns*

Below: **J.-C. Guirard de Montarnal, 26 rue Louis-Blanc, 1906.** *Apart from side bays half the width of the three central ones, the building has no other subtleties.*

to obtain permission for development (the building was a commercial speculation), it seems probable that, once the building permit had been granted in May 1904, Chedanne took the opportunity to make improvements.

The marvel of the facade at 124 rue Réaumur is that, once the initial decision to change from three to four bays had been made, comparatively few vital details needed to be altered. All that was required was: doubling the main stanchions for better loading capacity on wider bays; curving the corner posts of the bay windows where they act as brackets, and continuing them down to first-floor level and then curving them again, sideways, to provide vertical continuity; and introducing slightly curved soffits above and below the bay windows. The only decoration needed is supplied by the contrast between the riveted verticals and the sheet steel spandrels. The result is one of the first masterpieces of Modern architecture.

Chedanne's building was not illustrated in the magazines and was ignored by contemporary critics; its revolutionary character must have been too great a puzzle for them. Two subsequent garment factories by architects whose work was elsewhere much less radical do, however, show its influence. In 1906 Guirard de Montarnal designed the factory 100,000 Chemises at 26 rue Louis Blanc, 10e, a simple exposed metal frame filled with glazing (it is now the local police bureau), and in 1913 Jacques Hermant

Left: **Jean-Marie Boussard, Central Téléphonique, 46 rue du Louvre, 1891.** *Curved ends of grey brick and stone contrast with the curtain-walled north elevation, with Ionic capitals to the brick piers the only classical detail.*

Opposite: **Joseph Bouvard, former barracks, 4 rue de Schomberg, 1883.** *An early example of an exposed iron frame, complete with brackets to support the iron beams of the ground-floor arcade. Some of the three-storey buildings have since been converted into six-storey flats.*

Left: **Jean-Marie Boussard, Central Téléphonique, 46 rue du Louvre, 1891.** *Boussard's work is always full of character, as here with highly decorative iron in the telephone equipment halls.*

produced, at 12 rue Gaillon, 2e, a facade entirely of riveted metal but with a central bay window. Neither building, however, has the timeless elegance of 124 rue Réaumur.

Iron Framing for Other Uses

Of earlier framed structures, Julien Guadet's Hôtel des Postes, 1880, has been described in Chapter Four. The adjoining Central Téléphonique, 46 rue du Louvre, 1er, 1891 was by Jean-Marie Boussard (1844–1923), an original if slightly eccentric architect. The ground-floor elliptical arches and the grey pilastered brickwork are typical of his robust detailing. The north facade, facing the Hôtel des Postes, is a glazed curtain wall, its iron-framed bays reflecting the iron structure (floors as well as columns and beams) behind. Fire-resistance and good daylight without sun were the main functional requirements. The curved corner bays were altered during construction from the original design, with a corbelled projection introduced at third-floor level and, above this, two storeys in place of the single one with arched windows shown on the original drawings. From the way in which the curtain walling was simplified at the top, this variation appears original rather than a later alteration.

As architect to the Ministère des Postes et Télégraphes, in 1896 J.-M. Boussard designed the Administration des Postes at 40 boulevard de Port Royal, 5e, in which the framed structure is expressed externally as square bays filled with large windows in brick surrounds. The top floor is a later addition, but otherwise there appears to have been little external alteration, remarkable in that at first glance one could easily date the building as from the 1930s.

In 1883 Joseph Bouvard (1840–1920) was responsible for the design of a group of three-storey barracks for the Caserne Garde Républicaine at 4 rue de Schomberg, 4e, which utilised a structure of exposed cast-iron box columns, made up of plates and angle-irons tied together with wrought-iron wall plates. These are infilled with patterned red, yellow and black brickwork, with large windows in the centre of each bay, over a mainly recessed ground floor. In 1998 it was partly converted into six-storey flats by replacing the two main floors by three of lesser height and adding two visually lightweight storeys above. Bouvard's *groupe-scolaire* at 10–12 rue Saint-Lambert, 1891, similar in design, will be described with other schools in Chapter Seven. These examples of what the French called *pans de fer* (exposed iron framing with non-structural infill) are obviously derived from Viollet-le-Duc's coloured perspective of an exposed iron frame in his *Entretien XVIII*.[15]

The SNCF railway offices at 144 rue du Faubourg Saint-Denis, 10e (1889), by Adrien Gouny (extended behind in 1898), are illustrative of the application to semi-commercial use of the

The Triumph of Iron   113

Opposite: **Henri-Paul Nénot, offices, 40 rue de l'Arcade, 1904.** *The upper part of the two-storey base acts as a transition between stone below and brick above, while the canopied clock and bold corner cartouche provide a focus.*

Below: **Adrien Gouny, SNCF offices, 144 rue du faubourg Saint-Denis, 1889.** *Red brick surrounds to the delicately detailed iron-framed windows highlight the white brick piers, with further contrast provided by stone and faience.*

design methodology stemming from both Viollet-le-Duc and Labrouste, where external appearance, although at first glance 'traditional', is closely derived from non-traditional construction adapted to new functional requirements. As in Guadet's Hôtel des Postes, Gouny used masonry (in this case a mixture of brick and stone) to clad an iron-framed building. The metal is clearly shown and delicately detailed, notably in the spandrel panels and second-floor beams, the third-floor colonnettes, the metal capitals (slightly Greek without being classical) and the iron lintels they support. Similarly decorative are the iron ties that indicate the positions of cross beams, the entire ensemble complemented by the careful placing of contrasting red and white brickwork to create a whole that is light-hearted yet elegant.

A more individualistic but less innovative, purpose-built office building for the Compagnie des Wagons-Lits at 40 rue de l'Arcade, 8e (1904), by Henri-Paul Nénot, is faced mainly in brick, with a corner tower and stepped gables that seek inspiration in sixteenth-century chateaux for eight storeys of offices.

La Samaritaine and the Decorative Use of Iron

As already mentioned in Chapter Two, La Samaritaine is the period's *Grand Magasin* of greatest technical and decorative interest. It was built over a considerable period of time as its owner, Ernest Cognacq, assembled the site. Frantz Jourdain

Right: **Frantz Jourdain,
La Samaritaine, 1905.**
*The rue de la Monnaie facade
in 2006, the building empty
with a modern ground floor
and canopy. Above the first
floor, the original yellow
panels still have their floral
decoration.*

Below: **Frantz Jourdain,
La Samaritaine, 1905.**
*The original entrance, rue
de la Monnaie.*

(1847–1935), polemicist and founder of the Salon d'Automne, being appointed architect in 1883, was first employed to alter and improve the various existing buildings acquired. The main new building, at 17–19 rue de la Monnaie, 1er, was started in 1905 and extended when adjoining buildings could be demolished, to form a complete island block known as Magasin no 2 that was finally completed by 1910.

Iron construction was essential to complete each section as quickly as possible, nearly 500 workers being employed in day and night shifts. Jourdain was the *Maître d'Oeuvre* throughout, taking full responsibility for the design, including the installation of services. Ventilation ducting was encased within the interior columns, those on the facade containing heating and hot water pipes. Electrically controlled sun blinds were also installed, while the hollow box columns and beams on the rue de la Monnaie elevation were faced with yellow enamelled panels to provide an easily cleanable and impervious surface. The floral decoration relates more to the bucolic tradition of the boutique artists than to Art Nouveau.

The title panel 'Samaritaine' – designed by Eugène Grasset – over the centre was originally repeated round the base of the two corner cupolas (fantastic versions of those at Au Printemps), with rather coarse ironwork echoing that of the column capitals, now removed, on the rue de la Monnaie facade. The two cupolas

were demolished when the present river frontage designed by Henri Sauvage was built in 1926–8. A good deal of the curled ironwork (the word 'curvilinear' would imply a greater delicacy) has since been removed, but what remains is no match for the elegant use of wrought iron for balustrading and glazed entrance canopies (or *marquises*) that flourished during the Belle Epoque – whether based on eighteenth-century Rococo precedent or simplified under Art Nouveau influence. Rather, it relates more closely to the central hall of the Grand Palais and its staircase, completed five years earlier to a design by Albert Louvet.

Au Printemps and La Samaritaine both exhibited interesting uses of structural and decorative iron. These appear also as minor themes in the next chapter, which is devoted to the various stylistic attempts by architects to find a 'new art'. Many of the buildings described in Chapter Seven, 'The Social Aspect', built within stringent financial constraints and leading the way to a new art by a more organic route, also make use of exposed iron, while Chapter Eight, 'Towards a New Architecture', will show how the structural use of iron was gradually superseded by concrete, a more flexible material with better thermal properties.

1   Louis Rousselet, *L'Exposition universelle de 1889*, Paris, 1895, quoted in 'Palais des Machines Paris 1889' by Stuart Durant, *Lost Masterpieces*, Phaidon Press, London, 1999.

Right: **Frantz Jourdain, La Samaritaine, 1905.** *One of the two corner cupolas, which were demolished in 1926.*

2   David van Zanten, *Designing Paris*, MIT Press, Cambridge, MA and London, 1987, pp 83–98 and 234–46, and Allan Braham, *The Architecture of the French Enlightenment*, Thames and Hudson, London, 1980, p 113.

3   David van Zanten, *op cit*, pp 8–16.

4   Eugène Viollet-le-Duc, *Lectures on Architecture*, translated by B. Bucknell, Sampson Low, Marston, Searle & Rivington, London, 1881, Lecture XX, p 438.

5   Allan Braham, *op cit*, p 254.

6   Gare Saint-Lazare 1837, 1851–3, 1885–9 : Gare d'Austerlitz 1840–3, rebuilt 1866–9 : Gare du Nord 1842–6, rebuilt 1861–5 : Gare de Lyon 1847–52, enlarged 1895–1901 : Gare Montparnasse 1848–52, rebuilt 1961–9 : Gare de l'Est 1849–50

7   Undated letter from Jean Béraud to Constant Coquelin, Patrick Offenstadt, *Jean Béraud: catalogue raisonée*, Taschen, Cologne, 1999, p 336.

8   Albert de Lapparent, *Le siècle du fer*, Librairie F Savy, Paris, 1890, pp 95–6.

9   Stuart Durant, 'Palais des Machines, Paris 1889', in *Lost Masterpieces*, Phaidon Press, London, 1999: illustrations 29 and 30 show comparative sections of St Pancras and Palais des Machines.

10 Paul Chemetov and Bernard Marrey, *Architectures à Paris 1848–1914*, Dunod/Bordas, Paris, 1984, p 117.

11 Hugues Fiblec, *Paul Friesé*, Institut Français d'Architecture/ Editions Norma, Paris, 1991, pp 70–1 and 102–15.

12 Rue Réaumur: a list of the principal commercial structures is given here as this information is not easily available in print. South side: 61–3, P. Jouannin and E. Singery, 1898; 69, E. Pergod 1897–8; 91, J.-C. Guirard de Montarnal, 1897, (altered 1920); 93, L. Bonnenfant and L. Destors, 1896–8; 95, E. Menuel, 1898; 97, C. Devillard and P. Jolivald, 1900; 101, A. Walwein, 1898; 103, J.-J. Despras, 1896; 105, C. Ruzé 1898; 107, A. LeVoisvenel, 1897; 111-7, J. Mélard, 1896; 119, G. Cahn-Bousson, 1899; 121, C. Ruzé, 1900.
North side: 82, F. Constant-Bernard, 1896; 108-110, E. Wattier, 1898; 116, A. Waldwein, 1896; 118, J.-C. Guirard de Montarnal, 1898; 122, J.-J. Despras, 1897–8; 124, G. Chedanne, 1904–5; 126, A. LeVoisvenel, 1899; 128, A. Gautrin, 1896; 130, J.-C. Guirard de Montarnal, 1898; 132–4, J. Hermant ,1899.

13 Paul Chemetov and Bernard Marrey, *op cit*, p 123.

14 *La construction moderne*, 21 March 1900: already quoted as note 5, Chapter Two.

15 Bruno Foucart, *Viollet-le-Duc*, Editions de la Réunion des Musées Nationaux, Paris, 1980, p 27.

6 The Search for a New Art

The *Fin de Siècle*

The conservative nature of architecture at the 1900 International Exhibition, compared with that of 1889, both in respect to its nostalgia for Old Paris and its reliance on the Beaux-Arts classical tradition, can be explained partly by reaction against the Haussmannian regimentation of standard blocks and the extent of domination by mechanisation celebrated in the Palais des Machines.

Moreover, the 1890s, the decade separating the two exhibitions, was a time of political, social and artistic ferment generally. The expansion in international communications increased awareness of events going on elsewhere in the world, resulting not only in anxiety as to what political and social unrest might bring, but also knowledge of the latest developments in architecture – most apparent in the growth of illustrated magazines devoted to design. The architectural profession was, therefore, inevitably divided between backward glances at established customs and wide-ranging attempts to find a new art suitable for the coming century.

As has been seen in the case of garment factories and department stores, new building types posed design problems which inevitably brought with them their own appropriate changes in architectural form, and the next chapter will show that the increased construction of low-rental flats in the following decade would do the same.

The *Immeuble* and its Facade

The majority of Parisian architects were still mainly engaged in the design of middle-class *immeubles*. Modifications in internal planning resulting from changes in lifestyle have already been described in Chapter Three and, as indicated there, decoration within the apartments was mainly the concern of the occupants. The comparative standardisation of interior decoration, in so far as it was supplied by the developer, was determined by the residents' wishes to move to new accommodation providing a neutral background for their own possessions.[1]

The principal change in the basic form of apartment blocks was an increase in height, allowed by revisions to the building regulations to be described shortly. In elevational design terms, this resulted in buildings of six or seven floors of equal importance, plus a mansard roof – the latter usually, but not always, containing the maids' bedrooms. The standard Beaux-Arts treatment, based on Renaissance precedent, was a ground floor (the 'base') supporting the 'order' (usually two storeys high), with or without columns or pilasters and originally representing the most important rooms, the whole completed by an 'attic'

Opposite: **Jules Lavirotte, 29 avenue Rapp, 1900–1.** *Designed to advertise the client's wares, the building's decoration is particularly lavish.*

Left: **Octave de Courtois-Suffit, 134 rue du Faubourg Poissonnière, 1896.** *The vertical division is basically a two-storey base, three-storey 'order' and attic, but with medieval overtones and exposed iron lintels and tie-beam plates.*

Below: **Jean-Marie Boussard, 17 rue des Bernardins, 1890.** *The facade reads as five floors plus a top arcade above a cornice, which is emphasised by a stone frieze half a storey high. The iron balconies appear to be hanging in front.*

storey above the cornice. This configuration had already been uncomfortably stretched to cope with a standard Haussmannian block of five floors and became increasingly unsuitable as the upper floors became more desirable. A new way of organising facades was obviously required.

This chapter will therefore treat the *immeubles* as a backcloth, against which architects could conduct their experiments in search of an *art nouveau*. What form or forms this would eventually take was not yet clear, and the style now known as Art Nouveau was only one approach to the problem of adaptation to changing economic and cultural needs.

The Continued Influence of Viollet-le-Duc

Some architects, especially those whose practices included school or church work in addition to *immeubles*, and whose design approach was therefore orientated away from Beaux-Arts classicism, were influenced by Viollet-le-Duc's interest in the expression of combining iron and masonry: a rational approach to apartment blocks where fire-resistant construction, good thermal insulation and the provision of walls containing numerous chimney flues were all essential.

134 rue du Faubourg Poissonnière, 10e, 1896, by Octave de Courtois-Suffit (1856–1902), presents a facade seven stories high plus mansard, with windows lighting two apartments per floor – a

Right: **Georges Balleyguier, 23 avenue Rapp, 1898.** *Finished in stone, but with iron lintels, the six main floors are of equal height with no clear division into base and 'order', although there is an attic.*

Below: **Georges Balleyguier, 23 avenue Rapp, 1898.** *The framed structure has resulted in thin internal partitions and an exceptionally open living area, aided by a very large galerie with bay window.*

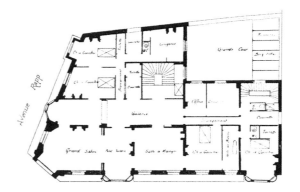

typical infill block. The provision of a continuous balcony on heavy corbels at second-floor level and a small cornice above the fourth floor, with further heavy brackets supporting projecting conservatories, is the nearest approach made to the traditional Beaux-Arts configuration of a two-storey base, a central three-storey 'order' and attic. The wide bracket or keystone of the arch above the entrance at *entresol* level acknowledges the party wall between apartments, although this is basically only a partition, as the chimneys are located either on the end walls or at the centre of each apartment between the two front rooms. All the windows have exposed iron lintels (as does the entrance door, supported here by stone corbels, an arrangement typical of medieval stone lintelled doors), while the decorative iron tie-plates indicate the position of iron cross beams.

The smaller block at 17 rue des Bernardins, 5e, 1890 by Jean-Marie Boussard, using his favourite grey brick, is a slightly lower-rental equivalent in that the facade clearly displays two apartments per floor, each two rooms wide, while the fairly solid stone arcade at ground level (partly altered) is echoed by a recessed arcade for the fifth-floor apartments. Boussard applied three-dimensional 'decoration' to his flat surface by adding cantilevered iron balconies, paired in the centre to make a symmetrical composition out of an even number of bays, the balustrades providing ornamental lightness.

Like Courtois-Suffit's building in rue du Faubourg Poissonière, 23 avenue Rapp, 7e, 1898, by Georges Balleyguier (1855–1944) has seven storeys plus a mansard, but is located on a corner site in a more fashionable area. It has only one large apartment per floor, planned around a central *galerie*, with a suite of reception rooms on the corner and five bedrooms. (The maids' rooms, of course, are in the roof.) The most unusual aspect of the plan is the almost complete absence of thick internal walls, except where containing chimney flues, the structure being largely framed. In other words, this is an expensive building, but not conventionally *grand luxe* in appearance.

The six main storeys are roughly of equal importance, although the fifth and sixth (which are slightly recessed) are of reduced height. Horizontal balconies connect bay windows with curved sides on the second, third and fifth floors, and there is no attempt to provide the equivalent of an 'order' of three or more floors. Indeed, the corner is treated as two three-storey units of equal height, one on top of the other. The window pediment above these is the only glance towards classicism and nearly all the windows have metal lintels. Three-sided bays at first-floor level are of exposed metal framing with red and yellow brick infill: a note of deference to Viollet-le-Duc. This is a remarkably original building, yet despite its prominent site it does not seem to have been published since first built. The elevational treatment

Right: **Emmanuel Brun,
1 rue Rousselet, c 1904.**
*A traditional vertical sub-
division, using a wide variety
of colours and materials, and
topped by projecting eaves
supported by iron brackets.*

Left: **Joseph Charlet and
Fernand Perrin, 43 rue
des Couronnes, c 1905.**
*Obviously a cheaper building
than 1 rue Rousselet, but
equally colourful.*

Right: **Charles Plumet,
151 rue Legendre, 1891.**
*Two flats per floor, with bay
windows at each end, resulting in a symmetrical block,
the composition tied together
by the second-floor balcony.*

generally shows a complete break with the Haussmannian 'ordinance' of repetitive bays, being freely composed with a form determined by the apartment plan. The nicely detailed chemist's shop on the corner may well be by Balleyguier, too.

More conventional in form, having the traditional two-storey base, three-storey 'order' plus attic and mansard, but showing Viollet-le-Duc's influence in their polychromy, are 1 rue Rousselet, 7e, by Emmanuel Brun (*b* 1864)[2] and 43 rue des Couronnes, 20e, by Joseph Charlet (*b* 1863) and Fernand Perrin (*b* 1873), both built about 1904. A forceful design, 1 rue Rousselet has perhaps too many motifs and materials, not least its large and small blocks of stone, white and red brick, blue ceramic tiles, exposed iron lintels, iron bay windows with brick spandrels, and arches with at least five designs of keystone. By contrast, the cheaper 43 rue des Couronnes was necessarily simpler and therefore more successful. Here the decoration is restricted to red and white patterned brickwork, blue and red tiling, a stone doorway and brackets, and a shop (Bar Floréal) – the last acknowledging the arrival of Art Nouveau at the other, smarter, end of Paris.

Plumet and His Followers
Charles Plumet (1861–1928) studied under Eugène Bruneau (*b* 1836) – a pupil of Henri Labrouste – and also under Anatole de

Baudot (1834–1915), who was a pupil of both Labrouste and Viollet-le-Duc and who lectured at the Musée des Monuments Français.

During the Belle Epoque, Plumet was regarded by his younger colleagues as the leader of a new movement, essentially within the French tradition but more innovative, encompassing both the Gothic and Classical Rationalist tendencies within the Ecole des Beaux-Arts. Similarly, his furniture designs – produced in partnership with Tony Selmersheim – were related both to the Arts and Crafts movement and to Art Nouveau, rejecting historicism but seeking forms and a style that would be suitable for mass production.

Plumet's earlier buildings – starting with 151 rue Legendre, 17e, of 1891, up to 67 avenue Raymond-Poincaré, 16e, of 1894–5 – are typical of *immeubles* relying on Gothic influence, being of simple rectangular forms in polychrome brickwork, with a limited use of stone where allowed by the budget. Both rue Legendre and avenue Raymond-Poincaré have standard-width windows with slightly arched heads, while the ground and first floors are faced with stone. Each has a continuous balcony at second-floor level with, at either end, a square stone 'bow-window' three storeys high, either enclosed with elliptical arches or as an open loggia with semi-Corinthian columns and stone balustrades. There is another continuous balcony on the fifth floor, and the

Left: **Charles Plumet, 50 avenue Victor-Hugo, 1900.** *With curved arches throughout – to windows, entrance and loggia – the facade reads as four plus one storeys vertically, with the top floor and attic recessed behind a stone balustrade.*

Below: **Léon Benouville, 17 and 19 boulevard Pasteur, 1897.** *Five floors and a cornice carrying a continuous balcony above, with just a string course at the first floor. The curvilinear balustrades and stone details are full of delights.*

building is completed by a dentilled cornice and a mansard roof with gabled dormers.

At the later building, the brick is a softer colour and the open loggias, being at the fourth rather than the second floor, would be less top-heavy had Plumet not then (to emphasise the centre line on this, a wider frontage with central entrance below) repeated the loggia in the centre, cantilevered out on moulded brackets. The wrought iron balustrades on both buildings are of a simple rectangular design, with the stone balustrading at avenue Raymond-Poincaré showing the influence of Curvilinear Gothic.

His next two apartment blocks, 36 rue de Tocqueville, 17e (1897), and his first fully mature work, 50 avenue Victor-Hugo, 16e (1900), show a softening of form by greater use of curves, made easier by substituting stone for brick and eschewing period detail. The projecting 'bow-windows' are supported on brackets, which at rue de Tocqueville are ogee curves supporting a flat plane into which an elliptical arch is cut. At avenue Victor-Hugo the projecting bays have canted angles and the brackets have become curved planes integral with the arches over. All the windows here have elliptical heads and, as introduced at rue de Tocqueville, there is a continuous arcade at the fourth floor (supported on arches without capitals), though the iron railings now have Rococo curves. Perhaps the only unsuccessful element is that of five curved arches, like separate stone dormers,

surrounding the fifth-floor windows, which recede from view behind the stone balustrade.

Léon Benouville (1860–1903), the son of an artist and educated at the Ecole des Arts et Manufactures, was also a protégé of de Baudot, but in addition to this direct link with Viollet-le-Duc he also worked as an architect both for the Monuments Historiques and for the dioceses of Perpignan and Lyons. His own buildings (not many, due to his early death) were infused with his love of Gothic and an understanding of its logic. Charles Knight wrote in an obituary article, '*He had a high ideal which he pursued ceaselessly: the truth in art.*' [3]

His 34 rue de Tocqueville, 1897, provides an interesting contrast with its contemporary by Plumet next door. Apart from the arched windows in the side bays at first and fourth floors it is strictly rectangular, and even the curvilinear balustrading (both wrought iron and stone) is medieval in inspiration. The structure is simple and clearly expressed, the only windows without arches being those in the 'bow-windows' at the third and fourth floors, which have exposed iron lintels and mullions. 17–19 boulevard Pasteur, 15e, of the same date, is even simpler. Particularly happy is the honest, craftsman-like way in which the canted bays at second to fourth floors are supported by a shallow square projection at first floor, and by the double ogee that makes the transition above the first-floor window.

Right: **Charles Plumet,
36 rue de Tocqueville,
and Léon Benouville, 34
rue de Tocqueville, both
1897.** *No 36 (rising over the
white van) is the lighter in
appearance, with no 34 (on
the right) more sober and
medieval in influence: typical
of the difference between the
architects' work.*

Left: **Léon Benouville, 46 rue Spontini, 1899.** *Below a top floor recessed behind a continuous balustrade are five floors of near equal height, with any sense of base and 'order' all but removed.*

Opposite: **Louis Sorel, 48 boulevard Raspail and 29 rue de Sèvres, 1909–12.** *At the corner, strength is given by solid end bays to both elevations, otherwise they alternate single windows with angled bays or bows.*

Right: **Louis Sorel, 7 rue Le Tasse, 1904–5.** *A little red brick on the main floors contrasts with white and green brick behind the fourth-floor loggia.*

At 46 rue Spontini, 16e (1899), there is a subtle interplay of brick and stone of the same colour, as well as of metal lintels and blind casings, the latter – which are set below the window arches – appearing to interweave between brick piers that have a satisfying variation in width, related to the room sizes behind. The narrow, strongly vertical windows are balanced by the horizontal stone copings at windowsill level. Perhaps only the polygonal corner turret and the curved brackets, with their carved bosses, that support the corner projection at second-floor level reveal the building's Gothic origins. There is no other decoration, apart from a minimum amount of wrought iron – and this in the *nouveau riche 'seizième'*! As Charles Knight wrote, *'he looked for a means of harmonious and simple lines and didn't consider decoration in itself but as a consequence of construction, to which it had to be subordinate'*.[4]

Plumet's interest in the design of simple furniture was shared by Benouville and by Louis Sorel (1867–1934), both of whom were concerned with the possibilities of mass production. Sorel (who had been a pupil of Charles Genuys at the Ecole des Arts Décoratifs and also of Emile Vaudremer, both followers of Viollet-le-Duc) was responsible for two larger and later *immeubles*

that continued the Plumet style into the new century. 7 rue le Tasse, 16e (1904–5), containing *grand luxe* apartments facing across to the Eiffel Tower, has a facade very similar to Plumet's 50 avenue Victor-Hugo, including elliptically headed windows and a projecting arched arcade at fourth-floor level. The usual mansard roof and dormers, however, are here replaced by two set-back floors with continuous balconies, because in this block the maids' bedrooms were located in a rear wing as an extension of each apartment. The fortunate occupants of the top flats, rather than the maids, now had the best outlook.

Sorel's very large block at the corner of 48 boulevard Raspail and 29 rue de Sèvres, 6e (1909–12), is more original. The delicately minimal use of brickwork, which lightens the top storeys, and the bracketing out of the angled bays over single windows at first-floor level show Sorel's debt to Benouville. Its picturesque silhouette, satisfying contrast of horizontal and vertical elements, and subtle use of canted and slightly curving projections combine to create one of the most successful examples of the sort of design treatment for a large multi-storey building that the City of Paris was keen to promote – as must now be discussed.

Left: **Louis Sorel, 48 boulevard Raspail and 29 rue de Sèvres, 1909–12.**
A decorative frieze below a continuous balcony acts as a cornice, above which the two recessed floors include a little brick into what below had been an all-stone facade.

Below: **Louis Sorel, 48 boulevard Raspail and 29 rue de Sèvres, 1909–12.**
All the windows are arched, while the balconnets have simple lattice balustrades with decorated centres.

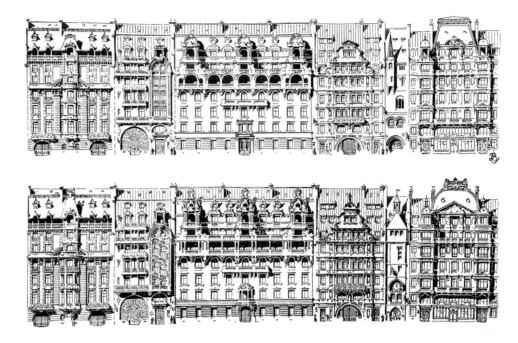

Camillo Sitte and Louis Bonnier

The ideas of the Austrian architect Camillo Sitte – as expounded in his book *City Planning according to Artistic Principles* of 1889, and translated into French by Camille Martin in 1902[5] – were influencing architects searching for a new urban architecture. Sitte devoted one chapter to the 'meagre and unimaginative character of modern city plans' and criticised the boredom of long undeviating boulevards. Eugène Hénard (1849–1923), who produced traffic studies from 1903 onwards proposing additional and wider boulevards to cater for automobiles, tried to mitigate the destruction these would cause to the existing dense fabric by setting new buildings at an angle of 45 degrees to the boulevards (*alignement brisé*) or, if parallel, setting alternate blocks back behind forecourts (*boulevard à redans*), in either case planting trees in the gaps.

Camillo Sitte had remarked that the increased size and repetitive nature of new urban structures could hardly be designed any more in an 'artistically effective manner'. The City's chief *architecte-voyer*, Louis Bonnier (1856–1946) – who was in sympathy with Camillo Sitte's theories and who had himself designed picturesque buildings in Normandy from 1893 onwards in what became known as the 'balneal' or bathing resort style – was principally responsible for a change in the building regulations in 1902. Previous alterations to the regulations had been made in 1882, 1884 and 1893, to allow greater heights on the wider streets and to permit permanent projections in the form of 'bow-windows', which had previously been theoretically demountable like glazed pavement café terraces.

Building regulations prevented the 'bow-windows' favoured by Bonnier being taken down to ground level, and architects had to provide brackets or consoles to support them. The problems of integrating these with the bays and of relating the consoles to the 'base' were usually best met if the latter was two storeys high. The illustrations in this chapter show varying degrees of success.

In 1896 Louis Bonnier produced drawings, based on a mélange of current building styles, to show how a more picturesque townscape might be achieved, with particular attention paid to the upper floors and roofline. His aim, while accepting the increased scale of new building, was to render it more humane by picturesque composition and varied detail. In the event, property developers accepted with alacrity the increased floor areas that the revised regulations allowed, while still keeping to the front facade building line, broken only by bays that were generally enclosed rather than designed as loggias – projecting balconies and open colonnades being considered unsuitable for the Parisian climate.

To encourage property developers to commission more imaginative designs, a Concours de Façades was instituted in

Right: **Louis Bonnier,
drawings of the building
height regulations.** *Major
changes to the regulations
controlling building heights
were made in both 1882 and
1902 – right and far right
respectively.*

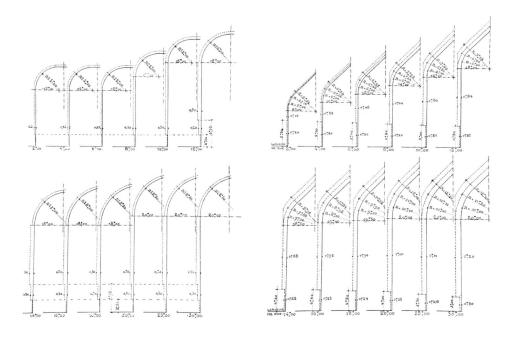

December 1897, with six prizes being awarded each year. The successful proprietors were exempted from half the highway maintenance tax; the architects only got a gold medal, but presumably it was good professional publicity. Although the City's juries were intentionally eclectic in their selections, variation in design being one of the main objectives of the competition, the result was inevitably an emphasis on external treatment unrelated to the building behind. Even so, the designs still had to fulfil building codes that controlled elements such as a building's height or the minimum dimensions of its internal courtyards. The diagrams drawn by Louis Bonnier (taken from *L'architecture*, 1903) show how facade heights were related to street widths – in both sets of drawings the solid lines represent the main building envelope and the dotted lines the limits of bays and other projections.

Art Nouveau

The decorative style known as Art Nouveau is almost the only aspect of Belle Epoque architecture to have been exhaustively studied, and for this reason the following section will only be a brief introduction. It is now generally thought that the two main sources of the style were the growing interest in Japanese art at the time and the English Arts and Crafts movement of the 1870s and early 1880s. *'Japonisme'* was introduced to France in the 1860s, and print albums and fans were being sold cheaply in Parisian department stores by the 1880s. Woodcuts, in particular, were a decisive influence on the Impressionists and the Nabis, affecting subject matter, colour and composition in most mediums, but especially in lithography. On the other hand, E. W. Godwin's Japanese-style furniture, first shown at the 1878 International Exhibition, was too rectangular and austere for French taste.

Samuel Bing (born Siegfried Bing in Hamburg in 1838), a dealer in Oriental objects who had founded a magazine *Le Japon artistique* in 1888, opened a gallery in Paris in December 1895, showing furniture and wallpapers by English and French designers, as well as glass by Louis Tiffany and Emile Gallé. He called the gallery L'Art Nouveau Bing. He employed Louis Bonnier to transform the existing building (since demolished), Bonnier's work showing in this instance a strong Japanese influence. Before approaching Bonnier, Bing had consulted the Belgians Henry Van de Velde (1863–1957), a painter who had just started to practise architecture, and the architect Victor Horta (1861–1947), who had recently completed the Tassel House (1893) in Brussels. With its interweaving linear decoration and exposed ironwork, the staircase of the Tassel House was the first and possibly the finest example of the Art Nouveau architectural style.

Left: **Hector Guimard, Ecole du Sacré-Cœur, 9 avenue de la Frillière, 1895.** *V-columns to what was once an open ground floor continue to support Guimard's original facade, with its clearly expressed structure.*

Right: **Hector Guimard, Castel Béranger, 14 rue La Fontaine, 1895.** *The entrance gate, with its 'whip-lash line' derived from Horta. Note also the elegance and perfect placement of the carving on the wide keystone and side columns.*

Horta had visited Paris for the 1889 'Triumph of Iron', had used English wallpapers and almost certainly knew Gallé's and Tiffany's glass. The publication in the 1890s of internationally available magazines devoted to art and design was also an important factor in the rapid growth of Art Nouveau as an accepted style. As an example, *The Studio*, founded in 1893, was published in French as well as English. In its early years it illustrated furniture and wallpapers by Voysey, houses by Norman Shaw, Mackmurdo and Baillie Scott, as well as Plumet's furniture. From 1901 onwards, it promoted the Secessionist work of the Austrians Josef Hoffmann and J. M. Olbrich and the German Peter Behrens.

Guimard and Other Art Nouveau Architects

Hector Guimard (1867–1942) is today the best known internationally of those Belle Epoque architects whose work was based on the teachings of Viollet-le-Duc. He studied first at the Ecole des Arts Décoratifs, where his teacher Charles Genuys (later Inspecteur-général des Monuments Historiques) introduced him to Viollet-le-Duc's analysis of medieval architecture, and taught him the principles of functional and asymmetric planning and picturesque composition. When he went on to the Ecole des Beaux-Arts he chose the atelier of Gustave Raulin, who had restored the cathedral at Angers and in

his own work applied Rationalist principles to the design of workshops and schools.

Guimard's first works, a series of private houses built in the early 1890s, show these influences, as does the Ecole du Sacré-Coeur, 9 avenue de la Frillière, 16e, designed in 1895 and now converted into flats. Built at the back of a restricted site, it effectively has three blank walls, only the long front wall having large windows for the classrooms on the first and second floors. The ground floor was left open in order to maximise the open-air playground area, the wall above being supported on V-columns derived from Viollet-le-Duc's design for a market, illustrated in his *Entretiens*[6] (see Chapter Four). The structure is clearly expressed throughout.

The first-floor triple windows, for example, have iron colonnettes that provide intermediate support for the lintels. On the second floor, the colonnettes are replaced by thin brick piers that support half-arches at the sides with a lintel over the centre, a curious device. The first-floor construction is of brick arches about a metre wide, resting on iron joists spanning front to back with stone infill on either side to provide an angled bed. These joists and the front iron beam are fully exposed.

The contemporary, seven-storey, middle-income apartment block at 14 rue La Fontaine, 16e (known as Castel Béranger), is also strictly rectangular on plan, with load-bearing cross walls at

Below: **Hector Guimard, Castel Béranger, 14 rue La Fontaine, 1895.** *The three cast-iron motifs on the balcony show Guimard's interest in mass production, fully utilised in his Métro station entrances. The blind box has delicate cut-outs.*

Above: **Hector Guimard, Castel Béranger, 14 rue La Fontaine, 1895.** *The mixture of materials and the picturesque composition illustrate Guimard's interest in the medieval, prior to his conversion to Art Nouveau.*

The Search for a New Art   133

Above: **Hector Guimard, 17–19 rue La Fontaine, 1911.** *The comparatively simple treatment of the uninterrupted seven-storey facade (plus recessed floors above) suits the building's size perfectly.*

Left: **Hector Guimard, Immeuble Jassedé, 142 avenue de Versailles, 1905.** *The building's quirky assemblage of windows and balconies is carefully balanced at the corner.*

Right: **Hector Guimard, Métro entrance, Porte Dauphine, 1902.** *The elegantly sculpted columns branch out to support the welcoming* marquise.

about four-metre centres. With its polychromatic mixture of rubble and ashlar stone and brick infill, its blue-painted windows having either stone arches or iron lintels, and its picturesque silhouette with one stone bay taken up as a gabled projection to ensure asymmetry (rationally redundant on a building with a central entrance), both the planning and the elevational treatment are, in general, typical of the more medieval-inspired Parisian buildings of the 1880s and early 1890s. Guimard himself said, in 1899, that he was only applying the theory of Viollet-le-Duc, but without being fascinated by medieval forms.[7] In the same year as obtaining permission for this design (1895), Guimard visited Brussels, where he met Victor Horta and saw his recently built Tassel House and its famous staircase. On returning to Paris, he revised the detailing of both the external ironwork – including the entrance gate – and the interiors in the new style.

Guimard's next major work, possibly his most original, was the series of Métro entrances, where railings and, occasionally, canopies were economically and speedily created by combining a small range of cast-iron elements, based on vegetable and skeletal forms and painted green to resemble patinated bronze. Like the Castel Béranger – derided as the *'castel dérangé'* by Parisians – the Métro entrances were thought by many to be unsuited to their environment, and at the place de l'Opéra the

City insisted on another architect designing a stone balustrade.

At the Immeuble Jassedé, 142 avenue de Versailles, 16e, designed 10 years later than Castel Béranger, Guimard renounced colour in favour of a mixture of cream stone and white brick, but provided elaboration in an arbitrarily varied treatment of balconies, corner bows and window heads – the latter having either stone arches or straight lintels with additional curved metal hoods. In 1911 he designed a group of apartment blocks at 17–19 rue La Fontaine and 8–10 rue Agar, infinitely simpler in treatment. Here, wide shallow arched windows, some slightly bowed, are set in a plain expanse of ashlar stone, the only Art Nouveau detailing being the curvilinear iron balconies, painted black, and the Flamboyant Gothic arches to the entrance doors. (Guimard's frontage to the café-bar has unfortunately been recently obscured by a, hopefully temporary, glazed enclosure.)

The preference for polychromy on the part of some architects, in contrast to the Parisian tradition of rendering or stone, was greatly assisted by Alexandre Bigot (1862–1927), whose chemical researches enabled him to manufacture glazed faience in a variety of forms and colours. This provided an impermeable facing material, its appearance unaffected by time or weather. The simplest application was in the form of square or rectangular patterned tiles completely covering a facade, already illustrated in Chapter Three as a facing to the studios at 31 rue

Campagne-Premier. Bigot could also produce larger, irregularly shaped ceramic elements for architects requiring more sculpturally elaborate surfaces.

Bigot was the client for 29 avenue Rapp, 7e (1901), an *immeuble* designed as an advertisement for his wares by Jules Lavirotte (1864–1924). Here the two lower floors are load-bearing stone, but the structure above is lightweight concrete (the Cottancin system, *ciment-armé*, to be described in Chapter Eight), entirely covered with faience. Quite apart from the sexual symbolism read into this facade by Salvador Dali and others (which would make it highly unsuitable for a block of family apartments), the general effect is of a jumble of overloaded decorative elements piled on top of one another. Despite this, it was one of three buildings by Lavirotte awarded a prize in the Concours de Façades.

An infinitely more effective use of large-scale sculptural decoration provided by Bigot's faience is at 14 rue d'Abbeville, 10e, also 1901, by Edouard Autant (1872–1964), an elegant composition of three wide bays. The structure is also Cottancin's *ciment armé*, but here the white and green coloured faience is contrasted with pink brickwork, while the strongly moulded central bay – which firmly unites the main floors (the 'order') with the base – is assisted in this central emphasis by the plain surface and delicate wrought-iron balconies of the side bays, and the division of their wide windows into pairs by a central mullion. This is a classically symmetrical facade, but without the usual traditional details.

A few other architects without Guimard's or Autant's design ability produced comparatively undistinguished *immeubles*, vaguely Art Nouveau in character. Guimard went on to design an expensive house for himself and his rich American wife at 122 avenue Mozart, 16e, in 1909–12, where all the rooms are curved in plan, containing curvilinear furniture of his own design. His later work however, like Horta's, was completely different in character, and after the war he became far more interested in the possibilities of prefabrication. Being an essentially decorative style, the success of Art Nouveau always depended on exceptionally original and talented architects able to work closely with the very best craftsmen, which therefore made it unsuited to the changed economic conditions of the twentieth century. Even the 'undulating whiplash line', the most famous decorative component used by Horta at the Tassel House (probably emanating from Mackmurdo's graphic work), only appears in Parisian architecture in the entrance to the Castel Béranger.

French Crafts and the Roccoco

All the architects in search of a new art, whose work has so far been mentioned, derived their approach basically from Gothic

Left: **Edouard Autant, 14 rue d'Abbeville, 1901.** *The classical composition combined with graceful Art Nouveau detailing contrasts significantly with the Baroque excesses of the building's left-hand neighbour.*

Below: **Georges Sinell, 7–11 rue Edmond-Valentin, 1898.** *Simplified Rococo forms are here sensibly adapted to modern requirements.*

precedent, but Plumet's later buildings contain curvilinear elements relating to French eighteenthth-century architecture, while Lavirotte designed several Parisian buildings in a style closely related to Rococo.

The French industrial economy of the 1890s did not keep pace with expansion by its rivals, Germany, the USA, and Britain. Instead, the government turned its attention to encouraging the export of crafts, particularly those producing luxury items. The eighteenth century was recalled as the last time when what was thought to be a specifically French art in furniture and decoration, the Rococo, had existed. The restoration of national monuments by the Third Republic and the establishment of a new department of *objets d'art* at the Louvre, in 1894, provided architects looking for a new art based on national historical precedent with an alternative source to Gothic: one which related the architecture of *immeubles* to the decoration and furniture they contained, especially in the more fashionable *arrondissements*.

7–11 rue Edmond-Valentin, 7e, 1898, by Georges Sinell (1864–1927), is a typical example. The decorative motifs used are all derived from the eighteenth century, but the building form, with five residential floors of equal importance, is new. The wide windows to the principal rooms, double the standard casement width, the elliptical arches and curving transoms, and the use of

stone balusters and delicately curvilinear wrought-iron railings can be seen throughout the 16th and 17th *arrondissements* – the variation in window widths providing a simple means of breaking the monotonous rhythm of the Haussmannian ordinance.

Sinell's buildings were usually relatively simple in form. The use of Rococo curves, however, could be much more extreme – for example, at 26 rue de Clichy, 9e, 1895 by Albert LeVoisvenel, where all the windows are arched and the balconies serpentine. The decorative cresting over the high entrance arch (an excellent example of the vegetal facade sculpture of the period) makes a graceful transition from concave arched surround to convex balcony front. LeVoisvenel, a prolific commercial architect, always maintained a high standard in both the robust Beaux-Arts classical manner and Rococo-inspired delicacy.

Xavier Schoellkopf (1870–1911) only had time to design a few buildings in his comparatively short professional life, and these tended to combine the more fluid characteristics of Rococo and Art Nouveau. 29 boulevard de Courcelles, 8e, 1902, is the best-known example. Externally the building starts conventionally at ground level, with four elliptically arched openings in a 'base' of rusticated stone. Above, the windows – two wide and two narrow on each floor denoting major and minor rooms within – produce an asymmetrical design by emphasising the right-hand bay.

Other than the slightly arched examples on the third floor, the windows are of standard rectangular shape until you get to the fifth floor, although they are set within openings that, by curving outwards, support the *balconnets* of the windows above. Generously wide piers between the windows provide vertical emphasis, the extent of these plain areas accentuating the stone tendrils that emerge from their surface at the fourth floor, unfurling around the arched balconies on either side. These form a vestigial cornice and support columns which branch directly into the arches they carry, without capitals. The facade is crowned by arches protected by scalloped weather moulds, while a triple arch on the right – of which the centre is a horse-shoe – introduces an exotic note. The effect at roof level has become more recessive, as the original *oeil-de-boeuf* dormers have since been replaced by rectangular ones.

Schoellkopf admired the softness of semi-ruined buildings before restoration, and likened his modelling of stone and plaster surfaces to the continuity of human forms.[8] The soft and fine-grained cream limestone used in Paris lent itself to the delicate facade carving used by many Belle Epoque architects. Internally, the main staircases of *immeubles* could be similarly fluid in form – curved stairs and balustrades being traditional to French Rococo – and electric light fittings could be integrated into ceilings. Generally, however, apartments had to have rectangular rooms to accommodate the tenants' furniture. Both Rococo and Art Nouveau were essentially expensive styles unless considerably diluted.

Flat and Recessed Facades

The flowing forms of Rococo and Art Nouveau lent themselves to the more sculptural facade treatment advocated by Louis Bonnier. In contrast, two examples of completely flat facades are given here. The first, 106 rue de l'Université, 7e, 1905, contains large and expensive apartments in the most traditionally aristocratic of Parisian *arrondissements*. It was designed by Ernest Sanson (1836–1918), or possibly his son Maurice (1864–1917), architects who specialised in housing the very rich, and it is a rare example of a sensible application of design principles established for the local *hôtels particuliers* adapted to a seven-storey building, where the five main floors of apartments are of equal value. This would only work where the rooms behind the facade are of appropriate scale.

11*bis* rue Georges-Saché, 14e, 1910 by Paul Vasseur, quite clearly reveals its composition of two apartments per floor, each with two interconnecting reception rooms of equal size. Apart from the use of continuous balconies on three floors, to provide visual balance between vertical and horizontal elements, delicate variations in surface treatment – of which the arches linking the

Right: **Frédéric Henry, 97–9 rue de Prony, 1906.** *The horizontal string courses at second and fifth floor levels unify these paired buildings.*

Below: **Paul Legriel, 170 rue de la Convention, 1901.** *A rich but not grandiose entrance, whose square proportion makes it all the more welcoming.*

second- and third-floor windows and the slight curving outwards of the wall plane to support the horizontal projections are only two examples – reflect the greatest credit on this little known architect. Paul Legriel's ability to provide rich detail where appropriate may be seen in the entrance door to 170 rue de la Convention, 15e, an otherwise very simple rectangular building which received a prize in the Concours de Façades in 1901.

An equally straightforward but slightly more modelled facade at 97–9 rue de Prony, 17e, 1906, by Frédéric Henry (1867–1939) is obviously that of two paired buildings, each having one apartment per floor with three front-facing rooms. Stone balustrading is introduced only where additional visual weight is required: over the twinned entrances and to emphasise the horizontal string course at second-floor level, which ties the two halves of the composition together. The stone mullions between the pairs of first-floor windows convert into voussoirs supporting the second-floor triangular bays above. The arches there provide a similar function for the upper bays, which are gently bowed. These are then carried up to the sixth floor, drawing attention away from the central party wall. The general effect is not dissimilar to Guimard's 21 rue La Fontaine, designed five years later with, if anything, even less period detail.

A similar amount of modelling, but with a more traditional composition, can be seen at 3 rue Louis-Boilly, 16e, 1912–14 by Charles Labro, included here as a more Rococo variant on 106 rue

Right: **Charles Labro,
3 rue Louis-Boilly, 1912
–14.** *The gently projecting
curved window heads are
echoed by the pedimented
gables over the fifth-floor
windows, glimpsed here
above the upper balcony.*

Left: **Raymond Barbaud and Edouard Bauhain, 5 rue Lalo, 1906.** *The building has a simple elegance, with square windows and two storeys of stone, the remainder in white brick. The central second-floor balcony acts as a focus.*

Below: **Adolphe Bocage,
15 rue de Téhéran, 1910.**
*Complete with well-placed
sculpture, the curved bays
with small side windows are
typical of Bocage.*

Below: **Charles Lefebvre,
83–5 rue Blomet, 1908.**
*The slight curves of the stone
corners contrast with the
homely wooden railings, the
ground-floor gates strengthening the domestic character.*

de l'Université and as an example of successful integration of
sculptural decoration at entrance and first-floor levels where its
detail can be easily seen from the street. 15 rue de Téhéran, 8e,
1910 by Adolphe Bocage is almost identical in size and
composition, yet its character is more static and the window
detailing is typical of its architect.

On wider sites, a greater degree of modelling could
sometimes be advantageously achieved by a central recessed
forecourt, providing more flats with a street frontage. A good
example can be found at 5 rue Lalo, 16e, 1906, by Raymond
Barbaud (1860–1927) and Edouard Bauhain (*b* 1864), where a
simple window element is repeated over seven storeys, with
minor variations in arch and lintel treatment – the latter in
coloured tiles on a stone and white brick elevation. The central
second-floor stone balustrade is all that is needed to tie the
composition together.

83–5 rue Blomet, 15e, 1908, by Charles Lefebvre, is smaller
in scale and more colourful because of the yellow brick (with stone
dressings) and the wooden railings, an unusual and homely
feature. This seems to be the only one of the many buildings by
Lefebvre in such a relaxed domestic style. The eclectic nature of
Second Empire architecture, where elements of various period
styles were often combined in one building, was replaced during
the Belle Epoque by the use by a single architect of several

Left: **André Granet, 30 avenue Marceau, 1913 –16.** *The recessed plan serves the avenue rather than the internal planning, while the building's picturesque qualities are emphasised by the elaborately carved gable.*

disparate manners in different buildings, as he explored the possibilities of finding a 'new art' suited to each project.

30 avenue Marceau, 8e, 1913–16, by André Granet (1881–1974), is probably unique in having a recessed facade not for functional reasons, but to provide an extreme example of the picturesque ensemble recommended by Louis Bonnier. Here everything builds up to the central gable, a *tour de force* of decorative sculpture.

The domestic character of 83–5 rue Blomet may also be seen in many buildings in the less fashionable residential *arrondissements*, and represents the nearest that Parisian architects got to the English Arts and Crafts movement. There is only space for one more here: 54 rue de Tolbiac, 13e, 1913 by J. Basset. This has two flats per floor, with the larger reception room in each flat having a curved bay that provides the necessary three-dimensional relief. The gridiron railings and the pagoda roofs above the bays (used in several buildings by Plumet in the 1890s) are typical of the style. This building by Basset appears never to have been illustrated in any publication, either when built or since, and his name does not appear in existing literature.[9]

The same applies to 7 rue Gerbert, 15e, 1912, completed 1919, by Albert Prugnaud, and at least 10 other buildings included in this chapter appear never to have been illustrated either. 7 rue Gerbert consists of seven equal floors of apartments in cheerful yellow brick enlivened with a few courses of glazed blue brick above the stone piers at the base. The ground floor being in domestic use, it is not of sufficient height to provide visual strength to the stone in relation to the five floors of brickwork above, so Prugnaud continued the piers up about a metre above floor level, curving them very slightly outwards to support a plain coping of just the right size. At the corner, the coping curves upwards slightly, so as to support – with the semi-circular arch below it – the curved brick corner above.

These are only two of the subtleties of this delightful building. Particularly happy is the proportion of the main entrance, where the coping, echoing the outward curve of the bowed balconies above, also rises to shield the welcoming carved head over the elliptical doorway, a late example of a great period in French decorative sculpture. (Unfortunately, restoration work prevented photography of this building.)

Curved Corners

Haussmann's new avenues, frequently crossing existing streets diagonally, created a tradition of sharp-cornered buildings, which gave their architects the chance to create curved angles, often crowned by domes and usually containing circular salons. To end this chapter, here are three examples dating from the final years of the Belle Epoque.

Left: **Charles Adda, 6 place de Mexico, 1912.** *The curve of the* place *and the angles of the side streets clearly informed the overall form of the building.*

Below: **Joseph Charlet and Fernand Perrin, 18 place Adolphe-Chérioux, date unknown.** *The rich variation in surface treatment, accomplished without fussiness, is a splendid achievement.*

6 place de Mexico, 16e, 1912 by Charles Adda (1873–1938), because it faces a circular *place*, itself has a concave main facade which can then merge with the side street elevations by positioning circular salons on the corners. The domes in this case are too small and their surface is fragmented by the insertion of arched dormers, but Adda had to allow for eight floors of apartments, each with a view of the Eiffel Tower down the opposite street. The principal interest of this building is in how he has done this within a traditional Beaux-Arts envelope, using mainly repetitive rectangular windows and balconies, and allowing the building's sculptural form to provide the main interest.

In contrast, at 18 place Adolphe-Chérioux, 15e by Joseph Charlet (*b* 1863) and Fernand Perrin (*b* 1873), where a garden square meets the busy local shopping street at right angles, the ground-floor bar follows the diagonal street corner line, but above it the circular salons of the paired apartments create a Borrominesque serpentine curve. The bedroom windows in the return elevations are simply repetitive, but in order to celebrate the corner's Baroque movement, the architects introduced minor differences in the salons' window treatment on every floor.

The former Hôtel Mercédès (now offices) at 9 rue de Presbourg, 16e, 1903 by Georges Chedanne, follows the gentle curve of the street with a curved corner at one end and a gabled return at the other, but the facade is highly modelled by curved bow windows, above which are open porches at fifth-floor level and pavilion roofs above. The overall envelope is further softened by all the windows having elliptical arched heads, while the sculptural decoration was carefully placed by Chedanne to emphasise important elements in the construction.

The 1889 and 1900 Exhibitions were both centred on the Champs de Mars, between the Eiffel Tower and the Ecole Militaire. After the 1900 Exhibition closed, the central area became a permanent public park, but avenues were laid out on either side, with high apartment blocks on their outer sides (usually eight storeys) and lower *immeubles* and individual houses on the inside, looking out over the park. These avenues are an excellent place to study the more expensive domestic architecture of the years immediately before and after the First World War.

There is a particularly fine example at 15 avenue Emile-Deschanel, 7e, 1909, by Georges Guyon *et fils*, which represents the grandest Beaux-Arts classical style, but here skilfully adapted to a multi-storey apartment block to create a pleasing relationship between straight and curved planes. Just as Charlet and Perrin's expensive building at place Adolphe-Chérioux contrasts in treatment with their petit-bourgeois 43 rue des Couronnes (illustrated earlier in this chapter), so also does Georges Guyon's

Left: **Georges Chedanne, Hôtel Mercédès, 9 rue de Presbourg, 1903.** *The curved plan erupts at the top of the building into a medieval riot of turrets.*

Right: **Georges Chedanne, Hôtel Mercédès, 9 rue de Presbourg, 1903.** *Drivers in goggles: all the sculptures are related to motoring.*

very expensive 15 avenue Emile-Deschanel appear completely different from his other domestic buildings – and not only because he was joined here by his son Maurice, recently graduated from the Ecole des Beaux-Arts. More importantly, it was because many of his earlier buildings had been designed for occupation by the working class. For reasons to be described in the next chapter, this sector of society has been largely ignored in this book so far.

This chapter has briefly described 35 buildings, 'variations on a theme' by architects searching for a new art. This number could easily have been increased to 300, such is the wealth of generally unknown apartment blocks of architectural value, which can easily pass unnoticed in Paris's traffic-filled streets and tree-lined avenues. While these were being built, other architects had been engaged in the design of buildings erected with public or philanthropic money, where the combination of new design problems and economic stringency led the way to a new architecture. This is the subject of the next chapter.

1   G. Soulier, *L'Art decoratif*, IV, 1902, pp 98–9: '*L'architecte a compris très justement que si moderne que veuille être une maison on ne peut demander au locataire de renouveler tout son mobilier afin d'être digne d'y entrer*'.

2   Emmanuel Brun should not be confused with Emmanuel Brune (1836–86); nine other architects called Brun are listed in the *Dictionnaire par noms d'architecture …*, 1876–1899, see Bibliography.

3   *L'Architecture*, XVII, n 11, 1909, pp 98–9.

4   *Ibid.*

5   According to G. R. and C. C. Collins, *Camillo Sitte: The Birth of Modern Town Planning*, Phaidon Press, London, 1965, Martin's volume was poorly translated, German examples being replaced by French or Belgian ones and emphasising medieval towns while suppressing Baroque examples.

6   E. Viollet-le-Duc, *Lectures*, translated by B. Bucknall, Sampson Low, London, 1881, vol 2, pp 63–5.

7   Letter from Guimard to L. C. Boileau, quoted by the latter in *L'Architecture*, 1899, p 122: '*Je n'ai fait qu'appliquer la théorie de Viollet-le-Duc, mais sans être fasciné par les formes du moyen âge.*'

8   Quoted in an anonymous article in *L'Art décoratif*, 1900, p 324: '*Les yeux, la bouche, que l'on peut comparer à des fenêtres percées dans une façade, ne sont pas troués à l'emporte-pièce, mais adoucis par les formes arrondies ou en pentes.*'

9   Basset's name will be included in *Dictionnaire, par noms d'architectes, des constructions élevées à Paris aux XIXe et XXe siècles, 1900–1914*, when published.

7 The Social Aspect

The Workers' Living Conditions

The poor may be 'always with us' but in cities, in past centuries, they lived mainly in slums – since demolished. In Paris it was only during the Belle Epoque that the state, aided by the church and a few rich philanthropists, came to realise that the living conditions of the working class must be improved. The following brief notes are given as the background to the architectural consequences of this reform.

After 1870 the *banlieue*, the suburban towns mainly to the north of the city, became the centre of industrialisation. (The factories and housing there are outside the geographical scope of this book.) Due to the rise in rents resulting from Haussmann's improvements, workers in light industry in the city centre were no longer able to live next to their work and, as already stated, they mostly settled in Belleville and other areas in the outer *arrondissements*.

Trade unions had been legalised in 1884 and had 140,000 members by 1890 and over 400,000 by 1902. A Trades Union confederation was formed in 1895. There were economic recessions in 1889 and 1892 and in 1902 and 1908, so that for many workers periods of overwork were interspersed with stretches of unemployment. The first *Bourse de Travail* (labour exchange) was founded in 1886. Industrial work was limited to an 11-hour day for women and adolescents in 1892, but 12 hours for men continued to be legal until 1904. By 1900 a 10-hour day had become usual, but for workers in central Paris commuting time lengthened this.

The wives' role in the family also increased in importance at this time, due to the husbands' long absence from home. Strikes in favour of an eight-hour day occurred in 1890 and 1906, and the construction of the 1900 Exhibition and the Métro were delayed by strikes, but it was only in 1906 that employers were finally forced to give workers one day off per week.

In 1891 Pope Leo XIII had issued his encyclical *Rerum Novarum*, demanding active government sponsorship of social improvement. This led to the political movement known as Ralliement, basically a union of republicans, monarchists and the church against the socialists – the first socialist Deputies (members of the National Assembly) having been elected in 1893, a year of strikes and riots. Despite this *rapprochement*, the monasteries were closed and their property sequestered in 1901, although the money thus gained by the state was in theory used to help finance workers' pension schemes introduced in 1910.

Opposite: **Emile Vaudremer, Lycée Buffon, 1885–90.** *The large overall scale of the building is complemented by the robustness of the stone base and string courses at eye level.*

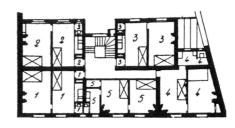

Below: **Wilbrod Chabrol, 45 rue Jeanne-d'Arc, 1888.** *Each unit consisted of two small rooms, a small kitchen or a kitchen recess, and a WC.*

Left: **Wilbrod Chabrol, 45 rue Jeanne-d'Arc, 1888.** *The earliest and most basic of* habitations à bon marché.

The Workers' Social Life

Small local cafés, referred to briefly in Chapter Two, were the centres of the workers' social life, taking the place of the traditional village cafés familiar to immigrants from the country and helping to reconcile them to city life. They provided space for sociability not possible in cramped living quarters. These cafés were centred around the owner's counter, where he and his wife welcomed both new and established customers. Heavy drinking among the working class was due largely to the sociability of pub culture and the lack of communal space elsewhere, but the Belle Epoque also saw the debut of football and cycle racing as both participant and spectator sports.

Unlike the city cafés – frequented by bourgeois men, visitors and prostitutes – the local ones were used by wives and grandmothers as well as male workers. All the local centres in Paris still have cafés with this type of life, but unfortunately almost entirely 'modernised' in décor. Only the more prosperous workers patronised the Montmartre cafés-concerts where classes mingled, but the comparatively poor had their own music halls. Summer and Sunday outings were mainly by train to places on the Seine north-west of Paris: Argenteuil, Asnières and the Grande Jatte.

The very poor had no homes: they either lived in the shanty towns or, if they could afford it, slept in *dortoirs* (dormitories), paying three francs a night for a separate cubicle or 15 centimes, payable in advance, for a bed in the common dormitory. Showers were provided, but no other accommodation.

Habitations à Bon Marché (HBMs)

Despite the improvements to public hygiene – including extensive slum clearances and the provision of water and drainage, carried out under Napoléon III and continued by the Third Republic, which also reformed street cleaning and refuse collection – there was a typhoid epidemic in 1882, followed by cholera in 1884 when 989 people died, and again in 1892 with 906 dead. Tuberculosis was rife and was clearly related to the continuance of defective housing: about a quarter of the population was housed in buildings with occupancy of more than two persons per room.

The city compiled a register of unhealthy buildings, and some idea of the extent of the problem can be gained from the fact that this took from 1882 to 1900 to complete. Outside the centre, conditions were even worse. Surrounding the city, and separating it from the factories and multi-storey housing of the industrial suburbs, were shanty towns built mainly of packing cases. The least unhygienic were those on the southern edge, built by workers' cooperatives, which had breeze block walls, a sink in every unit and a shared outside WC.

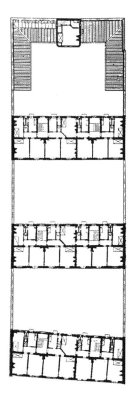

Left: **Georges Guyon, 5 rue Jeanne-d'Arc, 1899.**
The tie bars to cross beams and the undulating first-floor cornice are just two of this facade's felicitous details.

Right: **Georges Guyon, 5 rue Jeanne-d'Arc, 1899.**
Here, each unit of one to three rooms had a separate kitchen and a WC opening off the hall.

The first attempt to provide reasonable housing for workers was the Cité Napoléon, 1852, five-storey buildings of one- and two-room units entered from balconies around a central staircase – a somewhat prison-like arrangement. There was one WC on each floor, but water was only obtainable from a fountain at ground level.

Other schemes followed, also funded by public money, but the only interesting one to be built before the Belle Epoque, remarkable in its combination of home and workplace, was the privately financed rue des Immeubles Industriels, 11e, 1872–3, architect Emile Lemenil (1832–1913), which combined three floors of iron-framed workshops for the furniture trades with two-roomed flats constructed in masonry on another three floors above. The basement contained machinery producing compressed air for the workshops and the flats were provided with gas and water.

It was not until 1888[1] that the Societé Philanthropique, which had previously helped the creation of clinics and hospitals, was able to purchase a small site for its first purpose-built block of workers' flats at 45 rue Jeanne-d'Arc, 13e, architect Wilbrod Chabrol (1835–1919), an eight-storey structure with shops at street level and five flats on each upper floor. These had two rooms and either a kitchen recess or kitchenette and a WC. There was such a rental demand that Chabrol was asked to design a second block at 65 boulevard de Grenelle, 15e ,where the flats had three rooms, one for parents and one for children of each sex. (All the *habitations à bon marché* were for rental, available to those unable to afford the cheaper commercially built *immeubles*.)

The Groupe des Maisons Ouvrières, later financed anonymously by Mme Lebaudy, built its first scheme at 5 rue Jeanne-d'Arc in 1889, to designs by the architect Georges Guyon. Situated on a deep site, it consists of three parallel blocks separated by courtyards planted with trees, the rear courtyard incorporating a laundry area with children's playroom adjacent, a covered drying area and communal showers. There were 72 dwellings in all, each with three rooms, a kitchen and a WC. The rooms were slightly larger than at no 45: the largest being about 14 feet by 11, rather than 12 feet by 8. Space was saved by restricting load-bearing internal walls to those between flats, with only lightweight partitions between rooms, while any necessary structural strengthening was provided by iron cross beams – the external tie plates for these forming a decorative feature of the street elevation.

These early *habitations à bon marché* were of brick or rubble stone construction, with standard casement windows usually having exposed iron lintels. Georges Guyon's have a carefully composed elevational treatment. At 5 rue Jeanne-d'Arc, the wide

Left: **Georges Guyon, 10 rue de la Croix-Faubin, 1904–6.** *The street facade is finished in rubble stone mixed with buff and blue brick, producing a homely atmosphere.*

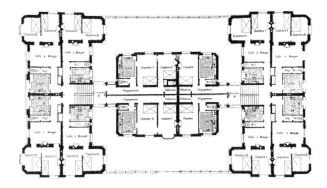

Above: **Henri Provensal,
HBM, rue du Marché-
Popincourt, 1907.** *On
an island site it was possible
to provide an open aspect to
every room.*

Right: **Henri Provensal,
HBM, rue du Marché-
Popincourt, 1907.** *The
building is well constructed,
with stone-faced wings containing central bays in brick
and simple wrought iron
railings to the balconies.*

buff brick piers provide a restful surface between the paired
windows, with their central mullions of stone and buff and red
brick, and patterned brickwork between the sills and lintels. The
piers' vertical emphasis is counteracted by strong stone
horizontals above first- and fifth-floor windows, the light stone
emphasised by dark brick above and below it. The first floor's
stone arched form undulates at a level near enough for passers-by
to appreciate its elegance, while the fifth floor's straight
dentilling, combined with the projecting eaves a storey higher,
ensures that the whole sixth floor serves as an 'attic'.

At 10 rue de la Croix-Faubin, 11e, of 1904–6, he used a
polychromatic mixture of dark rubble stone, and buff and blue
glazed brick. Being a longer-term investment than the cheaper
commercial housing built for rent, it made sense for the
philanthropically financed *habitations à bon marché* to be built of
better-quality materials and forms of construction, resulting in
lower maintenance costs.

In 1904 the Fondation Rothschild was set up for *'the
improvement of the material existence of workers'*. It immediately
held an architectural competition for an island site in the rue de
Prague, 12e, appointing the first, second, fourth and fifth prize-
winners to undertake, as a team under the supervision of H.-P.
Nénot, the design of all its projects – amounting to a total of
1125 dwellings between 1907 and 1913. The first prizewinner,

Augustin Rey (1864–1934), had made a detailed study of the
relationship between tuberculosis and ventilation, cleanliness
and even poor lighting. The second prizewinner, Henri Provensal,
(1868–1934) was appointed joint architect with Rey, but when
Rey left in 1906, it appears Provensal took over sole responsibility
for the design of all the foundation's subsequent projects. Like
Rey, he also had studied the beneficial effects of better daylighting
to habitable rooms.

The effects of their researches can be seen in the more
open planning of the Fondation Rothschild's schemes, for
example the first to be built, at rue du Marché-Popincourt, 11e.
There were 12 flats per floor (six per staircase) of one to three
rooms, kitchen and WC, and apart from four kitchens every room
receives good daylight and has an outward view. Showers and a
laundry were on the ground floor, which was otherwise devoted
to shops. At the competition site on the rue de Prague – the third
project to be built, containing 321 dwellings – the provision of
communal facilities was considerable, including showers, laundry,
a crèche for three- to six-year-olds, workshops, and educational
facilities for cooking, dressmaking and childcare. Electricity, gas
and water were provided in all flats.

As in private apartments, every bedroom had a fireplace,
although the provision of so many flues was an expensive item of
construction and restricted planning. Brick construction was used

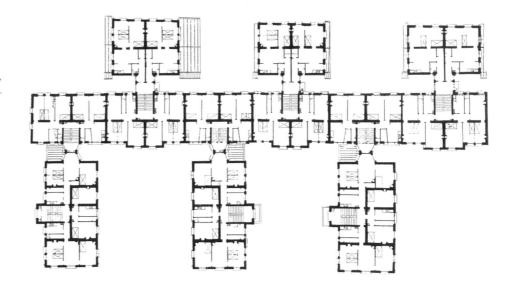

Right: **Henri Provensal,
HBM, rue Bargue, 1907
– 12.** *The dining rooms (les
salles commune)* provide
direct access to the bedrooms,
reducing wasteful circulation.

Below: **Henri Provensal,
HBM, rue Bargue, 1907
– 12.** *Smaller wings in red
and cream brick, each with
their own pitched roof, mask
the extent of the continuous
spine block behind.*

throughout – combined with some stone on the earlier schemes –
and the external treatment was generally straightforward, with
variations expressing directly the room layouts within. The most
attractive of Provensal's schemes is probably that at rue Bargue,
15e, 1907–12, due to its simple elevational treatment and open
overall plan. As the site was between two streets, Provensal was
able to provide a long spine block with garden forecourts between
projecting wings.

The Fondation Rothschild's architects were much
influenced by the first scheme designed by Henri Sauvage
(1873–1932) for the Societé des Logements Hygiéniques à Bon
Marché (founded by the architect Frantz Jourdain) at 7 rue de
Tretaigne, 18e, 1903–4. Here, the emphasis on hygiene led to the
use of a wood/cement composite flooring with coved skirtings,
washable wall-coverings and a complete absence of any
mouldings which might harbour dust. The treatment of the front
elevation is as functional as the internal finishes, with living
rooms having V-shaped bays to draw in the maximum amount of
light from the narrow street and to provide views along it. Next
to these, the kitchen windows have a projecting larder below the
sill, a standard provision at the time but unseen in bourgeois
blocks because their kitchens overlooked internal courtyards.

A co-operative shop, a 'hygienic' restaurant, and an evening
school with stage and library were provided at ground level,

Left and above: **Henri Sauvage, 7 rue de Trétaigne, 1903–4.** *Art Nouveau doors and delicate balconet railings are almost the sole decoration in this simple facade, the living room windows above angled for a view down the street.*

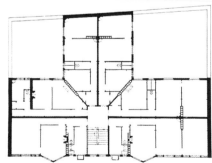

Above: **Henri Sauvage, 7 rue de Trétaigne, 1903–4** *The concrete structure saved space, but the restricted site still resulted in four out of the six flats being at the back.*

Left: **Henri Sauvage, 13 rue Hippolyte-Maindron, 1905–6.** *A straightforward facade of yellow brickwork and iron lintels, with projecting eaves above the fifth and again the recessed sixth floor, prove that decoration is not always needed to produce a distinguished building.*

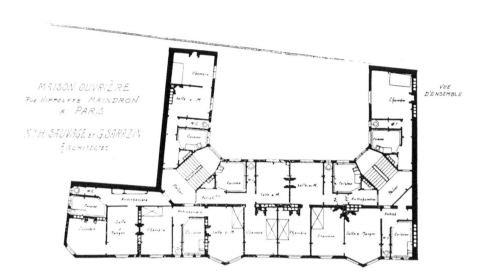

Right: **Henri Sauvage, 13 rue Hippolyte-Maindron, 1905–6.** *Two staircases give access to one single-room and six two-room units per floor, all with their own kitchens and WCs.*

where the communal showers were also situated. A flat roof at the top for clothes drying and plants was later replaced by a mansard storey, because of the demand for more flats. The four upper floors contained six family flats each, while the fifth floor was given over to smaller flats and single rooms for unmarried workers. Sauvage's Art Nouveau background during his earlier years at Nancy[2] may be seen in the entrance door and staircase balustrade. And although the flats were very simply treated internally, they all had specially designed hammered-copper fireplaces and the plain walls were set off by stencilled floral friezes in fresh colours. Externally, the painted frame with brick infill 'panels' was substituted for the ceramic tile facing proposed, as this was too expensive.

The most attractive externally of Sauvage's HBMs is that at the corner of 13 rue Hippolyte-Maindron and 20 rue Severo, 14e, 1905–6, where the treatment is a simpler version of rue de Trétaigne, incorporating vertical windows with exposed iron lintels, and triple windows in the kitchens with larders recessed behind concrete grilles. (The side lights of the triple windows have higher sills because they abut kitchen fittings.) The V-shaped bays support a square bay on the top floor, the whole in a plain surface of buff brickwork. The strong verticals are capped by two levels of projecting eaves, the top floor being slightly recessed. The appearance of this block is, in fact, very similar to the courtyard elevations of many of the elaborately expensive, stone-faced *immeubles* in the 'west-end', except that there the courtyard walls are usually faced with white glazed bricks to reflect daylight.

Now that most privately owned Parisian buildings have electronic security entrance systems instead of a concierge, it has become increasingly difficult to gain access to entrance halls, staircases or internal courtyards. Many of the latter, particularly in the largest and most luxurious blocks, were frequently treated 'architecturally', in keeping with the front facades. Even in the petit-bourgeois blocks erected by developers, where this would not have been economically feasible, the fronts were usually faced with carved stone – the architectural equivalent of always wearing one's best clothes in public. As such, Sauvage's achievement at rue Hippolyte-Maindron is all the more laudable, creating the highest-quality architecture by purely abstract means and almost wholly in buff brickwork. To find an equivalent in French architecture one has to go back to Ledoux or Boullée.

Georges Vaudoyer's (1877–1947) 72 rue de la Colonie, 13e, of 1911, for the Fondation Singer-Polignac is similar in feeling, with two blocks of polychrome brickwork and a projecting roof, but this being what was then on the city's edge, the rear half of the site could be devoted to individual garden plots, a rare luxury in Paris.

Left: **Georges Vaudoyer, 72 rue de la Colonie, 1911.** *With four colours of brick and perfectly considered proportions, even simple apartments for workers can enjoy a sense of nobility*

Below: **Auguste Labussière, 5–15 rue de la Saïda, 1912 –13.** *Concrete-framed flats for large families on an open site, with the red patterning and blue inserts around the top floor the only nod to Arts and Crafts styling.*

Left: **Auguste Labussière, 63–5 rue de l'Amiral Roussin, 1907.** *Part bird's-eye perspective and part axonometric, this drawing shows the overall scale of the development*

Opposite: **Auguste Labussière, 63–5 rue de l'Amiral Roussin, 1907.** *The formal symmetrical layout may have been suggested by the position of the street opposite, but it also facilitated good lighting to every flat.*

Below: **Auguste Labussière, 63–5 rue de l'Amiral Roussin, 1907.** *A combined kitchen/dining room provides each flat's only communal space, although the bedrooms are also large enough for sitting or study.*

The Groupe des Maisons Ouvrières' later schemes, for which the architect was Auguste Labussière (1863–1956), were on a larger scale (130 to 360 dwellings), facilitating the provision of greater open space, especially on sites away from the centre. At 5 rue Ernest-Lefèvre, 20e, 1905, and 124 avenue Daumesnil, 12e, 1907, there were spacious central courtyards, while at 6 rue de Cronstadt, 15e, 1913, where the site is wide but not deep, the provision of a U-shaped block converts the street into a square.

Planning of individual flats was also improved: for example, at rue de l'Amiral Roussin, 15e, 1907, each flat had a dining-kitchen, three bedrooms and a WC and shower. The dining-kitchen, used as the family living room, had continuous fixed fittings along one wall, with a tiled worktop between the cooker and the stone sink, all installed without gaps for reasons of hygiene and appearance. With a number of cupboards and a ventilated larder also included, it compared favourably with private *immeubles*, where the most basic of fitted kitchens was used only by the servants.

The most advanced of Labussière's housing schemes in external aspect is probably that at 5 rue de la Saïda, 15e (1913), which was built for large and, therefore, especially disadvantaged families on a spacious site. The dining-kitchen (called a *salle commune*) provides direct access to the three double bedrooms, thereby reducing otherwise unusable circulation space. As at

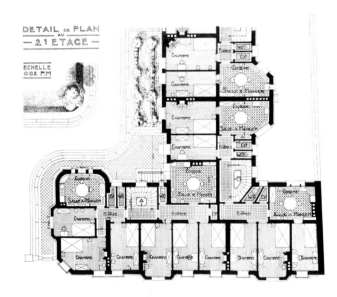

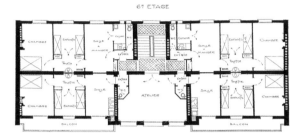

Below: **Labussière and Longery, Hostel, 94 rue de Charonne, 1910–11.** *A massive stone entrance screen gives way to decorative brickwork above.*

Sauvage's rue de Trétaigne, the concrete frame is exposed and painted, the only decoration being the patterned brickwork on the top floor.

Less well-known, because more conventional in appearance, is 155 boulevard Davout, 20e, 1911 by Edmond Delaire (1856–1921), the only block built of what was intended to be a *'cité-jardin'*. This has load-bearing brick walls and thin concrete floor slabs resting on beams with a suspended ceiling below, the space between filled with sound insulation. The plan shows one centrally placed radiator in each flat, as well as WCs and wash basins but no baths.[3]

Accommodation for Single Workers

About 30 per cent of the Parisian population at this time was single, with many young male workers from the provinces, while the girls were mostly in domestic service, living in the *immeubles* where they worked. The HBMs, however, were intended mainly for large families, with only a few single rooms available at rue de Trétaigne and rue de l'Amiral Roussin.

In 1910 the Fondation Lebaudy (as the Groupe des Maisons Ouvrières later became known) built a hostel of 743 rooms for single men at 94 rue de Charonne, 11e, designed by the architects Labussière and Longery. The ground floor contained a restaurant, reading and smoking rooms, a hairdresser, locker

Above: **Joseph Charlet and Fernand Perrin, 41 avenue René Coty, 1908.** *A hostel for single mothers, with colourful brickwork and large windows.*

Above: **Eugène Bliault, Telephonists' hostel, 41 rue de Lille, 1906.** *A telephonist in her bed-sitting room, with three upright chairs, a water jug and basin, and a candlestick on the bed-side table.*

room, a washroom and showers – the latter having their own entrance, presumably for non-residents. The hostel was sold to the Salvation Army in 1918 which still maintains it, thought it is now only for women and called the Palais de la Femme! The buff brickwork is enlivened by blue and orange patterning, while Mme Lebaudy features (anonymously, of course) in the stone bas-relief over the entrance.

As telephone exchanges were not yet fully automatic, callers had to be connected by telephonists, and many of these young ladies were accommodated in the Maison des Dames des Postes, Télégraphes et Téléphones at 41 rue de Lille, 7e, 1906, by the architect Eugène Bliault (*b* 1866). Each upper floor had 18 bedrooms, sharing two WCs and two baths or showers. The vaulted dining room on the ground floor, with its mosaic floor, can still be seen, as it is now a fashionable restaurant – Le Télégraphe. A reading room was also provided, and a small garden, while the dining room had tables for four, suggesting that meal times were the main opportunity for socialising.

Another charitable organisation, the Fondation Louise Koppe, built two homes for expectant mothers. The second and larger of these, at 41 avenue René Coty, 14e, 1908, by Joseph Charlet and Fernand Perrin, is a cheerful building. The light brickwork is enlivened by patterning in a darker red, while the wide windows illuminate dormitories on the upper floors and the refectory and play space below.

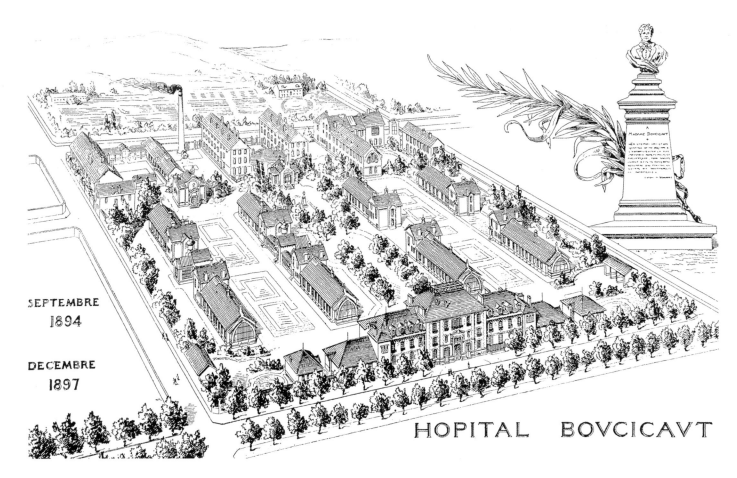

SEPTEMBRE
1894

DECEMBRE
1897

HOPITAL BOVCICAVT

Health and Hospitals

Diseases related to poor housing conditions have already been mentioned in this chapter. As described in Chapter One, Haussmann had, with the assistance of Belgrand, already provided the city with sewers and two sources of water. These measures helped to eliminate the problem of typhoid, but a series of cholera epidemics was only solved when Dr Adrien Proust – father of the novelist and Professor of Hygiene at the faculty of medicine – succeeded in organising a proper *cordon sanitaire* to prevent cholera entering Europe. Its success was celebrated in 1903, the same year the International Office of Public Hygiene opened in Paris.

The nineteenth century has been described as the heroic age of French medicine, the most famous scientist of the time, and the one with the most influence on hospital design, being the chemist Louis Pasteur (1822–95), director of scientific studies at the Ecole Normale. Pasteur had discovered that living forms could multiply in the absence of oxygen, leading him to the study of infectious diseases that culminated in the introduction of immunisation by inoculation in 1879. Joseph Lister's discovery of the antiseptic and the aseptic treatment of wounds was based on

Pasteur's researches, and Pasteur's assistant and successor Dr Roux dispensed the first course of microbiology and immunology in the world from the Institut Pasteur, founded in 1887.

The Hôpital Pasteur was first opened in 1900 and extended in 1928 and 1988: like most hospitals in central Paris it has been rebuilt to a much higher density to keep pace with medical requirements. The only architecturally unaltered portion of these buildings is the crypt in the Institut Pasteur – designed by Charles Girault in 1897 – a Byzantine-style domed chamber in marble and mosaic containing Pasteur's tomb (at the time of writing, not open to the public).[4]

The least altered surviving hospital of the Belle Epoque is the Hôpital Boucicault, 62–80 rue de la Convention, 15e (founded by Mme Boucicault, owner of the Magasins du Bon Marché), which Alphonse and Georges Legros won in competition in 1894 and completed in 1897. Recent rebuilding has been mainly confined to the surgical and service blocks, but to the same domestic scale as the original. The plan was dictated by the need for cross-ventilation ('Nightingale' wards) and strict separation of contagious diseases, reflecting Pasteur's and Roux's understanding of bacteria and the propagation of microbes in ambient air. The separate buildings are joined by underground corridors, 3.5 metres wide, for use by service trolleys. The hospital was originally intended for long-stay care, but is now used for micro-surgery.

Two other hospitals retaining much of their original architecture are Armand Trousseau, 20e, 1896–1901 by Alexandre Maistrasse and Marcel Berger; and Cochin, 13e, doubled in size in 1903 onwards by Paul Renaud and Justin Rochet. Their surviving buildings of the period are in a simple brick vernacular style, sheltering under projecting eaves, similar in character to the Fondation Louise Koppe.

The other most famous scientist of the time was Marie Curie (1867–1934), the discoverer of radium, who carried out much of her work in outbuildings owned by the Sorbonne – the present Institut Curie by H.-P. Nénot only being completed in 1914. Sharing its research facilities with the Institut Pasteur, the Institut Curie was housed in a group of simple brick buildings, their economic form and construction no doubt meeting with Mme Curie's approval.

Each *arrondissement* had its local clinic, mostly for children. A remarkable example is the Dispensaire Jouye-Rouve-Taniès, designed by Louis Bonnier at 190 rue des Pyrénées, 20e, 1902–4, intended for the treatment of tuberculosis and featuring open-air terraces, covered over in 1980. (The building is now used for social services.) Externally, it is in Bonnier's Normandy style, ensuring a summer holiday atmosphere. Construction is of rubble stone with cast-iron lintels, the arrangement of windows clearly expressing the function of the rooms within – including the stepped windows of the entrance staircase, whose tiled canopy has a rustic air as was doubtless intended.

Public Education

The modernisation of Paris with regard to public hygiene had been a priority under Haussmann's direction, but improvements in public education only became an essential element in government programmes once the Third Republic had been established – largely because France felt itself inferior to Prussia in this respect.

Jules Ferry, who was Ministre de l'Instruction Publique in 1879–81 and 1882–3, was the principal politician responsible for this reform, under which primary education became free, obligatory and lay – priests being ousted from teaching in state schools. (It should be noted that French anti-clericalism was concerned with the church's reactionary politics rather than with religion itself.) In Paris only about a third of married couples had

Above: **Louis Bonnier, former Clinic, 190 rue des Pyrénées, 1902–4.** *A seaside holiday atmosphere for children suffering from tuberculosis.*

Above: **Joseph Bouvard,**
***Groupe Scolaire,* 10–**
12 rue Saint-Lambert,
1891–2. *The polychromatic*
brickwork of the main facades
gives way to an exposed iron
frame, visible in the main
classroom wing behind.

Left: **Félix Narjoux,**
***Groupe Scolaire,* 41 rue**
de Tanger, 1876. *The*
mixture of brick and stone
with iron lintels and tie-plates,
and the provision of two wide
windows per classroom, make
this a typical school design.

children, but many new schools were needed to cater for the ever increasing number of immigrant families pouring into the city from the provinces and elsewhere.

Primary Schools

Some small nursery schools (*écoles maternelles)*, usually with just one classroom and a separate playroom (for use in wet weather as well as for meals and washing), were built as separate units, but the majority were part of a *groupe scolaire* composed of an infants' school and separate primary schools for boys and girls. The *groupe scolaire* at 41 rue de Tanger, 19e, by school design specialist Félix Narjoux (1836–91), has been described as '*the archetype, by its site, planning and style, of Parisian primary schools of the beginning of the Third Republic',*[5] and although early in date (1876) it varied very little from many other primary schools built 25 to 30 years later.

The three schools as first built were separated from one another by open playgrounds, the single-storey infants' school being at the rear and sharing an access gallery with the girls' school. The primary schools each had two upper floors of classrooms over a covered ground-floor play area, and all the schools had teachers' flats above them. The classrooms, ranged on one side of a corridor and cross-ventilated through it, are represented on the facades by two windows each. (The school as

described was extended by Roch Rozier in 1911, when adjoining land became available.) A feature of all the school plans – as well as those of the hospitals – is the clear differentiation between 'served' and 'servant' spaces, a separation characteristic of Beaux-Arts rationalism. (Louis Kahn, who attached such importance to this philosophy, spent part of his early working life in the office of Paul Cret, who had been a Beaux-Arts student.)

Narjoux was a pupil of Viollet-le-Duc, and all these schools show the influence of his insistence on the rational expression of function and structure. The structure at rue de Tanger consists of stone piers with iron cross-beams that support brick vaulting. The beams are indicated by decorative iron tie-plates on the facades, with the non-loadbearing panels below the windows being of brick in two colours. In this case the windows have either brick arches or stone lintels, although in some schools exposed iron lintels were also used.

Only two schools, those at 10–12 rue Saint-Lambert, 15e (1891–2, by Joseph Bouvard), and 40 rue Manin, 19e (1900, by Louis-Paul Nessi), had a complete iron frame, in both cases exposed externally. Even when architects better known for designing in the classical Beaux-Arts manner were brought in, their schools conformed to the rationalist pattern -– hardly surprising in view of the detailed functional brief and strict budget to which they had to work.

Below: **Louis Bonnier, Groupe scolaire, 25 rue Rouelle, 1910–12.** *The ground floor is mainly devoted to open and covered play areas for boys, girls and infants, only the latter also having classrooms there.*

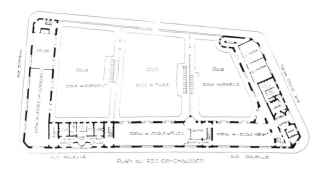

Above: **Louis Bonnier, Groupe scolaire, 25 rue Rouelle, 1910–12.** *An Arts and Crafts brickwork exterior, but the massing and use of exposed concrete are more modern.*

Below: **Louis Bonnier, Groupe scolaire, 25 rue Rouelle, 1910–12.** *The blue brick patterning and coloured mosaic around the entrances suggest the seeds of Art Deco.*

The most notable, if atypical, *groupe scolaire* of the Belle Epoque is that by Louis Bonnier (Joseph Bouvard's successor as Directeur-Général des Services Architecturales de la Ville de Paris) at 25 rue Rouelle, 15e, 1910–12. A continuous block envelops three sides of an island site, with upper-floor classrooms facing inwards onto a large open play area. The infants' school is large, with six classrooms on two floors, while the junior schools are on two to three floors, with the teachers' flats above treated as corner towers. Located next to the concierges' dwellings, the entrances are set within porches – the infants having their own, while that for the junior schools contains two separate doors.

Bonnier's interest in picturesque composition is facilitated by the functionalist expression of internal volumes and uses: for example, there are arched windows to the loggia-like covered play areas on the ground floor, while simple large rectangles light the classrooms. Small rooms have narrow windows, while those on staircases are stepped, the living rooms in the teachers' flats given special attention with curved bays. In this school concrete, not iron, was used for lintels, beams and floors. Externally, the only purely decorative elements are the areas of red brick patterning and the curved inset porches, where mosaic – whose patterning prefigures Art Deco – introduces blue and white into an exterior otherwise of pale buff and red. (The Tricolor flies from the entrances of all state schools.)

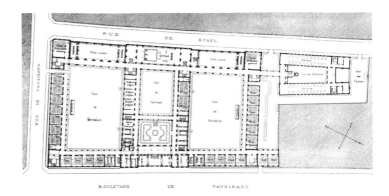

Above: **Émile Vaudremer,
Lycée Buffon, 1885–90.**
*Three courts surrounded by
open cloisters, each giving
onto classrooms on three sides,
with two covered play areas,
a gymnasium and a separate
refectory block on the fourth.*

Left: **Emile Vaudremer,
Lycée Buffon, 1885–90.**
*A new school for a new age,
but with plenty of traditional
stonework – see also page 148.*

Secondary Education

State institutions for secondary education (*collèges* and *lycées*) were usually much larger than the *groupes scolaires*, in both scale and the number of pupils they catered for. A Commission des Bâtiments des Lycées et Colleges was set up to allocate places to a greatly increased number of secondary school pupils, including – after the Camille Sée law was passed in 1881 – girls who previously had had no secondary educational facilities provided, except by convent schools where the emphasis was on training them as mothers.

Because of the sudden expansion in school places, many *lycées* were housed in old buildings. One of the most impressive of the new ones, however, was the Lycée Buffon, 16 boulevard Pasteur, 15e of 1885–90, by Emile Vaudremer (1829–1914). He had been second Premier Prix de Rome in 1854[6] and was joint Architecte des Edifices Religieux de la Ville de Paris with Victor Baltard, designer of the famous iron central market of Les Halles – now destroyed. Despite his years in Rome, Vaudremer had absorbed Viollet-le-Duc's love of Gothic architecture, as the Lycée Buffon shows. Catering for 800 pupils, the central portion of three to four storeys – surrounding a garden court and behind it a gymnasium court – contains all the administrative and communal rooms, apart from the refectories and kitchens which are in a separate building off one corner of the site.

On each side are much larger recreation courts, lined on three sides by two-storey cloisters which have stone arcades at ground level and columns supporting timber beams on the upper floor – on the model of Romanesque monasteries in the Midi. The elevational treatment generally, based on two structural bays per classroom, is of load-bearing stone and brick (with further brick walls between classrooms to provide good sound insulation), and iron cross-beams with brick vaulting. Windows either have stone arches or a stone lintel supported by small iron sections under it, the construction similar to Narjoux's rue de Tanger school of 13 years earlier.

Both schools are typical of the sensibly designed, carefully detailed and well-built schools erected all over Paris during the Third Republic, and many are still in use today. Indeed, after apartment blocks, they are the building type from this period of which the largest number survive. That the Lycée Buffon is among the finest of these is due to the superiority of Vaudremer's artistic talent, and to the combination within the building of the Classical and Gothic traditions of the Ecole des Beaux-Arts – the first in its form and the second in its structural coherence.

Function and Simplicity

The Lycée Jules-Ferry, 77 boulevard de Clichy, 9e, 1913 by Pierre Paquet (1875–1959), has much in common with the Lycée

Right: **Pierre Paquet,
Lycée Jules-Ferry, 1913.**
*The flatness of the brick facing
and almost flush windows
seems a little tame compared
with the Lycée Buffon, but is
lifted by the bold entrance.*

Buffon in its use of repetitive structural bays, two per classroom. Well lit by large rectangular windows, the classrooms are all located on one side of a corridor (in this case on the street side to reduce traffic noise), proving the continuing relevance of the formal mode a quarter century later. The difference is in the structure, which here is a concrete frame with lightweight non-structural partitions that provide total flexibility in planning and re-planning.

The external concrete walls are faced with brick (a mixture of buff and red). Only the ground-floor arches are perhaps reminiscent of the past: otherwise, although designed before the First World War, this is very obviously a twentieth-century building. Its forms were derived from functional rather than historical precedent, and simply treated – as would befit a society where neither craftsmen nor money for over-elaborate form or rich decoration were usually any longer available.

The illustrations to Chapters Six and Seven will have shown the gradual move towards greater functional and formal simplicity in both private and public architecture during the Belle Epoque, and this adaptation to changing needs – reflecting also international influences – will be the subject of the last chapter, whose title is that of the English translation of Le Corbusier's *Vers une architecture* of 1923.

1   For comparison, some dates of social housing in London include: Model dwellings by Henry Roberts, Holborn, 1849; Columbia Road, E2, for Baroness Burdett-Coutts, 1860; Peabody Trust estates from 1870; and LCC housing, Vincent Street, Westminster, 1897–1902.

2   See *Art Nouveau Architecture*, ed Frank Russell, Academy Editions, London, 1983, pp 121–4.

3   For a complete list of *habitations à bon marché* see *Le logement social à Paris 1850–1930* by Marie-Jeanne Dumont, Mardaga, Liège, 1991, pp 167–9.

4   Illustration in *La construction moderne*, 23 January 1897 (pl 39) also reproduced as pl 116 in *Dictionnaire par noms d'architectes …, 1876-1899*, Vol II.

5   Anne-Marie Châtelet, *Paris à l'école*, Editions du Pavillon de l'Arsenal, Picard éditeur, Paris, 1993: '*par sa localisation, ses dispositions et son style, l'archétype des écoles primaires parisiennes des débuts de la IIIe République*'.

6   Vaudremer went to Rome in place of A.-S. Diet, who had been first prizewinner the previous year, but having married was ineligible as a *pensionnaire*.

8 Towards a New Architecture

Paris as an International Centre

The last chapter was mainly concerned with how the French authorities and Parisian architects addressed the problem of ameliorating working-class living conditions. To turn to the larger picture, Chapter One mentioned briefly the effect on Parisian culture of the influx of foreign artists and writers after 1900, establishing Paris for the next half-century as the world centre for art. (New York was to take over for the latter part of the century, but until then architectural influence continued to stem from Europe, many American architects having studied at the Ecole des Beaux-Arts.)

The more cosmopolitan atmosphere, accompanied by a greater ease of travel and the dissemination of the latest ideas through the technical press, when combined with a greater scale of building work requiring new forms of construction, served to keep Paris at the centre of architectural development. It was here that French engineers led the way in the development of reinforced concrete, and the Rational tradition within the Ecole des Beaux-Arts helped to show French architects how to adapt to the new materials.

Choisy: Structure and Form

The two most influential books on architecture published during the Belle Epoque were Julien Guadet's *Eléments et théorie de l'Architecture*, to which reference has already been made, published as a whole in 1902, but based on the lectures Guadet had been giving at the Ecole des Beaux-Arts since being appointed Professor of Theory in 1894; and Auguste Choisy's *Histoire de l'Architecture* published in 1899. Choisy (1841–1909) was Ingénieur-en-chef des Ponts et Chaussées and his book was a history of architectural form mainly, although not solely, as a logical consequence of structural technique. His greatest praise was given to Greek and Gothic architecture (he acclaimed the latter as *'the most astonishing logical achievement in the art'*)[1]. The modern Parisian building he most respected was Labrouste's iron reading room at the Bibliothèque Nationale.

His admiration for the simplicity of Greek ornament and construction, which he described as *'the sign of a sure art, master of its means and certain of its effects'*,[2] was of considerable influence at a time when Art Nouveau was the fashionable decorative style. His ideas held particular sway with the many architects (as seen in the last chapter) who were trying to produce a simpler more functional architecture, but one which might still have an abstract beauty – a quality Choisy found in Greek architecture. In contrast, he thought Roman buildings essentially utilitarian in

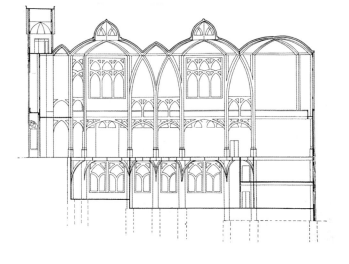

Left: **Anatole de Baudot, Eglise Saint-Jean de Montmartre, 1897–1904.** *The thin walls and columns are even more apparent in plan, and the city authorities were so concerned they halted construction for three years.*

comparison.[3] His study of the role of the asymmetrical entrance route (which Viollet-le-Duc had called the *mise en scène*) in Greek temple site planning, probably his greatest contribution to the future of architectural composition, did not have much immediate influence in France, due to the emphasis on strict symmetry in Beaux-Arts teaching. It was, however, taken up by Le Corbusier in the 1920s.

The Development of Reinforced Concrete: Cottancin and Hennebique

Despite the triumph of iron at the 1889 Exhibition, several French engineers were busy developing reinforced concrete. They included Paul Cottancin (1865–1928), who showed floors in ribbed concrete at the 1889 Exhibition, and François Hennebique (1842–1921). In 1880 Hennebique patented the first concrete slab reinforced with round rods, and followed this in 1892 with the first beam in which the upper and lower reinforcing rods were connected by stirrups. The disastrous fire at the Bazar de la Charité in 1897, with 135 deaths, emphasised the need for fireproof construction, and both Cottancin and Hennebique patented their own construction systems.

Cottancin's *ciment armé*, incorporating special perforated bricks reinforced with steel rods, set in a mixture of sand and cement (but no gravel), was adopted by Anatole de Baudot

(1834–1915) in his buildings, including the church of Saint-Jean-l'Evangéliste, 19 rue des Abbesses, 18e (usually called Saint-Jean de Montmartre), designed in 1897. Construction was halted for three years in 1899, when only the crypt and the concrete frame of the church were complete, because the city authorities were concerned at the thin structural sections used: columns 500 mm square and the floor of the church only 70 mm thick. The vaulted roof consists of two 70 mm-thick layers of *ciment armé*, with clinker insulation between. Although the Gothic inspiration for the structural forms is clear, particularly the ribbed vaulting (de Baudot was a disciple of Viollet-le-Duc), the effect of the interlocking ribs recalls the Baroque of Guarino Guarini, who had used a similar form of construction, in stone, in his only Parisian church, Sainte-Anne-la-Royale, in 1662.[4]

De Baudot used brick as the main external material, contrasting where the frame is exposed with a facing of very small ceramic tiles. These were manufactured by Alexandre Bigot (see Chapter Six), whose tiles were particularly popular with architects requiring a decorative and weatherproof surface for exposed concrete construction.[5] De Baudot shows, in this church, a mastery of spatial integration achieved with structural probity. Like Viollet-le-Duc and Guadet, he was not concerned with 'style' and this, together with the fact that he was responsible for comparatively few buildings, has resulted in his remaining less

Above: **Anatole de Baudot,
Eglise Saint-Jean de
Montmartre, 1897–1904.**
*The small structural sections
and the gallery balustrades
give a lacy effect with both
Gothic and Moorish overtones.*

Right: **Anatole de Baudot,
Eglise Saint-Jean de
Montmartre, 1897–1904.**
*Externally, the rather austere
facade in red brick seems
foreign to Paris and rarely
attracts the tourists visiting
Montmartre. This interesting
architect has been much
undervalued.*

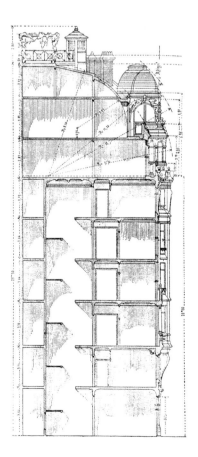

Below: **Edouard Arnaud, 1 rue Danton, 1899–1900.** *The section indicates how the thin concrete structure ensured the maximum number of floors and usability of space on a restricted site. The client's penthouse had a roof garden with turret access.*

Above: **Edouard Arnaud, 1 rue Danton, 1899–1900.** *A contemporary perspective drawing from,* L'Architecture moderne, *1901. The decorated facade gives little indication that this is a concrete structure faced with painted rendering.*

well-known than some of the more publicised exponents of Art Nouveau. De Baudot did not approve of such styles, writing: *'We are blinded on one side by the prestige of ancient forms and on the other by the exaggeration and puerile pretension of creating new forms purely for the sake of fantasy. This is not a new style that society really needs.'* [6]

The reduction in space taken up by concrete structures, in comparison with traditional masonry, was of obvious advantage in commercial buildings, and François Hennebique was the client for the first office and apartment building erected using his system. This was at 1 rue Danton, 6e, in 1899–1900, by Edouard Arnaud (1864–1943), who was himself an engineer as well as an architect. Hennebique's system of reinforced concrete was simpler and quicker to construct than Cottancin's and eventually superseded it. 1 rue Danton contained Hennebique's own office and apartment on the upper floors, with lettable accommodation below, and the whole structure, including the elevations which are rendered and painted, was in concrete.

Comparison of the section with that of a traditional Parisian apartment block will show how Arnaud was able to achieve an additional floor as well as more flexible floor areas. Despite the reduced thickness of their walls, however, his elevations continued to imitate stone forms. The contemporary perspective drawing from *La construction moderne*, 1901, unintentionally underlines the transitional nature of the Belle Epoque, the first complete use of a new structural technique contrasting with the lingering eclecticism of the architectural details (it would be difficult to say in what 'style') and with the ladies' long skirts and parasols – all in an apparently traffic-free street.

The first example of a department store constructed in Hennebique's system was Maison Potin at 140 rue de Rennes, 6e, 1902, by Paul Auscher (1866–1932), where the plan again reflects the effect of a light and flexible structure. The original interior, since altered, was elegantly detailed in a mixture of concrete and metal.[7] In contrast, the confectionery of the facades – particularly the corner tower, which has been likened to Salvador Dali's 'edible architecture' – gives no indication of a concrete structure behind the stone and rendering.

A More Cosmopolitan Architecture: François le Cœur

In 1908 the Ministère des Postes et Télégraphes commissioned François Le Cœur (1872–1934) to design an administration building in the Cité Martignac, 111 rue de Grenelle, 7e, of eight storeys plus basement. Apart from the traditionally designed ground floor (load-bearing stone with arched windows), it is constructed in *ciment armé*, using reinforced facing brick for the piers between the windows. The upper floors are set back in stages: on the top floor is a staff restaurant, a crèche (300 women worked in the building), a quiet sitting room and a roof terrace. François Le Cœur had studied under de Baudot and been

Right: **Paul Auscher, Maison Potin, 140 rue de Rennes, 1902.** *Apart from the top two floors which are rendered, the building is faced with stone and has a corner tower that might best be described as a concrete pâtisserie.*

Below: **François Le Cœur, Postal administration building, Cité Martignac, 1908.** *Including a crèche, a staff restaurant and a roof terrace at the top, this building is modern in every way.*

Left: **François Le Cœur, Central Téléphonique, 2 rue Bergère, 1911.** *Clear spanning hollow floors without projecting beams ensure a maximum usable volume on every floor.*

Below: **François Le Cœur, Central Téléphonique, 2 rue Bergère, 1911.** *A typical floor plan, showing the simple distribution of uses between the three wings.*

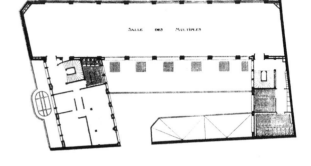

Below: **François Le Cœur, Central Téléphonique, 2 rue Bergère, 1911.** *A solid brick end to the equipment halls, the wall curving out at the top in the form of a concrete cove.*

assistant to Benouville, and his father Charles Le Cœur had been a pupil of Labrouste, so he had impeccable Rationalist credentials. The Cité Martignac was his first building, which may account for the hesitancy of the ground-floor treatment and some awkwardness of proportion.

Le Cœur's successive designs for the Central Téléphonique, 17 rue du Faubourg Poissonnière/2 rue Bergère, 9e, commenced in 1911, show him gradually overcoming these shortcomings and simplifying his details. The plan is straightforward, with the long elevation occupied by three floors of halls – housing the equipment and telephonists – lit from both sides and having hollow concrete floors that span front to back. The external walls, of reinforced brickwork, are also hollow, to contain the heating and ventilation systems. The elevations are beautifully detailed, for example: the vertical grooving in the concrete columns; the battered brick spandrel panels and perfectly cut brick arching over the windows; and the exquisite wrought ironwork (including the clock) made by Szabo to Le Cœur's designs.

The junction between the office block facing the rue du Faubourg Poissonnière and the wing containing the equipment halls, where the cornice above the cove of the main wing runs into the lower of the two penthouse cornices, is well managed – with the main horizontal emphasis provided by a cantilevered

Right: **François Le Cœur,
Central Téléphonique, 2
rue Bergère, 1911.** *The
central of the three windows
in the end wall with its
elegant wrought-iron grille:
a museum piece in itself.*

balcony on the floor below. The building was attacked in the press as being in the *'style Boche'* – Behrens' turbine factory in Berlin of 1909–10 being the most obvious inspiration – although the use of brickwork may have been influenced by Dutch architecture, for example Berlage's work of around 1900. The post office at the south-west corner was added after 1918.

Brickwork was again used as a facing material by Le Cœur in a low-cost apartment block, built in 1911–12 at 72–4 boulevard Vincent-Auriol, 13e. Here reddish-brown brick contrasts with white-painted concrete, which includes slender balconies and columns. The balcony and window ironwork is of the simplest rectangular pattern, somewhat reminiscent of Mackintosh. The combination of functional design, modern construction, international influence and French Rationalism is such that anyone trying to guess the date of this building might well choose a period after the Second World War rather than before the First.

French Style: Plumet and Auburtin

Marcel Auburtin (1872–1926) was the son of Emile Auburtin (1838–99), whose school designs are too early to be included in this book. Marcel produced architecture that was recognisably both 'Modern' and 'French', described at the time as *'la tendance Auburtin'*. His girls' school at 21 rue de Pontoise, 5e, 1910–11, would certainly have been accepted as French in style, being

Above: **Charles Plumet,
Studio house, 21 rue
Octave-Feuillet, 1908.**
*Windows of every size but,
studio north light aside, all
unified by rounded reveals.*

Right and above: **Auguste
Perret, 119 avenue de
Wagram, 1902.** *An elegant
symmetrical facade and a well-
contrived plan, illustrating
Perret's mastery of design even
in this early work.*

obviously derived from Plumet. The rounded brick reveals to the arched windows soften the warm coloured facade, which has a carefully balanced asymmetrical arrangement of windows, with the staircase window acting as a pivot. The overall emphasis, however, is best illustrated by the slight projection of the bay containing the large ground-floor arch and raised attic, which combines a total absence of period detail with an avant-garde composition.

This is derived from the slightly earlier large studio house by Plumet at 21 rue Octave-Feuillet, 16e, 1908, Plumet's most original design. Its entirely functional facade includes a low service door contrasting with a high entrance arch, and windows of varying shape and size that light the large and small salons on the ground floor and the two bedrooms – with a dressing room between – on the first. Only the top-floor studio window is rectangular, in keeping with the room's more workaday use as an artist's *atelier*.

The Development of Concrete Design: Perret and Others

The simple elliptical arches used by Plumet and Auburtin also occur on the ground and fourth floors of 119 avenue de Wagram, 17e, 1902 by Auguste Perret (1874–1954). Perret's father Claude was a builder, exiled to Belgium after the Commune, but following his return he formed a contracting firm with his three young sons Auguste, Gustave and Claude, specialising in reinforced concrete. Auguste studied at the Ecole des Beaux-Arts as a pupil of Julien Guadet and was a friend of Guadet's architect son Paul.

119 avenue de Wagram is, at first sight, reminiscent of Schoellkopf's 29 boulevard de Courcelles designed in the same year – not least in its contrast of sculptural garlands against an otherwise plain stone surface – although it is two storeys higher and its symmetrical facade and strong cornice line above the fifth floor make it much more conventionally classical in form. The originality of the facade treatment lies in the elimination of a traditional 'base', the five main floors being a continuous plain surface broken only by the projecting end bays. These have concave 'responds', curving gently out from the flat plane at pavement level to produce the most successful solution to the design problem of integrating bays and their supports into an overall facade – mentioned in Chapter Six. The fifth floor, with its square windows and circular columns, then acts as an arcaded frieze, but one which is also given the character of a pergola by the carved garlands trailing from it and the 'leaf' capitals on the columns. Above this are a slightly curved set-back floor and a further large apartment in the mansard roof.

The structure behind this stone facade is of reinforced concrete, providing thinner structural walls than would otherwise

Left: **Auguste Perret, 25*bis* rue Benjamin Franklin, 1903–4.** *As the ground floor is mostly glass, the building reads as seven floors starting from pavement level, plus two more set back, in an essentially vertical composition.*

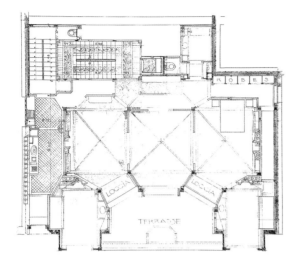

be necessary, while the dining rooms have a completely glazed 'bow-window' wall to the court. Many details of the planning, for example the central *galerie* and the octagonal bedroom, are strictly Beaux-Arts.

Without doubt, the most famous early concrete building in Paris is the apartment block at 25*bis* rue Benjamin Franklin, 16e, designed in 1903–4 by Auguste Perret, and constructed by his family building firm using the Hennebique system. The plan was determined by a legal requirement prohibiting windows to the rear, so that there are effectively three party walls, the staircase at the rear of the building receiving daylight solely through a wall of hexagonal glass bricks.

The recessed form made it possible for all six habitable rooms to have windows on the front elevation – an additional advantage as this gives the best views across to the Eiffel Tower. The slenderness of the concrete columns and the thin panel walls provided maximum floor space. In what is basically a two-living-room, three-bedroom apartment, the three main rooms and the hall, or *galerie*, can all become one space if desired, by the provision of wide door openings – the furthest 'open planning' had been taken in Paris up to that time.[8] Perret's Beaux-Arts training shows itself in the planning, however, with each spatial component – despite the open plan – being a discrete and symmetrical entity.

Externally, the concrete frame, although covered with Bigot's tiles as a permanent finish, is clearly expressed by slightly recessing the non-structural panels and covering them with patterned rather than plain tiles. The patterning is of chestnut leaves, while on the sixth floor bunches of grapes appear to hang over a trellis – an example of the emphasis on vegetation as a decorative motif noticeable also in Guimard's work. Some of the curved forms on the upper floors – such as the fish-scale tiles flowing over small projections at the side of the loggias on the sixth floor, the slightly arched dormer windows above, and uncertainty in what to do with adjacent exposed rainwater pipes – are the only signs of hesitancy in developing a new idiom.

The emphasis on vertical lines marks a complete break with the Beaux-Arts tradition of facades composed of load-bearing base, 'order' and 'attic'. The strictly rectangular frame also signals Perret's realisation that simple, re-usable timber shuttering would provide the most economical form of construction in this new material. At the same time, the combination of small-scale framed units and delicate pattern provides an echo, which may be unconscious, of the *japonisme* fashionable in French painting and decoration during the previous 30 years.

Le Corbusier worked in Perret's *atelier* on the ground floor in 1908–9, and saw in this building the open plan, free facade and flat roof garden that he was to develop as three of the five

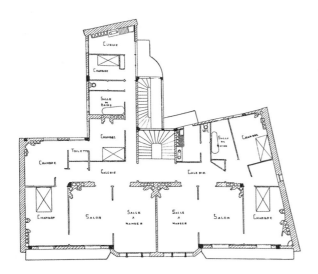

essentials in both his Dom-ino house design of 1914 and his Weissenhof housing of 1927.[9] Of the other two, the free-standing columns or *pilotis* have not been used, Perret's design method being to integrate the structure and dividing walls, while Le Corbusier's ribbon windows would have been not only contrary to the vertical emphasis of this building, but also unnecessary for the provision of uniform daylighting when wide floor-to-ceiling windows were installed. (The simple, tubular-framed 'netting' balustrade, later used by Le Corbusier, also made its first appearance here, after being tried out with slightly more elaboration at 119 avenue de Wagram.)

25 *bis* rue Benjamin Franklin is an exact contemporary with Sauvage's 7 rue de Trétaigne (see Chapter Seven) and, indeed, they would have been very similar in appearance, externally, had the ceramic facing originally intended by Sauvage not been omitted as a cost saving. As a result, the visual contrast between frame and panels is greater at rue de Trétaigne, although this was probably not Sauvage's intention; it would appear from a contemporary photograph that the brick spandrels at rue de Trétaigne were originally painted, but there is now no sign of this.

Compared with rue Benjamin Franklin, the plan of 15 avenue Perrichont, 16e, 1907, by architect-proprietor Joachim Richard (1869–1950), appears at first to be that of a typical *seizième* block of the period, with two apartments per floor, each

Left: **Paul Guadet, 138 boulevard Exelmans, 1912.** *An interesting rather than successful attempt at expressing the different types of apartment within the building. The balcony railings appear to have strayed from elsewhere.*

Right: **Paul Huillard and Louis Süe, 3*bis* and 5 rue Cassini, 1905 and 1906.** *No 5, on the right, displays a bold use of strongly coloured brick; a year later the same architects were using thin concrete sections to unify an original composition at 3bis.*

having a salon and adjacent dining room capable of combination into a large reception room, plus two to four bedrooms. One then notices that internal brickwork is mainly confined to the grouped chimney flues, and that there are small concrete columns within the wall thicknesses. In fact, the floors consist of concrete T-beams linked by hollow 'pots' that form a permanent shuttering and provide a level soffit for plastering below. It was realised at the time that this form of construction provided flexibility for future re-planning, as the position of internal partitions no longer depended on the existence of another wall or beam below.

The concrete frame is exposed externally with brick infill panels, the frame being painted at the rear and faced with ceramic tiles at the front – as also is the central brick bay. The proportions of the ceramic panels (particularly the ogee hoods over some first-floor windows) are not entirely happy, and the patterned brickwork is reminiscent of some of Richard's much earlier and very traditional apartment blocks in the 15th *arrondissement*. The slightly tentative aesthetic treatment externally suggests that Richard was experimenting with new techniques for the functional advantages they would provide: something which might have been more difficult if he had not himself been the client.

The house Julien Guadet's son Paul (1873–1931) designed for himself at 95 boulevard Murat, 16e, in 1912, is mainly known

for its extensive use of concrete – including the owner's bed! Unsurprisingly, this was built by the Perret brothers' contracting firm. Of more interest here, however, in that it shows the same architect using exposed concrete in a bourgeois apartment block, is 138 boulevard Exelmans, 16e, also of 1912. The elevational composition is curious rather than attractive, particularly its subdivision into the equivalent – totally without classical detailing – of base, 'order' (with the *étage noble* emphasised) and attic.

Two floors of *ateliers*, the bay width too narrow for visual comfort as at boulevard Murat, support four floors of apartments with two apartments per floor clearly expressed. The triangular bays are perhaps derived from 7 rue de Trétaigne, as is undoubtedly the elevational treatment that reflects the internal functions. Finally, there are three floors of artists' studios at the top. The joints of the concrete columns and beams are emphasised by tile inserts, and the straight vertical brick joints indicate that the panels are non-loadbearing. The wrought-iron balcony railings, on the other hand, show a lingering Art Nouveau influence.[10]

Another and much more successful small-scale use of concrete framing without period detailing is 3*bis* rue Cassini, 14e, the third of three adjacent studio houses designed by Paul Huillard (1875–1966) and Louis Süe (1875–1968) between 1903

Left: **Henri Sauvage, 26 rue Vavin, 1912.** *Covered with white glazed tiles with blue inserts, the wall curves out at each floor to accommodate plant troughs, a small open space opposite making the terraces more useful than most Parisian balconies.*

and 1906. Virtually identical in size and content, but for different painter clients, the change in external treatment within three years is remarkable. The first, no 7, is in stone, the staircase indicated by two stepped openings with an Ionic column between, and a broken pediment over the triple studio windows. No 5 is in brick, with a ground-floor arch marking the living room, then small windows for the bedrooms, while the studio is fully glazed. This house marks an intermediate stage, both in the reduction of plain surface and the elimination of inherited stylistic elements.

The concrete framing at 3 *bis* rue Cassini is used visually as a unifying device on a facade which appears to lighten as it rises, aided by the greater preponderance of dark grey brickwork at the base and by the filigree effect of the thin concrete struts between the studio windows.

A hitherto seemingly unillustrated *immeuble* in stone, but with painted exposed concrete lintels forming an essential part of the composition, is 16 rue de la Procession, 15e, 1913, by Théodore Lambert (*b* 1857). Apart from the curved hoods above the top windows and the nominal subdivision into base, 'order' and two-storey attic, this is clearly twentieth-century in character. The dark tiled spandrel panels provide contrast in tone, while the curved roof and its atelier windows add just the right character to the whole.

Facing Concrete Structures

Concrete needs a weather protection to prevent water penetration and maintain an acceptable appearance. At 7 rue de Trétaigne (see Chapter Seven), a cheap building, Sauvage had to use paint, while at 25 *bis* rue Benjamin Franklin, where rents were high, Perret could afford to cover his structure with Bigot's ceramic tiles. The buildings in this section show other methods of dealing with this problem.

Henri Sauvage's block at 26 rue Vavin, 6e, of 1912 is famed for its covering of white *Métropolitain* tiles and its set-back section. This building predates by 10 years his *habitations à bon marché* at rue des Amiraux, 18e, where the space under the setback flats is used for a swimming pool. At rue Vavin the internal space on the lower floors can only be used for storage, though this is economically affordable with luxury apartments. (These are not 'workers' flats' as has been erroneously stated in one book.) When Sauvage built on the adjoining site in 1924 (137 boulevard Raspail) he reverted to a vertical facade in the Parisian tradition. In 1908 Sauvage had designed a block of *habitations à bon marché* at 163 boulevard de l'Hôpital, 13e, which was completely faced with small faience tiles, but these have now been replaced by rendering and the roof has also been altered.

Henri Deneux (1874–1969), a pupil of Anatole de Baudot, was chief architect of the Monuments Historiques. His only

Left: **Henri Deneux, 185 rue Belliard, 1913.** *Here the tiles are applied directly to a concrete wall rather than a frame filled with panels, the darker tiles at ground level providing a visual base for this unique building.*

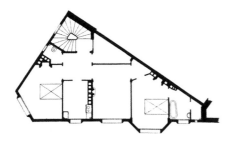

Above and opposite below:
Henri Deneux, 185 rue Belliard, 1913. *The plan and section both show how the thin concrete external walls save space on this small triangular site.*

Right: **Henri Sauvage, 126 rue de Provence, 1912.** *Furniture showroom, offices and design studio are all successfully unified in an elegantly proportioned facade which retains a human scale, helped by the warm colour.*

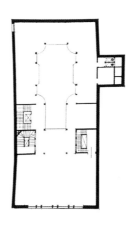

Right: **Henri Sauvage, 126 rue de Provence, 1912.** *Light from above was essential on a site enclosed by walls on three sides, hence the top-lit atrium at the rear of the showroom.*

Parisian building was a small apartment block, designed for himself in 1913, at 185 rue Belliard, 18e. The slender structure possible with *ciment armé* ensured maximum utilisation of space on a restricted triangular corner site. The elevations are completely faced with blue and white tiles set in cement, forming circular abstract patterns that suggest a Moorish influence and are curiously prophetic of the *Snail* paper cut-out of 1952 by Matisse. Matisse had visited Moorish Spain in 1910 and Morocco in 1912, while Perret's contracting firm was building in North Africa from 1908 – although he did not design there until 1916 onwards. Deneux's doorway, with its portrait of the architect above, is the only feature betraying his medieval interests.

The nearest concrete equivalent to Chedanne's metal masterpiece at 124 rue Réaumur, in both scale and commercial use, is probably the building designed by Henri Sauvage at 126 rue de Provence, 8e, in 1912, in that it is of similar size and the interior receives daylight either from the front elevation or from a central courtyard. The client was the furniture designer Louis Majorelle, for whom Sauvage had designed a house at Nancy 15 years before, in a style perhaps best described as a mixture of vernacular and Art Nouveau.[11]

The uses of Majorelle's new building were mixed: his showroom occupied the ground to second floors; the next three floors were let as offices; and Majorelle's *atelier* was at the top. On the elevation, the showroom windows are grouped to represent the single unit within (the narrow vertical side windows were not included in the original design), while the individual offices above each have their own window.

Sauvage improved on his original design here, using curved rather than angled 'bow-windows' on the central office floor only, with square windows above and below – the latter having stepped sills curved on plan, reflecting the curves above. The beaten metal window railings are a development of the metalwork at 7 rue de Trétaigne, although the original iron *marquise* has unfortunately disappeared. A penthouse floor has replaced the original low-pitched roof, probably when the building was converted for use as a bank in the 1920s.

Apart from the grey mosaic facing to the central mullions and dark grey granite on the ground floor, the concrete structure is faced with pink sandstone, providing a continuous surface equivalent to the tile facing at rue Vavin. This was a relatively new approach, quite unlike Sauvage's earlier rue de Trétaigne where there is a clear distinction between concrete structure and non-loadbearing infill – a feature of Perret's work from 1903 onwards. Apart from the window railings, all traces of Art Nouveau have been left behind; the pink and grey colouring provides a warm contrast to the usual Parisian cream stone and brick, but was not taken up by other architects.

Above: **Auguste Perret,
Théâtre des Champs-
Elysées, 1911–13.** *An
urbane exterior, relying on
Bourdelle's reliefs and the
gilded window frames to
provide a note of distinction.*

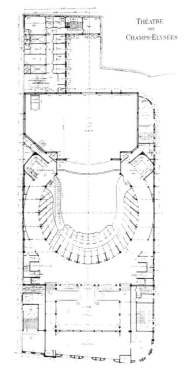

Right: **Auguste Perret,
Théâtre des Champs-
Elysées, 1911–13.** *As at
Garnier's Opéra, the space
allotted to audience circulation is extremely generous,
with the auditorium's circular
form evident on first entering
the foyer.*

The Théâtre des Champs-Elysées

The transformation which took place in some Parisian
architecture, despite apparent general continuity, during the
Belle Epoque might well be illustrated by comparing the
Sorbonne of 1881–1904 (see Chapter Four) with the Théâtre des
Champs-Elysées, 15 avenue Montagne, 8e, of 1911–14. The
history of the Théâtre's design[12] – with its changes of site and
architects, and the final emphasis on cost saving and speedy
completion – is of particular interest, reflecting the effect on the
architectural profession when government patronage began to be
replaced by private enterprise.

Roger Bouvard (1875–1961) – son of Joseph Bouvard and
the designer of both brick schools and Beaux-Arts classical stone
immeubles, two of which were awarded prizes in the Concours de
Façades – was appointed architect for the project in 1910,
producing his first design for another site for which the promoters
were unable to obtain the lease.

At the suggestion of the painter Maurice Denis, who with
the sculptor Antoine Bourdelle had also been commissioned to
work on the project by the client Gabriel Astruc, Bouvard was
later joined by the Belgian architect and furniture designer Henri
Van de Velde (1863–1957). Van de Velde subsequently took over
the design (Bouvard being relegated to dealing with practical
matters) and decided that the theatre should be constructed in

concrete rather than metal to save costs, with the Perret brothers
suggested as contractors.

In February 1911, Auguste Perret declared the design
impossible to construct in concrete and took over responsibility
for its redesign, enabling a contract to be signed with Perret
Frères at the end of March. Van de Velde resigned three months
later and there is little doubt that Auguste Perret must be
considered the building's true architect.

The slightly bland classic nature of the exterior reflects
Bouvard's original design – although Van de Velde and Bourdelle
also produced sketch elevations inferior to Perret's final solution.
Both in plan and section, however, the interior is a remarkably
logical and economic use of concrete construction applied to a
classical conception, using constant-sized rectangular beams and
circular columns – with eight slightly larger columns carrying the
circular dome – as well as bowstring trusses and cantilevered
balconies.

The geometry of the plan has a simplicity and tautness,
provided by the clear relation of the curved forms to the
rectangular frame, that evaded Garnier and Bernier in their
theatre plans. This neo-classical simplicity, which may reflect the
period's revived interest in the late eighteenth century, is given
additional lucidity and elegance by the absence of ornament. The
abstract flowing linear curves of the staircase balustrades, for

Right: **Auguste Perret, Théâtre des Champs-Elysées, 1911–13.** *The traditional red and gold auditorium, its sobriety more suitable for concerts and ballet than for the Opéra Comique style.*

Right: **Auguste Perret, Théâtre des Champs-Elysées, 1911–13.** *An extremely elegant shallow staircase, with the balustrade's flowing lines set off by white walls and the floor's inset marble panels.*

example, are a great improvement on René Binet's version at Le Printemps of 1910 -- now destroyed. Here, at the end of the Belle Epoque, Viollet-le-Duc's understanding of the structural logic of Gothic architecture and Labrouste's ability to adapt the essentials of Beaux-Arts classical teaching to modern needs, were combined. Writing much later, Perret stated: *'Architecture is the art of organising space expressed by means of construction.'* [13]

In addition to the sculptural bas-reliefs by Bourdelle and the decorative painting (for example the Grand Théâtre's ceiling) by Maurice Denis, further decorative painting by Roussel and Vuillard was carried out in the smaller theatre, La Comédie, at a later date. The integration of sculpture and painting with architecture was an essential part of the Beaux-Arts tradition, and this was its last major example. Perret and his brothers were members of the Cercle des Artistes de Passy, which included the painters Picabia, Gleizes and Duchamp-Villon, as well as the poet Apollinaire.

The Théâtre des Champs-Elysées was intended mainly for music and dance, and the opening season included the premières of Debussy's *Jeux* and of Stravinsky's and Nijinsky's *The Rite of Spring*. The abstract nature of the first (the Games of the title being played out within the music as well as by the dancers) has perhaps rather more in common with Perret's building than the primitivism which so enraged the *Rite*'s first-night audience. Such

outrage had already been seen at the 1905 Exhibition at the Salon d'Automne (founded in 1903 by the architect Frantz Jourdain), where the paintings by Matisse, Derain and Vlaminck led to their being called 'fauves', or wild beasts. (Picasso's *Les Demoiselles d'Avignon* of 1907 was not exhibited until 1916.)

The Emergence of Abstraction

Cézanne's retrospective of 1907 greatly influenced the young Braque, whose first one-man show at Kahnweiler's gallery in 1908 initiated the term 'Cubism'. Picasso's and Braque's Cubist work of 1910–12 was concerned basically with invention rather than representation, while Frantisek Kupka, who was living in Paris at the same time, was working on the first abstract paintings to be produced there. Mondrian arrived in Paris in 1911, and his drawings of Parisian buildings of 1912–13 immediately preceded his first purely abstract oval canvases.

This leads us back to the two artists connected with the Théâtre des Champs-Elysées: Henri Van de Velde and Maurice Denis. Van de Velde, whose rectangular furniture had been influenced by Mackintosh, was the director of the School of Arts and Crafts at Weimar from 1901 to 1914 (later moved by its subsequent director Walter Gropius to Dessau, where it was re-named the Bauhaus), while Denis' declaration in 1890 that, *'a picture is essentially a surface covered with colours arranged in a certain order*[14] helped pave the way to abstract art. Under the influence of Giotto's frescoes at Padua seen in 1907, the *fauvist* Matisse was, by the next year, writing in his *Notes d'un peintre* of the search for clarity and order.

The above discursion into contemporary painting is intended to underline the close international links between the arts in the Paris of 1900 to 1914, and also its artists' links with the past as well as with the foundation of an 'abstract' art more closely related to architecture. After the First World War, the new comparatively short-lived French 'style' to follow Art Nouveau was to stem from the Decorative Arts Exhibition of 1925, but Perret's Swiss pupil, the architect and painter Le Corbusier, having returned to Paris, was to develop a more revolutionary architecture based on a variety of historical precedents.[15] The illustrations in the second half of this book show Parisian architecture becoming increasingly 'abstract' in character as period motifs were forsaken.

Continuity and Change in Architecture:
Lessons of the Belle Epoque

The cessation of building in Paris brought about by the First World War has the effect of our seeing the Belle Epoque as a distinct historical period, although, as this book has hopefully shown, it was in many respects a successful conclusion to the nineteenth century as well as being the beginning of the age in which we still live: an age of adjustment to painfully swift change, resulting in a pluralistic architecture, there being as yet no consensus on the direction that architecture should take.

At the beginning of the new century, the Third Republic moved to Ralliement, a heroic effort to provide social cohesion, and Chapter Seven has shown how architects played their part in the development of an urban architecture designed for the mass of the population. They were able to do so through the Rational tradition within the Ecole des Beaux-Arts, which had – irrespective of medieval or classical bias – emphasised the tradition of fitness for purpose and a consequent lack of interest in passing fashion.

The vast building programme of the Haussmann era had combined new technical methods with traditional craftsmanship, a synthesis that was strengthened by the high standards of design inculcated by architectural education, which had produced a profession proud of its standing as artists as well as craftsmen.

Very many little- or un-known architects (there has only been space to introduce some in this book, although others will be mentioned in the Appendix) were designing economic but imaginative buildings for everyday use of a remarkably high standard. These could provide inspiration to all concerned with producing architecture today in similar, often straitened, conditions.

All this could not have been achieved without the French tradition of clarity and order emphasised earlier in Chapter Eight, strengthened by the ability to draw on the past for inspiration.

Continuity and Change in the City

The city as planned by Napoléon III and carried out under the supervision of Haussmann and his assistants one and a half centuries ago has proved to be beautiful, structurally enduring and adaptable – the latter because it was designed for a developing society that is still recognisable today. The provision of local centres and the mixture of residential and commercial uses have ensured the continuation of a lively use at street level, while from the start the wide avenues encouraged the provision of pavement cafés and strolling space. Some narrower streets, either partly or wholly pedestrianised, were also used for street markets.

The generally regular building height, combined with domestic use of the upper floors, has preserved a human scale, which only became lost in those areas rebuilt in the 1950s with individual high-rise blocks of flats or offices isolated from the street scene.

With this exception, the nineteenth-century city is still there, but it is important that the character of the individual 'ordinary' buildings, as well as its monuments, should be recognised and appreciated, not only to ensure that they are well cared for, but also so that those responsible for inserting new buildings into the existing fabric can fully understand its qualities.

The variety of Belle Epoque architecture proves that imitation is unnecessary, but that sensitivity is essential. Provided the City authorities can overcome the strangulating vehicular traffic, a problem which is being addressed elsewhere, there is no reason why the fabric of Paris should not continue to provide an ideal setting for a civilised city life and an object lesson to city builders everywhere.

1   A. Choisy, *Histoire de l'architecture*, Gauthier-Villars, Paris, 1899, p 600: *'La vie de l'architecture gothique s'arrête au 15e siècle. Son histoire a été du plus étonnant effort de la logique dans l'art.'*

2   *Ibid*, p 285: *'A l'époque hellénique l'ornement, aussi bien que la construction, a pour caractère cette simplicité qui est la marque d'un art mûr, maître de ses moyens, sûr de ses effets.'*

3   *Ibid*, p 512: *'De l'art grec, qui semble un culte désintéressé rendu aux idées d'harmonie et de beauté abstraite, nous passons à une architecture essentiellement utilitaire.'*

4   Illustrated in *Guarino Guarini and his Architecture*, by H. A. Meek, Yale University Press, Newhaven, CT and London, 1988, p 27. Demolished 1821, but de Baudot may have seen an illustration.

5   Notable examples of Bigot's ceramics not mentioned in previous chapters include 62 rue Boursault, 17e, by Simonet, and 6 rue de Hanovre, 2e, by Bocage (including staircase).

6   A. de Baudot, *L'Architecture: le passé, le présent*, Henri Laurens, Paris, 1916, p 3: *'Nous possédons bien ces éléments de rénovation, mais sans chercher à profiter des avantages qu'ils offrent en faveur de la conception et de la composition. Nous sommes aveuglés, d'un côté, par le prestige des formes anciennes, et de l'autre, par la vanteuse et puérile prétention de créer des nouvelles formes, sans autre direction que la fantaisie. Ce n'est pas un style nouveau dont la société actuelle a besoin.'*

7   The interior photograph in *Paris Art Nouveau*, by F. Borsi and E. Godoli, Marc Vokar, Paris, 1989, p 161, is of Maison Potin and not Grand Bazar de la rue de Rennes, as stated.

8   Some early examples of open planning include Norman Shaw's West House, Campden Hill Road, Kensington (1878); McKim, Mead & White's Isaac Bell House, Newport, RI (1881); Frank Lloyd Wright's Isidore Heller House, Chicago (1897); and the J. W. Hussa house, Chicago (1899).
    In Paris: Balleyguier's 23 avenue Rapp (1898) (see Chapter Six)

    and Bocage's 95 boulevard Raspail (1902) (see Chapter Four) have rooms connected by exceptionally wide folding doors. Pairs of rooms joined by folding doors occur in many eighteenth-century terrace houses in London, where the partitions between rooms were timber framed; there are fewer in the Bath terraces, because internal walls there were usually load-bearing.

9   William J. R. Curtis, *Le Corbusier, Ideas and Forms*, Phaidon, London and New York, 1986, p 69.

10 The only previously published illustration of 138 boulevard Exelmans, in Chemetov and Marrey's *Architectures à Paris 1848–1914*, Bordas, Paris, 1984, dates from before the authorship of the building was known.

11 Illustrated p 121, *Art Nouveau Architecture*, edited by Frank Russell, Academy Editions, London, 1979.

12 See 'Qui est l'architecte du Théâtre des Champs-Elysées?', by Bernard Marrey, *L'Architecture d'aujourd'hui*, July 1974, on which the brief summary given here is based.

13 *'L'architecture est l'art d'organiser l'espace, c'est par la construction qu'il s'exprime'* ('Contribution à une théorie de l'architecture'), see *Auguste Perret*, by Roberto Gargiani, Gallimard/Electa, Paris/Milan, 1994, p 38.

14 'Définition du Néo-traditionnisme' in *Art et critique*, August 1890; see also G. H. Hamilton, *Painting and Sculpture in Europe 1880–1940*, Penguin Books, Harmondsworth, 1967/1972, p 304.

15 The influence of the Parthenon and medieval monasteries on Le Corbusier are well-known examples: see also *The Mathematics of the Ideal Villa and Other Essays*, by Colin Rowe, MIT Press, Cambridge, MA, 1982, pp 4–28 (first published in *The Architectural Review*, March 1947), and 'A Paradoxical Avant-Garde, Le Corbusier's Villas of the 1920s' by Richard Etlin, *The Architectural Review*, January 1987.

75 Architects

The *Dictionnaire par noms d'architectes* by Anne Dugast and Isabelle Parizet (see Bibliography) lists 4871 architects who made building applications between 1876 and 1899 alone. The purpose of this appendix is to provide additional information about some of the architects included in Chapters One to Eight, and to list additional buildings for which there has not been space to include illustrations. This is for the convenience of those readers who may wish to look at further examples of Belle Epoque architecture. A selection of over 20 other excellent architects, for whose work there was no space in the main chapters, has been included: this could easily have been increased to 100, such is the high standard of work produced during the period.

The full names of architects are here recorded: elsewhere in the book only the given names by which they chose to be called are used. Only their principal Parisian buildings are listed, with important work elsewhere mentioned only if relevant. Dates for both architects and buildings are given when available and the buildings are all apartment blocks unless mentioned otherwise. Buildings illustrated are shown in bold letters.

Dates of diplomas are from the Ecole des Beaux-Arts (EBA) unless stated otherwise. The names of '*Patrons*' under whom those listed studied is also included, as this is essential background information. A list of the principal EBA *Patrons* is given in note three, Chapter Four.

Dates

Construction dates given are either dates of building applications or completion dates. Due to building sites being generally highly organised (although there were some strikes) and commercial pressure to complete, most of the *immeubles* seem to have been completed in about a year. Architects' birth and death dates have not always been possible to establish, especially as obituaries were not always published during the First World War, when many of the younger architects were killed.

CHARLES ADDA 1873–1938 (pupil of Laloux, diploma 1901). Simplified classical motifs intelligently adapted to multi-storey application and delicately detailed.

48 ave du Président-Wilson, 16e, 1908; 58 rue Bobillot, 13e, c 1911; **6 place de Mexico**, 16 rue de Sablons and 4 rue des Belles-Feuilles, 16e, 1912; 16 rue Ampère, 17e, 1913; House, 5 rue du Général-Appert, 16e (now Pakistani Embassy), no date.

GEORGES ALBENQUE 1877–1963 (pupil of Paulin and Guadet, dipl 1907) and EUGÈNE GONNOT 1879–1944 (pupil of Paulin and Maistrasse, dipl 1910). Included here for their attractive domestic work started at the end of the Belle Epoque and continued equally appropriately in the 1920s.

HBM 1 rue Henri Becque, 13e (won in competition), 1913–22; HBM 10 rue Ernest et Henri Rousselle, 13e, 1913–22; Artists' studios, 7 & 9 rue Antoine Chantin, 14e, 1914.

GEORGES BALLEYGUIER 1855–1944 (pupil of Ginain). Despite Ginain being a strict classicist, Balleyguier's detailing was usually original and applied to simple forms rationally related to function and structure.

24 rue Boccador, 8e, 1890; **23 ave Rapp**, 7e, 1898; 9 bd Raspail, 7e, 1901; Former Banque Société Générale, 6 rue de Sèvres, 6e, 1901–5.

(GEORGES) RAYMOND BARBAUD 1860–1927 (probably self-taught) and **J. P. EDOUARD BAUHAIN**, *b* 1864 (pupil of André and Laloux). Their work is of a consistently high standard, often having sparing but adroit use of sculptural decoration.

Syndicat de l'Epicerie Française, 12 rue de Renard, 4e, 1901; 74 ave Henri-Martin/199 ave Victor-Hugo, 16e, 1903; **5 rue Lalo**, 16e, 1906.

ANATOLE DE BAUDOT 1834–1915 (pupil of Labrouste and assistant of Viollet-le-Duc). Inspecteur-général des Edifices Diocésains; Professeur d'Architecture Française, Musée des Monuments Historiques 1887–1912. His first important concrete building was the Lycée Lakanal, Sceaux 1882–6. Author of *L'Architecture et le beton armé*, 1905, and *L'Architecture, le passé, le present*, published posthumously in 1916.

1 and 1*bis* rue de Pomereu, 16e, 1894 (design for single house on site 1892, illus in *Dictionnaire par noms d'architectes*, vol I), Lycée Victor-Hugo, 27 rue de Sévigné, 3e, 1896; **Eglise Saint-Jean-l'Evangeliste**, 19 rue des Abbesses, 18e, 1897–1904.

JULIEN (FRANÇOIS) BAYARD 1843–1929 (pupil of Questel). Buildings generally notable for complete absence of period motifs.

74 rue Jean-Jacques-Rousseau, 1er, 1884. 24 rue du Louvre, 1er, 1894 (with Ernest Bertrand). House, 10 rue Alphonse-de-Neuville, 17e, 1898 (two floors since added). 10 rue Puvis-de-Chavannes, 17e (date not known).

LÉON BENOUVILLE 1860–1903, born Rome, father a painter and friend of Corot, brother Pierre an architect. Studied Ecole des Arts et Manufactures, dipl 1884. Assistant to Charles Le Coeur. Architect, Edifices Diocésains, Perpignan and Lyons, also Monuments Historiques. Designed furniture; also workers' houses, Ardennes and Vosges. His early death robbed France of one of its best architects.

34 rue de Tocqueville, 17e, 1897; **17–19 bd Pasteur**, 15e, 1897; **46 rue Spontini**, 16e, 1899.

CHARLES BLANCHE 1863–1937 (pupil of Raulin), dipl 1891. His best *immeubles* are those in brick, with distinctive wood and iron bay windows, very domestic in character.

151 rue de Charonne, 11e, 1896; 18–20 ave Théophile-Gautier, 16e, 1899; 31–3 ave de Versailles, 16e, 1899–1901; 102 rue de Belleville, 19e, 1901; 101 rue de Sèvres, 6e, 1901; 210 rue du faubourg Saint-Denis, 10e, c 1901; 20 ave de Wagram, 8e, 1902; 7 rue Lekain, 16e, 1902–5; 62 rue des Vignes, 16e, 1908; 28–30 ave Théophile-Gautier, 16e, 1905; House, 17 quai Louis-Blériot, 16e, 1911; 3 rue Charles-Lamoureux, 16e, c 1911.

VICTOR (AUGUSTE) BLAVETTE, 1850–1933 (pupil of Constant-Dufeux and Ginain), dipl 1878, Prix de Rome 1879. Assistant to Dutert, Palais des Machines 1889. Professor of Theory, EBA, 1908. His sensibly designed buildings generally lack the over-elaboration associated with the Prix de Rome.

Groupe scolaire, 9 rue des Panoyaux, 20e, 1891; 114 bd Saint-Germain, 6e, 1898; Ecole, 146 ave Félix-Faure, 15e, 1906–9; 167 rue de Montmartre, 2e, 1909; Conservatoire de musique, 14 rue de Madrid, 8e, c 1909.

(F.) ADOLPHE BOCAGE 1860–1927 (pupil of Guadet). Before 1891 his early work, in partnership with J Brevet, appears unsure. The later buildings varied in treatment, the majority linked by use of elliptical curves counteracted by horizontal string courses. All are worth study for subtlety of composition and delicate 'placing' of decorative detail. Masterful domestic planning. 6 rue de Hanovre quite different in character because commercial. One of the best architects of the period.

91 ave Gambetta, 20e, 1891; 79 ave de Villiers, 17e, 1893, also no 89, 1895; 229–31 ave Gambetta, 20e, 1894; 66 rue de Reuilly, 12e, 1894–5; 4 chaussée de la Muette, 16e, 1901; 133 bd de Ménilmontant, 11e, 1902; **95 bd Raspail**/36 rue de Fleuris, 6e, 1902; 93 & 95 ave Gambetta, 20e, 1905–8 and 5–7 rue de la Chine, 20e, c 1909; Offices, 6 rue de Hanovre, 2e, 1908; 1–3 and 2 rue Charles-Dickens, 18e, 1908; **15 rue de Téhéran**, 8e, 1910; 6–10 ave Constant-Coquelin and 5–7 ave Daniel-Lesueur, 7e, 1913; 6 cité Malesherbes, 9e and 1 rue Moncey, 9e are undated, but look about 1913.

ÉMILE (EUGÈNE) BOIS 1875–1960 (pupil of Moyeaux), dipl 1899. Forcefully sculpted designs with good use of colour. His most prominent later building the Église Saint-Pierre-de-Chaillot, ave Marceau 1933.

166 rue de la Convention, 15e, 1912. 183 (also identical 188) rue de la Convention, 15e, 1913; Groupe scolaire, 50 rue Vauvenargues and 7 rue Georgette-Agutte, 18e, won in competition 1913, completed 1920; HBM 14 rue Abel, 12e, 1913–21.

LOUIS (BERNARD) BONNIER 1856–1946 (pupil of André and Moyeaux), dipl 1886. His father-in-law and son both architects. Assistant to Paul Sédille. Early practice on Normandy coast in rustic 'balneal' style. Architecte-voyer-en-chef, Ville de Paris. Inspecteur-général des Services d'Architecture et d'Aesthétique 1911. Despite his bureaucratic appointments he was a remarkable designer and draughtsman and exerted great artistic influence. Responsible for staircase balustrade at Dutert's Galerie de Paléontologie 1892–8 and for Samuel Bing's L'Art Nouveau Bing 1895, since demolished. His remarkable designs for pavilions at 1900 Exhibition are illustrated in Bernard Marrey's monograph (see Bibliography).

Dispensaire Jouye-Rouve-Taniès, 190 rue des Pyrénées, 20e, 1902–4; Groupe scolaire, **25 rue Rouelle/22 rue Sextius-Michel**, 15e, 1910–12; 67 rue des Meuniers, 12e (with his son Jacques), 1912–13; His swimming bath at the Butte-aux-Cailles, 5 place Verlaine, 13e, built 1922–4 was first designed in 1914.

JEAN-MARIE BOUSSARD 1844–1923 (pupil of Paccard) started practice in 1879. Most interesting early building 7–9 place des Ternes, 17e, 1881, planned round a circular court on an irregular site. Vigorous designs, often with Mannerist details and not afraid of being 'ugly'. Straightforward expression of iron and concrete construction, when used.

51 rue Pergolèse, 16e, 1886; **17 rue des Bernardins**, 5e, 1890; Administration des Postes (now Caisse Nationale), 4 rue Saint-Romain, 6e, 1890; **Central Téléphonique, 46 rue du Louvre**, 1er, 1891; 5 rue Dangeau, 16e, 1894. 41 & 45, 40–2 rue Ribéra, 16e, 1894; 4 rue Jean-Goujon, 8e, 1894; Administration des Postes, 40 bd de Port-Royal, 5e, 1896; 76 ave Mozart, 16e, 1896; Administration des Postes, 55 & 55bis ave de Saxe, 7e, 1899; 4–6 rue Jasmin, 16e, 1909–11.

JOSEPH (ANTOINE) BOUVARD 1840–1920 (pupil of Constant-Dufeux). Father of Roger Bouvard. Directeur-général des Services Architecturales de la Ville de Paris. Directeur, Services Architecturales, 1900 Exhibition (including design of Dôme Central). Despite administrative appointments, probably responsible for design of buildings attributed to him: he also designed railway stations at Marseilles and Saint-Etienne.

Caserne Garde Républicaine, 4 rue de Schomberg, 4e, 1883; Bourse de Travail, rue du Château-d'Eau, 10e, 1888–93; **Groupe scolaire, 10–12 rue Saint-Lambert**, 15e, 1891–2.

RAOUL BRANDON 1878–1941 (pupil of Defrasse, Laloux and Scellier de Gisors). Brothers Lionel and Daniel also architects. His early *immeubles* are the epitome of the late Belle Epoque style; later designed HBMs in partnership with his brothers and became a socialist Député in 1925.

1 rue Huysmans, 6e, 1909 (also no 2, 1919); 199 rue de Charenton, 12e, 1911; 172 ave du Maine, 14e, 1913.

ACHILLE CHAMPY 1868–1950 (probably self-taught). In practice 1902–35. Most of his work, although not of the highest rank, has considerable character, incorporating Romanesque, classical and Art Nouveau influences.

109 ave Ledru-Rollin, 11e, undated; 102–6 cour de Vincennes, 12e, 1903; 10 rue Belgrand, 20e, undated; 6 place Félix Eboué, 12e, 1904; 11bis place de la Nation, 11e, 1905; 68–72 bd de Picpus, 12e, 1905–7; 93 ave Philippe-Auguste, 11e, 1908; 21 ave Emile Deschanel, 7e, undated; 17–27 rue de la Folie Regnault, 20e, 1913.

JOSEPH CHARLET b 1863 and **FERNAND PERRIN** b 1873 (pupils of Guadet). Charlet was an architecte-voyer and worked in partnership with Calinaud and Michel 1896–1903. Excellent at large-scale compositions with delicately sculptured details set off by large areas of plain wall.

2 rue de Navarin, 9e, 1903 (Charlet and Michel); **43 rue des Couronnes**, 20e, 1905; 22–4 rue Charles-Baudelaire, 12e, 1908–10; **Maison Maternelle Louise Kopp, 41 ave René Coty**, 14e, 1908; **18 place Adolphe Chérioux**, 15e, undated.

GEORGES (PAUL) CHEDANNE 1861–1940 (pupil of Guadet), dipl 1887. Prix de Rome 1887 (measured the Pantheon). His buildings, while varying considerably in style, are all of the very highest quality. In addition to his Parisian work, he designed 'palace' hotels elsewhere and four embassies or legations abroad.

Former Elysée Palace Hotel, **103 ave des Champs-Elysées**, 8e, 1897–9; Former Hôtel Mercédès, **9 rue de Presbourg**, 16e, 1903; Garment factory, **124 rue Réaumur**, 2e, 1904.

LÉON CHESNAY b 1869 (pupil of Gerhardt and Redon), dipl 1898. Worked in a variety of manners and materials; his buildings all highly professional and worthy of close study.

4 rue d'Arsonval, 15e, undated; 84 bd Barbès, 18e, 1905; **23bis ave de Messine**, 8e and 7 rue de Messine, 8e, 1906; 85 rue de Courcelles, 8e, 1907; 128–30 rue Lecourbe, 15e, 1907; 4–10 rue Victor Duruy, 15e, 1909.

L.-A. OCTAVE DE COURTOIS-SUFFIT 1856–1902 (pupil of Pascal and of his stepfather Jules Suffit), dipl 1881. Second Prix de

Rome 1882. Viollet-le-Duc would appear to have been a stronger influence than the classicist Pascal. Original facade compositions with oversized brackets supporting bays and balconies.

134 rue du faubourg Poissonnière, 10e, 1896; Nursery school, 24 rue du Retrait, 19e, 1896; School, 20 rue des Cendriers, 20e, 1897; 190*ter* bd Malesherbes, 17e, 1898; 62*bis* rue de la Tour, 16e, 1901; 18 rue de Grenelle, 7e, 1902; 20*bis* rue Boissière, 16e, 1902.

LAURENT DOILLET 1861–1931 (pupil of Raulin). Well-composed designs whose visual interest arises mainly from careful contrast of brick and stone.

Groupe scolaire, 9 rue Bretonneau, 20e, 1897; Caserne des Pompiers, 47 rue Haxo, 20e, 1900–5; HBM, 23–5 rue Bobillot, 13e, 1913.

JEAN-CAMILLE FORMIGÉ 1845–1926 studied at Ecole des Arts Décoratifs and EBA (pupil of Laisné). Member of the Institut. Chief architect, Services Promenades et Jardins, Ville de Paris; chief architect, Monuments Historiques. Chief assistant to Théodore Ballu, 1881–5. Own practice 1887–1924. Designed Palais des Beaux-Arts, Palais des Industries and Dôme Central at 1889 Exhibition.

Monument Crématoire, cemetery of Père-Lachaise, 20e, 1887–9 (Romanesque); 6 rue Dufrenoy, 16e, 1900 (with Emmanuel Gonse); **Le Métro Aérien**, 1902–7; Manufacture Nationale des Gobelins, 42 ave des Gobelins, 13e, 1914.

PAUL (ÉMILE) FRIESÉ 1851–1917 (pupil of Coquart). Assistant to Jules Denfer (engineer) 1883–8. The monograph by Hugues Fiblec (see Bibliography) includes illustrations of his Usine Génératrice and the Bâtiment de l'Administration du Métro, quai de la Rapée, a masterpiece now demolished.

Usine Electrique de la Compagnie Parisienne de l'Air Comprimé, **132 quai de Jemmapes**, 10e, 1895–8; **Grand Magasin Aux trois Quartiers**, **20 rue Duphot**, 1e, 1898; 92 and 150 ave des Champs-Elysées, 8e, 1898–1900. Printing works, 20 rue Bergère, 9e, 1905; **Banque Franco-Suisse, 120 rue Lafayette**, 9e, 1908 (with Joseph Cassien-Bernard).
Electric sub-stations: 41 rue de Caumartin, 9e, 1903/1908; 135 bd de Grenelle, 15e, 1906; 14 ave Parmentier, 11e, 1908; 3 rue Rampon, 9e, 1908; **36 rue Jacques-Louvel-Tessier**, 10e, 1908; 6 rue Récamier, 7e, 1910. **31 bd Bourdon**, 4e, 1911; 2*bis* rue Michel-Ange, 16e, 1912.

CHARLES GENUYS 1852–1928 (pupil of Train). Second Prix de Rome 1879. Professor at Ecole des Arts Décoratifs. Designer of light fittings and carpets, his *immeubles* typical of understated sensible Belle Epoque buildings which haven't dated.

48 rue Saint-Ferdinand, 17e, 1893; 81 ave Victor-Hugo, 16e, 1897; 141 rue de la Pompe, 16e, 1899.

CHARLES (LOUIS) GIRAULT 1851–1932 (pupil of Daumet), dipl 1888. Prix de Rome 1880. Professor, EBA. Member of the Institut. The most accomplished classical architect of the Belle Epoque. Designed race-stands at Longchamp and various royal commissions at Brussels. Coordinating architect, Grand Palais, 8e, 1896.

12*bis* place Henri-Bergson, 8e, 1891; 36 ave Georges-Mandel, 16e, 1891 (he lived there); House, **14 rue Eugène-Flachat**, 17e, 1895; **Petit Palais**, 8e, 1896–1900. House, 21 rue Blanche, 9e, 1901–3.

(PAUL) ADRIEN GOUNY *b* 1852 (pupil of Daumet). Influenced by Viollet-le-Duc. Layered elevational treatment with polychromatic materials and exposed iron.

Offices, SNCF, **144 rue du faubourg Saint-Denis**, 10e, 1889, extended behind in rue d'Alsace in 1898, in a more prosaic style; House, 9 rue Fortuny, 17e, 1892.

ANDRÉ GRANET 1881–1974 (pupil of Redon). Son of Louis Granet (*b* 1852); son-in-law of Gustave Eiffel. Practising at the extreme end of the Belle Epoque, his work was the culmination of the most elegantly elaborate Belle Epoque style. (In the 1920s he became one of the founders of Art Deco.)

30 ave Marceau, 8e, 1913–16; 30–8 rue Desaix, 15e, 1914; 10–14 square Desaix, 15e, 1914 (both these consist of a group of identical *immeubles*, but with varied external treatment); 124 rue Lafayette, 10e, 1914–15.

HECTOR (GERMAIN) GUIMARD 1867–1942 (pupil of Genuys at Ecole des Arts Décoratifs and of Raulin at EBA). Professor at the former 1894–8. His interest in prefabrication, shown in his Métro entrance cast-iron balustrading was pursued after he had given up Art Nouveau. Brilliant publicist.

House, 34 rue Boileau, 16e, 1891; House, 41 rue Chardon-Lagache, 16e, 1893; **Castel Béranger, 14 rue La Fontaine**, 16e, 1894–5; Former Ecole du Sacré-Coeur, **9 ave de la Frillière**, 16e, 1895; House, 39 bd Exelmans, 16e, 1895. Métro entrances 1898–1901; **Immeuble Jassedé, 142 ave de Versailles**, 16e, 1905; Own house, 122 ave Mozart, 16e, 1909–12; **17–19 rue La Fontaine** and **8–10 rue Agar**, 16e, 1911; Synagogue, 10 rue Pavée, 3e, 1913; Offices, 10 rue de la Bretagne, 3e, 1914–19.

GEORGES GUYON (dates unrecorded) and son Maurice (*b* 1877, pupil of Paulin, dipl 1906). Excellent HBMs. The luxury *immeubles* from 1907 show Maurice's Beaux-Arts training. Georges was probably self-taught.

HBM **5 rue Jeanne d'Arc**, 13e, 1899; HBM **10 rue de la Croix-Faubin**, 11e, 1904–6; 21 & 25 rue Henri-Monnier, 9e, 1907; HBM 237 rue Saint-Charles, 15e, 1909; 15 ave Emile-Deschanel, 7e, 1909.

FRÉDÉRIC (ADRIEN) HENRY 1867–1939 (pupil of Daumet and Girault), dipl 1896. Hermant's assistant, Caserne des Célestins. Perhaps an architect's architect; it would be difficult to fault any of his simple buildings.

House (now offices) 14*bis*–16 rue de la Faisanderie, 16e, 1898–1901; 95 bd Exelmans, 16e, date unknown; **97–9 rue de Prony**, 17e, 1906; HBM 181–3 rue Belliard, 18e, 1914.

JACQUES HERMANT 1855–1930 (pupil of Vaudremer and Raulin). Second Prix de Rome 1880. Architecte-en-chef, Bâtiments Civils et Palais Nationaux, 1914–20. Early work in partnership with his father Achille. A large practice: highly competent designer of large public, commercial and private buildings.

Garment factory, **23 rue du Mail**, 2e, 1884; **Caserne des Célestins**, 4e, 1889–95; 19 ave MacMahon, 17e, 1898; Société Générale, 132 rue Réaumur, 2e, 1899–1901; Former Magasin Aux Classes Laborieuses, 85 rue du faubourg Saint-Martin, 10e, 1900 (only facade remains); 10 rue Georges-Berger, 17e, 1905 (Rococo); Salle Gaveau (concert hall), 45 rue de la Boétie, 8e, 1906; **Société Générale, 29 bd Haussmann**, 9e, 1906–19; 4 ave de New York, 16e, 1906; Garment factory, 12 rue Gaillon, 2e, 1912–13 (steel and glass facade).

PAUL (ÉMILE) HUILLARD 1875–1966 and **LOUIS SÜE** 1875-1968 (both pupils of Laloux), diplomas 1900. Practised separately after 1914, Süe mainly as a decorator.

Studio houses 240 & 242 bd Raspail, 14e, 1903; 7 rue Valentin-Haüy, 7e, 1904–6; **Studio houses, rue Cassini**, 14e, no 7, 1903, no 5, 1905, no 3*bis*, 1906; 3 rue Beaunier, 14e, 1907, top floors added 1910–12; 126 bd Montparnasse, 14e, c 1908; 229 bd Raspail, 14e, 1909; 23 ave Emile-Deschanel, 7e, date unknown.

FRANTZ (CALIXTE RAPHAEL FERDINAND MARIE) JOURDAIN 1847–1935 (pupil of Daumet 1867–70). Author of numerous books and articles; founded the Société des Logements Hygiéniques à Bon Marché in 1902, the Société du Nouveau Paris in 1903 with Chéret, Guimard, Rodin and Sauvage and the Salon d'Automne in 1905, its first show devoted to Cézanne and Gauguin. His use of exposed iron and polychromy shows his debt to Viollet-le-Duc and Sédille with the later addition of Art Nouveau.

9 rue Galilée, 16e, 1883 (in partnership with Henri Fivaz); Grand magasin **La Samaritaine**, rue de Rivoli/rue de la Monnaie, 1er, 1883–1910; 16 rue du Louvre, 1er, 1912; La Samaritaine Deluxe, 27 bd des Capucines, 2e, 1914–17.

CHARLES LABRO (dates unrecorded) engineering diploma from Ecole Centrale, despite this the strongest architectural influence would seem to be Art Nouveau, later superseded by Plumet and the Rococo.

15 rue des Ursulines, 5e, 1900; 6 rue de l'Abbaye, 6e, 1901; 147 rue du Chemin Vert, 11e, 1903; 133 rue Michel-Ange, 16e, 1910; **3–9 rue Louis-Boilly** and 19–21 bd Suchet, 16e, 1912–14; 8 ave Ingres, 16e, 1914.

AUGUSTE LABUSSIÈRE 1863–1956, engineering diploma from Ecole Centrale. Architecte-voyer, Ville de Paris. Architect, Fondation Lebaudy 1903–17.

HBM 5 rue Ernest-Lefèvre, 20e, 1905; HBM 124 ave Daumesnil, 12e, 1907; HBM **63–5 rue de l'Amiral-Roussin**, 15e, 1907; 9 rue Beudant, 17e, 1908; Armée de Salut (**Le Palais de la Femme**), 94 rue de Charonne, 11e, 1910–11 (with C. Longery); HBM **5–15 rue de la Saïda**, 15e, 1912–13; HBM 6 rue de Cronstadt, 15e, 1913; HBM 7 rue d'Annam, 20e, 1913.

VICTOR (ALEXANDRE FRÉDÉRIC) LALOUX 1850–1937 (pupil of André), dipl 1877, Prix de Rome 1878. Member of the Institut. Inspecteur-général des Bâtiments Civils. The most successful 'Patron' at the EBA in preparing his students for the Prix de Rome.

8 rue Danielle-Casanova, 1er, 1889; 81 ave Bosquet, 7e, 1892; **Gare and Hôtel d'Orsay**, 1898–1900; Rear extension, Crédit Lyonnais, 17 bd des Italiens, 9e, 1904–13 (with André Narjoux; interior since gutted); Laloux also designed the station, town hall and basilica of St Martin at Tours between 1885 and 1897).

THÉODORE LAMBERT *b* 1857 (pupil of André). Designer of Art Nouveau furniture and had an interior design firm in the late 1890s.

11 ave de Saxe/53 ave de Ségur, 7e, 1891 (with P Gélis-Didot); **16 rue de la Procession**, 15e, 1913.

JULES (AIMÉ) LAVIROTTE 1864–1924 (pupil of Blondel). His buildings a mixture of Art Nouveau, Mannerism, the Beaux-Arts version of Romanesque and Rococo.

151 rue de Grenelle, 7e, 1898. House, 12 rue Sédillot, 7e, 1899; 3 square Rapp, 7e, 1899; 134 rue de Grenelle, 7e, 1900; **29 ave Rapp**, 7e, 1901; 34 ave de Wagram (now the Ceramic Hotel), 8e, 1904; House, 23 ave de Messine, 8e, 1906 (the top floors added when converted into flats, originally it had a flat roof garden); 6 rue de Messine, 8e, 1907.

FRANÇOIS LE COEUR 1872–1934 (his father Charles Le Coeur a pupil of Labrouste). Studied at Ecole Centrale des Arts et Manufactures 1893–5 and attended de Baudot's course at the Trocadéro 1897–1900. Assistant to Benouville.

Hôtel des Postes, Cité Martignac, 111 rue de Grenelle, 7e, 1908; **Central Téléphonique, 2 rue Bergère**, 9e, 1911–14; **72–4 bd Vincent-Auriol**, 13e, 1911–12.

CHARLES LEFEBVRE 1867–1923 (pupil of Ginain) dipl 1893. A very large output maintaining a high standard: the following are only a small sample.

239 bd Péreire, 17e, 1897; 8 rue de Tocqueville/18 rue de la Terrasse, 17e, 1902; 31 rue de Courcelles, 8e, 1902; 1 ave du Président-Wilson, 16e, 1903; 1 and 7–9 ave Elysée-Reclus, 7e, 1907–8; **83–5 rue Blomet**, 15e, 1908; 1–3 ave Silvestre de Sacy, 7e, 1909; 5 rue Théodore de Banville, 17e, 1909; **170 bd Haussmann/33–5 rue de Courcelles**, 8e, 1909; 29 rue George-Sand, 16e, 1909; 140 ave Victor-Hugo, 16e, 1910–11; 11 rue Cernuschi, 17e, 1911; Offices, 19 bd de Strasbourg, 10e, c 1913.

LOUIS LEFRANC *b* 1865 (pupil of André). Slightly grim but very solid and characterful use of brick and stone.

5 bd de Reuilly, 12e, 1890; 7–9 bd du Temple, 3e, 1899–1902; 158 rue de Charonne, 11e, 1910; Société Théosophique, 4 square Rapp, 7e, 1912.

PAUL (AUGUSTE) LEGRIEL 1866–1936 (pupil of Raulin) dipl 1895. Avocat, Cour d'Appel 1893–7. Simply designed buildings with large windows, mostly square, and no period detail.

163 rue de la Convention, 15e, 1899; **170 rue de la Convention**, 15e, 1900; 64–6 rue Spontini, 16e, 1904; 8 rue Edouard-Fournier, 16e, c 1907; Offices, 3 rue Moncey, 9e, 1909–10; 23 ave Charles-Floquet, 7e, 1911.

ALBERT LEVOISVENEL *d* 1905. Probably self-taught, first recorded office address 1880. Like Charles Lefebvre, had a large practice producing excellent work. Again, only a small sample can be given.

Crèche and school, 13 & 15 rue des Bernardins, 5e, 1891; 36 ave Niel, 17e, 1894; **26–8 rue de Clichy**, 9e, 1895; 15 ave Victor-Hugo, 16e, 1896–8; Garment factory, 107 rue Réaumur, 2e, 1897; **1–3 *bis* quai aux Fleurs**, 4e, 1898; 116 rue de la Boétie, 8e, 1899; 105–7 ave Victor-Hugo, 16e, 1901; 21*ter* bd Diderot, 12e, 1902.

LOUIS (ISIDORE) MASSON-DETOURBET 1860–1930 (pupil of Ginain), dipl 1891. The three buildings given here are of totally individual character and unlike one another.

Extension, School of Commerce, 54 rue Condorcet, 9e, 1894 (neo-Greek); 35 ave d'Eylau, 16e, 1894 (interesting arrangement of balconies, rather reserved stone *immeuble*); Ecole Commerciale de la Chambre de Commerce de Paris, 3 rue Armand-Moisant, 15e, 1908 (brick with grouped classroom windows and ramped staircase windows).

JOSEPH (E.) CHARLES GUIRARD DE MONTARNAL 1867–1949 (pupil of Ginain). Mainly interesting as an example of a pupil of a strictly classical '*Maistre*'; struggled with only limited success to adapt Beaux-Arts tradition to new requirements.

2 rue Girardon, 18e, 1895; Garment factory, 91près rue Réaumur, 2e, 1897, but much modified 1920; Garment factory, 130 rue Réaumur, 2e, 1898; Garment factory, **118 rue Réaumur**, 2e, 1900; 100,000 Chemises garment factory, **26 rue Louis-Blanc**, 10e, 1906 (ground floor modern); Garment factory, 41 rue Greneta, 2e, 1909, top floor added 1913.

HENRI-PAUL NÉNOT 1853–1934 (pupil of Questel and Pascal). Assistant in Garnier's Opéra *agence*. Prix de Rome 1877. Member of the Institut. Inspecteur-général des Bâtiments Civils. Consulting architect, Fondation Rothschild, 1904. His immense success thoroughly deserved: his planning in particular exceptionally assured.

La Sorbonne, 5e, 1882–1901; 26–30 rue Guynemer, 6e, 1891 & 1897; 87 bd Saint-Michel, 5e, 1895; House, 15 rue de Lubeck, 16e, 1896; 32 ave Georges-Mandel, 16e, 1899; Offices, **40 rue de l'Arcade**, 8e, 1904; Offices, 2 rue Pillet-Will, 9e, 1902; Bank (Louis Dreyfus), 2 rue de la Banque, 2e, 1905; Reconstruction behind existing facades, Hôtel Meurice, rue du Mont Thabor, 1er, 1907–8; Garment factory, 18–20 rue du faubourg du Temple, 11e, 1909; Institut d'Océanographie, 195 rue Saint-Jacques, 5e, 1910; Offices, rue and place Edouard VII, 9e, 1911 (complete street: interiors gutted recently); Offices (Compagnie Suez), 1 rue d'Astorg, 8e, 1912–13.

AUGUSTE PERRET 1874–1954 (pupil of Bernier, Paulin and Guadet), see Bibliography for literature devoted to him.

Offices, 10 rue du faubourg Poissonnière, 10e, 1898; **119 ave de Wagram**, 17e, 1902; 83 ave Niel, 17e, 1903–4. **25*bis* rue Benjamin-Franklin**, 16e, 1903–4; **Théâtre des Champs-Elysées**, 15 ave Montaigne, 8e, 1911–13.

CHARLES PLUMET 1861–1928 (pupil of Train and Bruneau at Ecole des Arts Décoratifs). Secretary and vice-president, Salon d'Automne. Designed furniture, shops and interiors in partnership with Tony Selmersheim (1871–1971).

151 rue Legendre, 17e, 1891; 33 rue Truffault, 17e, 1893; 67 ave Raymond-Poincaré, 16e, 1894–5; **36 rue de Tocqueville**, 17e, 1897; **50 ave Victor-Hugo**, 16e, 1900; 24 rue Paul-Valéry, 16e, 1904; 13–15 and **21 bd Lannes**, 16e, 1905–6; Studio house, **21 rue Octave-Feuillet**, 16e, 1908; 1 bd de Montmorency, 16e, 1912; 39 ave Victor-Hugo, 16e, 1912–13; Offices, 33 rue du Louvre, 2e, 1913–14.

(AMET) GEORGES (ALEXANDRE) PRADELLE 1865–1935 (pupil of Duray and Guadet). His work shows mixture of traditional and modern elements typical of the period.

5 rue de Luynes, 7e, 1904 (full-blown Beaux-Arts classicism); 112 quai de Jemmapes, 10e, 1907–8 (brick, with concrete balconies and bay windows); 5*bis* rue du Chemin-Vert, 11e, 1911 (stone and coloured mosaic, cantilevered concrete balconies).

HENRI PRESLIER (dates unknown) high standard of domestic work, currently unmentioned in available literature.

House, 27 (formerly 19*bis*) rue Raffet, 16e, 1908; 4 rue Erlanger, 16e, 1909; 3 rue René-Bazin, 16e, 1911; 5 rue du Colonel-Moll, 17e, 1911; 6 and 8 rue Huysmans, 6e, 1912; 67 rue de Tocqueville, 17e, 1913; 84 rue La Fontaine, 16e, undated.

HENRI PROVENSAL 1868–1934 (pupil of Duray and Guadet). Architect, Fondation Rothschild 1905–12, chief architect 1912–19 (designed HBMs for the Ville de Paris 1919–34).

HBM **rue du Marché-Popincourt**, 11e, 1907–8; HBM 117 rue de Belleville, 19e, 1907–8; HBM 8 rue de Prague, 12e, 1909; HBM **11 rue Bargue**, 15e, 1907–12; HBM 256 rue Marcadet, 18e, 1913–19.

ALBERT PRUGNAUD (dates unknown). An architect of *immeubles*, as was his brother Louis Prugnaud (*b* 1866). All Albert's buildings are worth seeing.

5 rue Dupont-des-Loges, 7e, 1896; 19 rue d'Edimbourg, 8e, 1902; 143 bd Raspail, 6e, 1906; 111 bd Exelmans, 16e, 1906; 12 rue Théodore de Banville, 17e, 1907; 68 rue Blomet, 15e, 1912; 32 rue Gassendi, 14e, 1914.

(CASIMIR) JOACHIM RICHARD 1869–1950 (pupil of Laloux). In partnership with Henri Audiger to 1907.

110 rue Saint-Charles, 15e, 1894; 114 rue Saint-Charles, 15e, undated, c 1900; 207 rue de la Croix-Nivert, 15e, 1903; **15 ave Perrichont**, 16e, 1907; House, 40 rue Boileau, 16e, 1907; 40 ave Félix-Faure, 15e, 1907; 136 ave Emile-Zola, 15e, 1911; 3–9 rue du Général Delestraint, 16e, 1912; House, 16 rue de Montevideo, 16e, 1914–15.

JOSEPH ROUS *b* 1863 (pupil of André). Professor of industrial design. Designed housing for the Assistance Publique.

HBM, 42–4 rue du Château des Rentiers, 13e, 1913; HBM, 128 & 133 rue de Clignancourt, 18e, 1914; HBM, 148–56 ave du Maine, 14e, 1914.

GABRIEL (EUGÈNE MARIE) RUPRICH-ROBERT 1859–1953 (his architect father Victor 1820–87). Inspecteur-général des Monuments Historiques, Architecte-en-chef du Gouvernement. Clear influence of Viollet-le-Duc.

10 rue d'Assas, 6e, 1888; Institut Catholique, 21 rue d'Assas, 1894–7; 50 ave de Ségur, 7e, 1900; Workshops, 210 rue du faubourg Saint-Antoine, 12e, 1905–6 (metal framed).

(PAUL) ERNEST SANSON 1836–1918 (pupil of Gilbert, Diet and Questel), his son **MAURICE SANSON** 1864–1917 (pupil of Daumet) in partnership with father 1900 and **RENÉ SERGENT** 1865–1927 (studied at Ecole Special under Trélat, dipl 1884 and

was later a professor there), assistant to Ernest Sanson 1884–99. All the work produced by them was in the best-quality luxury class and it is possible that all three were involved in its design.

The following work was signed by Ernest Sanson: House, 18 rue de Martignac, 7e, 1878; House, 2 place des Etats-Unis, 16e, 1886; House, 29 rue Galilée, 16e, 1892; House, 9 ave George V, 8e, 1893, completed by Sergent 1912 and almost certainly designed by him; 8 ave Marceau, 8e, 1893; 57 ave Montaigne, 8e, 1895; House, 11 place des Etats-Unis, 16e, 1895; 42–4 rue d'Anjou, 8e, 1899; 41 rue Boissière, 16e, 1899; Houses, 49 & 51 ave d'Iéna, 16e, 1897; **106 rue de l'Université,** 7e, 1905; House, 1 bd Delessert, 16e, 1911–20; also country châteaux and other Parisian mansions since demolished.
The following work signed by René Sergent: 59 rue de Varenne, 7e, 1904; 3, 5 and 5*bis* rue Le Tasse, 16e, 1904–8; House, 4 ave Emile Deschanel, 7e, 1908; House, 63 rue Monceau, 8e, 1911–14, now the Musée Nissim de Camondo. The mansions designed by these architects are illustrated in *Les Palais Parisiens de la Belle Epoque (see* Bibliography*)*.

FRANÇOIS SAULNIER *b* 1875 (pupil of Paulin). Frequent use of curved bays, but cannot be classed as Art Nouveau or Rococo.

68 rue de Vaugirard, 6e (date not known); 3 rue Cassini, 14e, 1906; 20–4 rue Pierre et Marie Curie, 5e, 1910 (interesting use of set-backs); **15 rue Gay-Lussac**, 5e, 1912.

HENRI SAUVAGE 1873–1932 (pupil of Pascal). In partnership with Claude Sarrazin to 1912. His Art Nouveau phase featured Louis Majorelle's villa at Nancy, 1898–1900, and a theatre for the dancer Loïe Fuller at the 1900 International Exhibition.

17 rue Damremont, 18e, 1902; HBM 1 rue Ferdinand-Flocon, 18e, 1903; HBM **7 rue de Trétaigne**, 18e, 1903–4; 22 and 22*bis* rue Langier, 17e, 1904; Galerie Argentine, 111 ave Victor-Hugo, 16e, 1904; 7 rue Danville, 14e, 1905; HBM **20 rue Severo/ 13 rue Hippolyte-Maidron**, 14e, 1905–6; HBM 163 bd de l'Hôpital, 13e, 1908; HBM 1 rue de la Chine, 20e, 1908; 29 rue de la Boétie, 8e, 1911; **26 rue Vavin**, 6e, 1912; Showroom and offices, **126 rue de Provence**, 8e, 1912–13.

(FRANÇOIS) XAVIER SCHOELLKOPF 1870–1911 (pupil of Guadet and Paulin).

92 ave de la République, 11e, 1898; 96 ave de la République, 11e, 1901; **29 bd de Courcelles**, 8e, 1902; 90 ave Parmentier, 11e, c 1909; 20*bis* rue d'Alésia, 14e, 1910 (This last building suggests that Schoellkopf might have moved from his Rococo phase to something simpler if he had lived longer.)

PAUL SÉDILLE 1836–1900 (pupil of Guénepin), his father Charles 1807–71. Architect, Bâtiments Civils. Chef d'installation, 1889 Exhibition. Forerunner of many younger architects in his use of exposed iron and absence of period ornament.

28 bd **Malesherbes**, 8e, 1870–2; 58 rue de Lisbonne, 8e, 1876; External escape balconies, Théâtre du Palais Royal, rue de Montpensier, 1er, 1880; House, 45 rue Boissière, 16e, 1880–2; Ceramic workshops, 4 rue de la Pierre-Levée, 11e, 1880–4; Grand Magasin, **Au Printemps**, 9e, 1882–9; 86 rue Jean-Pierre Timbaud, 11e, 1894; 30 rue Galilée, 16e, 1895.

ALBERT SÉLONIER 1858–1926. Probably self-taught. The following is just a brief selection of his enormous output.

234 bd Raspail, 14e, 1897; 108 bd du Montparnasse, 14e, 1897–8; 204 bd Raspail, 14e, 1898; 12 and 16 rue Alphonse-Daudet, 14e, 1898; 2 rue Dante, 5e, 1902; 146 rue de Courcelles, 17e, 1902; 73 bd de Grenelle, 15e, 1903; 45 rue Oberkampf, 11e, 1906; 4 rue Eugène-Labiche, 16e, 1907; 31 ave Hoche, 8e, 1909; 19 bd Delessert, 16e, 1910; 1 place du Panthéon, 5e, 1912; **25 rue Vernet**, 8e, 1913 (now Hôtel Vernet).

GEORGES SINELL 1864–1927. Exceptionally able at dealing with triangular corner sites. The later buildings simpler in treatment.

7–11 rue Edmond-Valentin, 7e, 1898; 6 rue Danton, 6e, 1903; 2 rue des Petits-Pères, 2e, 1903; 91 rue du Cherche-Midi, 6e, 1904; 49 rue Nollet, 17e, 1909; 64 rue de Saussure, 17e, 1911; 37 rue Vital, 16e, 1914; 106 rue de la Tour, 16e, 1914–19.

CHARLES STOULLIG *d* 1933. Another 'unknown' architect whose work has been largely unrecorded.

4 ave Marceau, 8e, 1895; 63 rue de la Boétie, 8e, 1896–7; 160 bd du Montparnasse, 14e, 1899–1900; 4 rue Largillière, 16e, 1903; 18 rue du Regard, 6e, 1905; 83 ave Henri Martin, 16e, 1908; 32 rue des Archives, 4e, 1911; 198 ave Victor-Hugo, 16e, 1914–19; 127 rue de la Faisanderie, 16e, date unknown.

(JOSEPH) ALBERT TOURNAIRE 1862–1958 (pupil of André) dipl 1883. Prix de Rome 1888. Member of the Institut. Architecte-en-chef, Ville de Paris. His buildings, somewhat mixed stylistically, have a good deal of character.

18–20 rue Fourcroy, 17e, 1898; 25–7 rue Pigalle, 9e, 1901; 4 rue des Frères Périer, 16e, 28 and 30 ave d'Eylau, 16e, unknown date; Extension to Palais de Justice, 4 bd du Palais and quai des Orfèvres, 1er, 1911–14.

PAUL VASSEUR *b* 1850 (pupil of Laisné). Sensible but understated designs.

Warehouse, 15–17 bd Ornano, 18e, 1884; 34 rue Guy-Môquet, 17e, 1892; 12 rue Pelouze, 8e, c 1899; **11***bis* **rue Georges-Saché**, 14e, 1910.

GEORGES (LÉON JEAN) VAUDOYER 1877–1947 (pupil of Marcel Lambert) dipl 1905. Great-nephew of Viollet-le-Duc, son of Alfred Vaudoyer (1846–1917), grandson of Léon and great-grandson of Antoine, both Prix de Rome, nephew of William

and cousin of Richard Bouwens van der Boijen! Equally able at designing bourgeois *immeubles* and *habitations à bon marché*.

2–6 rue Wurtz, 13e, date unknown; HBM 9 rue Laplace, 5e, 1909; 133 & 135 ave de Suffren, 7e, 1910; HBM **72 rue de la Colonie**, 13e, 1911; 3 rue Albert de Lapparent, 7e, 1910; 8 rue José-Maria de Heredia, 7e, c 1911; HBM 60 rue Vergniaud, 13e, 1913; HBM 18 rue Censier, 5e, 1914; HBM 14–18 rue Jobbé-Duval, 15e, 1914; HBM rue Ernest-Roche, 17e, 1913–21; 207 rue de Tolbiac, 13e, 1913–22.

(JOSEPH AUGUSTE) ÉMILE VAUDREMER 1829–1914 (pupil of Blouet and Gilbert) Prix de Rome 1854. Member of the Institut. Architecte des Edifices Religieux de la Ville de Paris. Professor, EBA. Only some of his later buildings can be given here.

Lycée Buffon, 16 bd Pasteur, 15e, 1885–90; Lycée Molière, 71 rue de Ranelagh, 16e, 1886–8; Eglise Grecque, rue Georges-Bizet, 16e, 1890; House, 12 rue Chardin, 16e, 1895; Groupe scolaire, place Dupleix, 15e, 1895–7; 27–33 ave Georges-Mandel, 16e, 1896–8 (half-timbered *immeuble*!); Eglise Saint-Antoine-des-Quinze-Vingts, 66 ave Ledru-Rollin, 12e, 1902–4.

L. VEBER (dates and forename unrecorded) and **RENÉ (MARIE FÉLIX) MICHAU** *b* 1873 (pupil of Pascal). This virtually unknown partnership produced many interestingly detailed *immeubles* at the end of the Belle Epoque.

16 place Félix-Eboué, 12e, 1905. 14 rue Nélaton, 15e, 1907; 28–32 rue Charles-Baudelaire, 12e, 1908; 32 ave de la Bourdonnais, 7e, 1910; 11*bis* ave Elisée-Reclus, 7e, 1910; 8, 10, 14 and 34 ave Charles-Floquet, 7e, 1911; 3 rue du Général-Lambert, 7e, 1912; 5 ave du Général Détrie, 7e, 1913; 6 and 8 rue Houdart de Lamotte, 15e, 1913; 3 rue François Coppée, 15e, 1913; 6 square Desaix, 15e, c 1914; 48 ave de Saxe, 7e, 1914–16; 194 rue de la Croix-Nivert, 15e, undated; 3 and 5 rue Hermel, 18e, undated.

PAUL (ALEXANDRE JOSEPH) WALLON 1845–1918 (pupil of Questel and Pascal) dipl 1876. Grandfather Henri and brother Charles both architects. Secretary, Société Centrale. His buildings have elegant and original variations on standard themes.

107–9 rue de Courcelles, 17e, 1896; 191 ave du Maine 14e, 1894–1900; Workshops, 6 rue d'Enghien, 10e, 1898; 71–3 bd Raspail, 6e, 1909; 86 ave de Breteuil, 7e, 1913; 12 rue Say, 9e, undated.

Bibliography

The principal sources of information for this book, in addition to those listed in the Select Bibliography, were as follows:

1   The author's walking researches, aided by the original practice of often inscribing the name of the architect and completion date on a stone, usually at first-floor level. (These inscriptions are sometimes now obscured by later shop fascias.)

2   Copies of *L'architecture* and *La construction moderne* illustrating many, though by no means all, of the most interesting Parisian buildings being proposed or built during the period.

3   The *Dictionnaire par noms d'architectes* (see Select Bibliography) prepared by Anne Dugast and Isabelle Parizet on behalf of the Commission des Travaux Historiques, of which five volumes covering the period 1876–99 have now been published. Further volumes for the period 1900–14 are in preparation. The listings are mainly based on applications for Building Permission: occasionally construction did not take place, or the building has since been demolished.

4   The following magazines, generally published monthly. (Articles therein, referring to specific subjects, are listed where appropriate in the Chapter Endnotes.)

L'architecture, 1888–1913, Librairie des Imprimeries Réunies, Paris.
La construction moderne, 1886–1929, Dujardin et Cie Editeurs, Paris.
L'art decoratif, 1898 onwards, Bureaux de l'Art Décoratif, Paris.
Art et décoration, 1888 onwards, Librairie Centrale des Beaux-Arts, Paris.
Revue des arts décoratifs 1901, etc, Bureaux de l'Art Décoratif, Paris.
The Studio was published from 1896 onwards in English and French, containing information on the latest in design in Britain, France, Austria and Germany.

CONTEMPORARY SOURCES: PRIMARY

de Baudot, Anatole. *L'architecture: le passé, le present*, Henri Laurens, Paris, 1916.

Blanc, Charles. *Grammaire des arts du dessin*, Jules Renouard, Paris, 1867.

Choisy, Auguste. *Histoire de l'architecture*, Gauthier-Villars, Paris, 1899.

Daly, César. *L'architecture privée au XIXe siècle*, Ducher et Cie, Paris, 1864.

Delaire, E. and D. de Penanrun. *Les architectes élèves de l'Ecole des Beaux-Arts*, Imprimerie Chaix, Paris, 1895 and 1907.

Dictionnaire de l'Académie des Beaux-Arts. Institut de France, Paris, 1884.

Garnier, Charles. *Le théâtre*, Paris, 1871.

Gelis-Didot, P. and T. Lambert. *La construction privée à la fin du XIXe siècle*, Librairies Imprimeries Réunies, Paris, 1893.

Guadet, Julien. *Eléments et théorie de l'architecture*, Aulanier et Cie, Paris, 1902.

Guimard, Hector. *An Architect's Opinion of Art Nouveau*, Architectural Record, New York, 2 June 1902.

Havard, Henri. *Les arts de l'ameublement: la décoration*, Librairie Ch Delagrave, Paris, 1928.

Lefol, G. *Immeubles modernes de Paris*, Ch Messin, Paris, 1912.

Lévy, A. *Maisons les plus remarquables construites à Paris de 1905 à 1914*, Librairie Centrale des Beaux-Arts, Paris, 1920.

Magne, Lucien. *L'Archtecture française du siècle*, Firmin-Didot, Paris, 1889.

Maisons les plus remarquables construites à Paris de 1905 à 1914, Librairie centrale des Beaux-Arts, A. Lévy éditeur, Paris, 1920.

Perks, Sidney. *Residential Flats of All Classes*, Batsford, London, 1905.

Planat, P. *Maisons de rapport, habitations à loyers*, Aulanier et Cie, Paris, 1895.

Planat, P. *Décors d'intérieurs*, Bibliothèque de la Construction Moderne, Paris, 1900.

Rémon, Georges. *Intérieurs modernes*, J. Rouan et Cie, Paris, 1900.

Rivoalen, E. *Maison modernes de rapport et de commerce*, Georges Flanchon, Paris, 1906.

Viollet-le-Duc, E. E. *Entretiens sur l'Architecture*, Paris, 1863–72 (2 vols). English translation by Benjamin Bucknall, *Lectures on Architecture*, Sampson Low, London, 1877.

CONTEMPORARY SOURCES: SECONDARY

Baedeker, Karl. *Paris and Environs*, Baedeker, Leipzig, 13th edn, 1898.

Baudelaire, Charles. *Le peintre de la vie moderne*, Figaro, Paris, 1863, translated by Jonathan Mayne, *The Painter of Modern Life*, Thames & Hudson, London, 1964.

Goncourt, Edmond de, translated by Robert Baldick. *Pages from the Goncourt Journal*, Oxford University Press, London and New York, 1962.

Proust, Marcel, translated by C.K. Scott Moncrieff and Terence Kilmartin. *Remembrance of Things Past*, Chatto and Windus, London, 1981, and Penguin Books, Harmondsworth, 1983.

Simond, Charles. *Paris de 1800 à 1900: tome III 1870–1900*, Librairie Plon, Paris, 1901.

Staffe, la Baronne. *Usages du monde. Régles du savoir-vivre dans la société moderne*, Havard fils, Paris, 1896.

Uzanne, Octave. *Les modes de Paris 1797–1897*, Paris, 1898.

Zola, Emile. *Pot-Bouille*, 1882, translated by Brian Nelson, *Pot Luck*, Oxford University Press, London, 1999.

Zola, Emile. *Au bonheur des dames*, 1883, translated by Brian Nelson, *The Ladies' Paradise*, Oxford University Press, London, 1995.

Zola, Emile. *L'Oeuvre*, 1886, translated by Thomas Walton, *The Masterpiece*, Paul Elek, London, 1950.

MODERN SOURCES: PRIMARY

Accolti Gil, Biagio. *Paris, vestibules de l'éclectisme*, De Luca Editore, Rome, and Vilo Editeur, Paris, 1982.

Banham, Reyner. *Theory and Design in the First Machine Age*, Architectural Press, London, 1960.

Barker, Michael. 'Paris: Belle Epoque Restaurants and Cafés', *Decorative Arts Society Journal* no 22, Antique Collectors' Club. Woodbridge, Suffolk, 1998.

Barré-Despond, Arlette. *Jourdain*, Rizzoli, New York, 1991.

Borsi, Franco and Ezio Godoli. *Paris Art Nouveau: architecture et décoration*, Marc Vokar Editeur, Paris, 1989.

Borsi, Franco and Ezio Godoli, translated by J. Elmes, *Paris 1900*, Granada Publishing, London,1978.

Britton, Karla. *Auguste Perret*, Phaidon Press, London, 2001.

Carreau-Vacher, Isabelle. *François Le Cœur: rigueur et Modernité*, Paris: Monuments Historiques, Paris, no 184, November 1992.

des Cars, Jean and Pierre Pinon. *Paris-Haussmann: le Paris d'Haussmann*, Pavillon de l'Arsenal/Picard éditeur, Paris, 1991.

Champigneulle, Bernard. *Perret*, Arts et Métiers Graphiques, Paris, 1959.

Châtelet, Anne-Marie. *Paris à l'école*, Pavillon de l'Arsenal/Picard éditeur, Paris, 1993.

Châtelet, Anne-Marie and others. *Paris Disegnata/Edificata: la Professionalità dell'architetto e la construzione della città nel 1900*, Lignori Editore, Naples, 1988.

Chemetov, Paul and Bernard Marrey. *Architectures à Paris 1848–1914*, Dunod/Bordas, Paris, 1984.

Chemetov, P. and M. J. Dumont and B. Marrey. *Paris-Banlieue 1919–1939*, Dunod/Bordas, Paris, 1989.

Clausen, Meredith L. *Frantz Jourdain and the Samaritaine: Art Nouveau Theory and Criticism*, EJ Brill, Leiden, 1987.

Cohen, Jean-Louis and Monique Eleb-Vidal. *Paris Architecture 1900–2000*, Editions Norma, Paris, 2000.

Colson, Jean and Marie-Christine Lauroa (ed). *Dictionnaire des Monuments de Paris*, Editions Hervas, Paris, 1992.

Crosnier-Leconte, Marie-Laure and others. *Victor Laloux, l'Architecte de la Gare d'Orsay*, Réunion des Musées Nationaux, Paris, 1987.

Culot, Maurice and Lise Grenier (ed). *Henri Sauvage 1873–1932*, Archives d'Architecture Moderne, Brussels, 1977.

Delorme, Jean-Claude and Philippe Chair. *L'Ecole de Paris: 10 architectes et leurs immeubles 1905–1937*, Editions du Moniteur, Paris, 1981 and 1990.

Denby, Elaine. *Grand Hotels: Reality and Illusion*, Reaktion Books, London, 1998.

Drexler, Arthur (ed). *Architecture of the Ecole des Beaux-Arts*, Secker and Warburg, London, 1977.

Dugast, Anne and Isabelle Parizet. *Dictionnaire par noms d'architectes des constructions élevées à Paris aux XIXe et XXe siècles. Période 1876–1899* (5 vols), Institut d'Histoire de Paris/Commission des Travaux Historiques, Paris, 1990–2003.

Dumont, Marie-Jeanne. *Le Logement Social à Paris 1850–1930: les habitations à bon marché*, Mardaga, Liège, 1991.

Durant, Stuart. 'Palais des Machines, Paris 1889', in *Lost Masterpieces*, Phaidon Press, London, 1999.

Egbert, Donald Drew. *The Beaux-Arts Tradition in French Architecture*, Princeton University Press, Princeton, NJ, and Guildford, Surrey, 1980.

Eleb-Vidal, Monique. *Architectures de la vie privée: maisons et mentalités XVIIe–XIXe siècles*, Archives d'Architecture Moderne, Brussels, 1989.

Eleb-Vidal, Monique with Anne Debarre Blanchard. *L'Invention de l'habitation moderne, Paris 1880–1950*, Hazan, Paris and Archives d'Architecture Moderne, Brussels, 1995.

Emery, Marc. *Un siècle d'architecture en France 1850–1950*, Horizons de France, Paris, 1971.

Evenson, Norma. *Paris: A Century of Change 1878–1978*, Yale University Press, New Haven, CT, 1979.

Fiblec, Hugues. *Paul Friesé 1851–1917*, Institut Français d'Architecture/Editions Norma, Paris, 1991.

Foucart, Bruno. *Viollet-le-Duc*, Editions de la Réunion des Musées Nationaux, Paris, 1980.

Gargiani, Roberto. *Auguste Perret, la théorie et l'oeuvre*, Gallimard/Electa, Paris/Milan, 1994.

Godoli, Ezio. *Hector Guimard*, Editori Laterza, Rome, 1992.

Gomez y Caceres, Georges and Marie-Ange de Pierredon. *Les décors des boutiques parisiennes*, Délégation à l'Action Artistique de la Ville de Paris, Paris, 1987.

Goy-Truffaut, Françoise. *Paris façade: un siècle de sculptures décoratives*, Hazan, Paris, 1989.

Gregotti, Vittorio (ed). *Perret: 25 bis rue Franklin*, Rassegna no 28, Milan, 1979.

Gregotti, Vittorio (ed). *Anatole de Baudot 1834–1915*, Rassegna no 68, Milan, 1996.

Hautecoeur, Louis. *Histoire de l'Architecture Classique en France, tome 7, 1848–1900*, Editions Picard, Paris, 1957.

Hitchcock, Henry-Russell. *Architecture: Nineteenth and Twentieth Centuries*, Penguin Books, Harmondsworth, 1958/1971.

Jacques, Annie. *La carrière de l'architecte au XIXe siècle*, Editions de la Réunion des Musées Nationaux, Paris, 1986.

Jullian, René. *Histoire de l'architecture en France de 1889 à nos jours. Un siècle de Modernité*, Philippe Sers, Paris, 1984.

Leclerc, Bénédicte. *Julien Guadet: l'Hôtel des Postes de Paris*, Monuments Historiques no 184, Paris, November 1992.

Le Coeur, Marc. *Charles Le Coeur*, Réunion des Musées Nationaux, Paris, 1996.

Lemoine, Bertrand. *L'architecture du fer: France XIXe siècle*, Collection Milieux, Paris, and Champ Vallon, Seyssel, 1986.

Loyer, François. *Paris XIXe siècle: l'immeuble et la rue*. Paris: Hazan, 1987. American edition: *Paris Nineteenth Century*, Architecture & Urbanism, Abbeville Press, New York, 1988.

Loyer, François. *France, Viollet-le-Duc to Tony Garnier: the passion for rationalism*, (in *Art Nouveau Architecture*, edited by Frank Russell), Academy Editions, London, 1979.

Loyer, François and Hélène Guéné. *Henri Sauvage: les immeubles à gradins*, Mardaga, Brussels, 1987.

Loyer, François. *Histoire de l'architecture française de la Révolution à nos jours*, Mengès, Editions du patrimoine, Paris, 1999.

Marrey, Bernard. *Louis Bonnier 1856–1946*, Mardaga, Brussels, 1988.

Marrey, Bernard. *Le fer à Paris, Architectures*, Picard Editeur and Pavillon de l'Arsenal, Paris, 1991.

Marrey, Bernard with Marie-Jeanne Dumont. *La brique à Paris*, Picard Editeur and Pavillon de l'Arsenal, Paris, 1991.

Marrey, Bernard and Franck Hammoutène. *Le béton à Paris*, Picard Editeur et Pavillon de l'Arsenal, Paris, 1999.

Marrey, Bernard. *Les grands magasins des origines à 1939*, Librairie Picard, Paris, 1979.

Marrey, Bernard. 'Qui est l'architecte du Théâtre des Champs-Elysées?', *L'Architecture d'aujourd'hui*, Paris, July 1974.

McClure, Bert and Bruno Régnier. *Architectural Walks in Paris*, La Découvert/Le Monde/Editions SOL, Paris, 1989.

Mead, Christopher Curtis. *Charles Garnier's Paris Opera*, MIT Press, Cambridge, MA and Architectural History Foundation, New York, 1991.

Meeks, Carroll L. V. *The Railway Station: an Architectural History*, Architectural Press/Yale University Press, London, 1957.

Middleton, Robin and David Watkin. *Neoclassical and Nineteenth Century Architecture*, Harry N Abrams Inc, New York, 1980.

Minnaert, Jean-Baptiste. *Henri Sauvage*, Editions Norma, Paris, 2002.

Olsen, Donald J. *The City as a Work of Art*. Princeton University Press/Yale University Press, New Haven and London, 1986.

Parissien, Steven. *Station to Station*, Weidenfeld and Nicolson, London, 1985.

Pevsner, Nikolaus. *A History of Building Types*, Thames and Hudson, London, 1976.

Pinchon, Jean-François. *Edouard Niermans, Architecte de la Café-Society*, Mardaga, Liège, 1991.

Pinchon, Jean-François. *Les palais d'argent: l'architecture bancaire en France de 1850 à 1930*, Réunion des Musées Nationaux, Paris, 1992.

Pinkney, D. H. *Napoleon III and the Rebuilding of Paris*, Princeton University Press, New Jersey, 1958.

Plum, Gilles. *Le Grand Palais: l'aventure du Palais des Beaux-Arts*, Réunion des Musées Nationaux, Paris, 1993.

Poisson, Georges and others. *Paris: Guide-Bleu*, Hachette-Guides-Bleus, Paris, 1992.

Rousset-Charny, Gérard. *Les Palais Parisiens de la Belle Epoque*, Délégation de l'Action Artistique de la Ville de Paris, Paris, 1990.

Seitz, Frédéric. *L'Ecole Spéciale d'Architecture 1865–1930: Une entreprise d'idée*, Picard, Paris, 1995.

Steiner, Frances H. *French Iron Architecture*, UMI Research Press, Ann Arbor, Michigan, 1984.

Sutcliffe, Anthony. *Paris: an Architectural History*, Yale University Press, New Haven, CT and London, 1993.

Sutcliffe, Anthony. *The Autumn of Central Paris, the defeat of town planning 1850–1970*, Edward Arnold, London, 1970.

Taylor, Brian Brace. 'Sauvage and Hygienic Housing or the Cleanliness Revolution in Paris', *Archithese* no 12, 'L'immeuble collectif 1900-11', Zurich, 1974.

Thiébaut, Philippe. *Guimard: l'Art Nouveau*, Découverts Gallimard/Réunion des Musées Nationaux, Paris, 1992.

White, Norval. *The Guide to the Architecture of Paris*, Charles Scribner's Sons/Macmillan Publishing Company, New York, 1991.

van Zanten, David. *Designing Paris: the Architecture of Duban, Labrouste, Duc and Vaudoyer*, MIT Press, Cambridge, MA, 1987.

van Zanten, David. *Building Paris: Architectural institutions and the transformation of the French capital 1830–70*, Cambridge University Press, Cambridge and New York, 1994.

MODERN SOURCES: SECONDARY

Abdy, Jane. *The French Poster: Chéret to Cappiello*, Studio Vista, London, 1969.

Arendt, Hannah. *The Human Condition*, University of Chicago Press, Chicago, 1958.

Benjamin, Walter. *Paris, capitale du XIXe siècle, le livre des Passages*, Les Editions du Cerf, Paris, 1989.

Bergdoll, Barry. *Léon Vaudoyer, Historicism in the Age of Industry*, Architectural History Foundation/MIT Press, Cambridge, MA, 1994.

Berlanstein, Lenard R. *The Working People of Paris 1871–1914*, John Hopkins University Press, Baltimore & London, 1984.

Burnand, Robert. *Paris 1900*, Librairie Hachette, Paris, 1951.

Carey, Frances and Antony Griffiths. *From Manet to Toulouse-Lautrec, French Lithographs 1860–1900*, British Museum Publications, London, 1978.

Chapman, Guy. *The Dreyfus Case: a reassessment*, Rupert Hart-Davis, London, 1955.

Chapman, Guy. *The Third Republic: first phase 1871–94*, Macmillan & Co, London, 1962.

Clark, T. J. *The Painting of Modern Life: Paris in the art of Manet and his followers*, Thames and Hudson, London, 1985.

Couperie, Pierre. *Paris through the Ages*, Cuénot, Paris, 1968; English translation, Barrie and Jenkins, London, 1970.

Distel, Anne and others. *Gustave Caillebotte, the Unknown Impressionist*, Ludion Press, Ghent/Royal Academy of Arts, London, 1996.

Dubbini, Renzo (ed). *Henri Labrouste*, Electa, Milan, 2000.

Duncan, Alastair. *Art Nouveau Furniture*, Thames and Hudson, London, 1982.

Durant, Stuart. *Ornament: a Survey of Decoration since 1830*, Macdonald and Co, London, 1986.

Giedion, Siegfried. *Building in France, Building in Iron, Building in Ferro-concrete* (originally published in German 1928), Getty Center for the History of Art and the Humanities, Santa Monica, CA, 1995.

Giedion, Siegfried. *Mechanisation takes Command*, Oxford University Press, 1948.

Gosling, Nigel. *Paris 1900–1914, The Miraculous Years*, Weidenfeld and Nicolson, London, 1978.

Granger, Frank. *Vitruvius on Architecture*, W. Heinemann Ltd, London, 1931.

Haine, W. Scott. *The World of the Paris Café: Sociability among the French Working Class 1789–1914*, The John Hopkins University Press, Baltimore and London, 1996.

Hamilton, George Heard. *Painting and Sculpture in Europe 1880–1940*, Penguin Books, Harmondsworth, 1967/1972.

Harriss, Joseph. *The Eiffel Tower: Symbol of an Age*, Paul Elek, London, 1976.

Hemmings, F. W. J. *Culture and Society in France 1848–98: Dissidents and Philistines*, Batsford, London, 1971.

Herbert, Robert L. *Impressionism: Art, Leisure and Parisian Society*, Yale University Press, New Haven, CT, and London, 1988.

Kinsman, Jane and others. *Paris in the Late Nineteenth Century*, Thames & Hudson, Melbourne, Australia/National Gallery of Australia, 1997.

Lafargue, Jacqueline and others. *Du Palais au Palace: les grands hôtels de voyageurs à Paris du XIXe siècle*, Paris Musées, Paris, 1998.

McMullen, R. *Degas, His Life, Times and Work*, Secker and Warburg, London, 1985.

Madsen, Stephen Tschudi. *Sources of Art Nouveau*, Da Capo Press, New York, 1975 (originally published Oslo, 1956).

Mandell, Richard D. *Paris 1900, the Great World's Fair*, University of Toronto Press, 1967.

Marrey, Bernard and Jean-Pierre Monnet. *La grande histoire des serres et des jardins d'hiver en France 1780–1900*, Graphite, Turin, 1984.

Offenstadt, Patrick. *Jean Béraud. The Belle Epoque: A Dream of Times Gone By*, Taschen, Cologne, 1999.

Oster, Daniel and Jean Goulemot. *La Vie Parisienne, anthologie des moeurs du XIXe Siècle*, Sand/Conti, Paris, 1989.

Pevsner, Nikolaus. *Pioneers of the Modern Movement, from William Morris to Walter Gropius*, Faber and Faber, London, 1936.

Painter, George D. *Marcel Proust* (2 vols), Chatto and Windus, London, 1959; Penguin Books, Harmondsworth, 1977.

Pevsner, Nikolaus. *A History of Building Types*, Thames and Hudson, London, 1976.

Poisson, Georges. *Histoire de l'architecture à Paris (nouvelle histoire de Paris)*, Bibliothèque de la Ville de Paris, Paris, 1997.

Rearick, Charles. *Pleasures of the Belle Epoque*, Yale University Press, New Haven, CT, and London, 1985.

Rheims, Maurice. *Nineteenth Century Sculpture*, translated by Robert E. Wolf, Thames and Hudson, London, 1977.

Ritchie, Andrew Carnduff. *Edouard Vuillard*, Museum of Modern Art, New York, 1954.

Rosenblum, Robert and others. *1900: Art at the Crossroads*, Royal Academy of Arts, London, 2000.

Rudorff, Raymond. *Belle Epoque, Paris in the Nineties*, Hamish Hamilton, London, 1972.

Schorske, Carl E. *Fin de Siècle Vienna, Politics and Culture*, Weidenfeld and Nicolson, London, 1980.

Shattuck, Roger. *The Banquet Years: The Arts in France 1885–1918*, Faber and Faber, London, 1959.

Silverman, Debora L. *Art Nouveau in Fin-de-Siècle France: Politics, Psychology and Style*, University of California Press, Berkeley, 1989.

Thomson, Richard. *Seurat*, Phaidon Press, Oxford, 1985.

Thomson, Richard. *The Troubled Republic: visual culture and social debate in France 1889–1900*, Yale University Press, New Haven, CT, and London, 2004.

Thornton, Peter. *Authentic Décor*, Weidenfeld and Nicolson, London, 1985.

Tulard, Jean and Alfred Fierro. *Almanach de Paris de 1789 à nos jours*, Encyclopædia Universalis, Paris, 1990.

Villoteau, Pierre. *La Vie Parisienne à la Belle Epoque*, Cercle de Bibliophile: Edito-Service SA, Geneva, 1968.

Watkins, Nicholas. *Bonnard: Colour and Light*, Tate Gallery Publishing, London, 1988.

Weisberg, Gabriel P. and others. *Japonisme: Japanese Influence on French Art 1854–1910*, Cleveland Museum of Art, 1975.

West, Shearer. *Fin de Siècle*, Bloomsbury Publishing, London, 1993.

Zeldin, Theodore. *France 1848–1945 Vol II Intellect, Taste and Anxiety*, Clarendon Press, Oxford, 1977.

Index

Figures in italics indicate captions

Acknowledgements

I am deeply indebted to the late M. Michel Fleury, Vice-President of the Commission du Vieux Paris and his successor M. François Loyer, for allowing me to consult information being collected by Mmes. Anne Dugast and Isabelle Parizet, not yet published, on new constructions receiving Building Permission between 1900 and 1914. The first series of their *Dictionnaire, par noms d'architectes, des constructions élevées à Paris, XIXe et XXe siècles* (covering the years 1876–1899) had already proved indispensable.

The staff of the following libraries have proved unfailingly helpful in my search for information on little-known buildings and architects: the London Library; the British Architectural Library (RIBA); the British Art Library (V&A); the Bibliothêque Historique de la Ville de Paris; and the Archives de Paris.

On behalf of Steve Gorton, Wiley-Academy and myself, I would like to thank the owners and occupiers of buildings where interior photography was allowed, especially a private apartment, whose owners must naturally remain anonymous. I would also like to thank a number of friends who have assisted me in various ways, particularly Michael Bloch, Valerie Chinchen, Elaine Denby, Stewart Easton, Francis King, Geoffrey Nunn and the late Dorothy Stroud.

Last, but very far from least, many thanks to Helen Castle and Abigail Grater for fostering a first-time author and providing me with so much patient help and advice.

Credits

All colour photographs are by Steve Gorton.

The drawings on pages 12, 13, 25, 72, 110 and 111 are by Roy Johnston.

Ownership or original publication of black and white contemporary illustrations, where known, are given below. (*'La Construction Moderne'* abbreviated to *'CM'* and *'L'Architecture'* to *'l'Arch.'*)

p 16: Cliché Bibliothéque Nationale; **pp.18-19**: *'Les Modes de Paris 1797-1897'*; **p29**: CM 1892-93 p.509; **p38**: Cliché Bibliothéque Nationale; **p39**: CM 1899, plate 56; **p40**: *Encyclopédie d'architecture* 1885; **p46**: Paris, Musée d'Orsay; **p51**: *'Maisons de rapport'* (P. Planat); **p52**: *l'Arch.* 1907, p18; **p56**: *'Immeubles modernes de Paris'* (G. Lefol); **p58**: Cliché Lausiaux, 1918, Commission du Vieux Paris; **p61** *'Maisons les plus remarquables construites à Paris de1905 à 1914*; **p70**: (Viollet-le-Duc) *'Lectures on Architecture'* (transl. B. Bucknall) vol.II, plate XXI. (Labrouste) *'Designing Paris'*(D. van Zanten; MIT Press); **p71**: CM 1886; **p74**: *'Maisons moderne de rapport'* (E. Rivoalen) liv.40; **p75**: *l'Arch.* 1906, p3; **p76**: CM 30 Aug. 1890; **p79**: *l'Arch.* 1900 plate 12; **p84**: l.l.-Viollet; **p95**: Roger-Viollet; **p96**: *CM* 22Dec.1900; **p98**: Studio Chevojan, Paris 1889; **p99**: *'Eléments et Théorie de l'Architecture'* (Guadet) vol. II, p371; **p105**: *l'Arch.*1900; **p106**: Archives d'Architecture du XXe siècle de l'Institut français d'Architecture, Paris; **p112**: *CM* 1 Apr.1893; **p121**: *l'Arch.* 1898; **p130**: l'Arch. 1897; **p131**: l'Arch. 1903; **p151**: *CM* 1901-02, p306; **pp153-154**: Fond. Rothschild; **p155**: Fonds Sauvage; **p157**: *'Monographies de bâtiments modernes'* (A. Ragnenet); **p160**: archives Fond. Lebaudy; **p162**: *CM* 1912, p533; **p163**: *l'Arch.* 1907, plate 26; **p164**: *CM* 25 June 1898; **p167**: *CM* 1912, p521; **p168**: *CM* 1889-90 plates 5 and 6; **p172**: *CM* 22Apr. 1905, p352; **p174**: (Perspective) *CM* 1901, plate 68, (Section) *CM* 1900, p328; **p176**: *'L'Architecture, le passé, le présent'* (A. de Baudot); **p179**: *CM* 1903-04, plate 28; **p181** Fonds. Perret; **p182**: *CM* 1908, plate 95; **pp186-187**: *'L'Architecture, le passé, le présent'* (A. de Baudot); **p188**: *l'Arch.* 1913, p160